Quaker Perspectives
in
Higher Education

Edited by:

Donn Weinholtz

Jeffrey Dudiak

Donald A. Smith

Full Media Services

http://www.fullmediaservices.com

Friends Association for Higher Education

http://www.quakerfahe.org

ISBN-13: 978-0-9960033-2-2

ISBN-10: 0-9660033-2-0

Contents

i

List of Figures

List of Tables

About the Authors

Abigail E. Adams is a sociocultural anthropologist, professor and chair at Central Connecticut State University. She did her doctoral work at the University of Virginia, researching the role of U.S. and Maya evangelical Christians during Guatemala's 36 years of civil war and counterinsurgency. She earned her master's degree in Latin American Studies from Stanford University and undergraduate degree from Haverford College in biology and anthropology. She leads Field Schools in Cultural Anthropology to Central America on a regular basis. Abigail and her family are members of Storrs Friends Meeting in Connecticut, and Abigail is an active member of the Friends Association for Higher Education.

Greg Barnes retired as director of the English Language Center at Drexel in 2001. Since that time, he has written on Quaker topics exclusively, as his personal ministry. He published *A Biography of Lillian and George Willoughby* (Edwin Mellen Press) in 2007 and *Philadelphia's Arch Street Meeting House: A Biography* (Quakerbridge Media) in 2012. He is currently at work on a centennial history of the American Friends Service Committee. A member of Central Philadelphia Monthly Meeting, he and his wife now live at Friends Riverfront, a Quaker experimental retirement community in old city, Philadelphia.

Doug Bennett served as President of Earlham College from 1997 to 2011. Previously he held positions at the American Council of Learned Societies, Reed College, and Temple University. Within the world of Friends he currently clerks AFSC's Friends Relations Committee, is a member of the Quaker United Nations Committee (NY), and a member of the General Board of FCNL. Previously he served on governing boards and committees for Haverford College, Friends Seminary (NYC), Germantown Friends School, and the Friends Association for Higher Education. A convinced Quaker, Doug is a member of First Friends Meeting in Richmond, Indiana. He now lives in Maine, and blogs about religious matters on riverviewfriend.wordpress.com.

Douglas Burks is a Professor of Biology at Wilmington College of Ohio where he has taught and done research with undergraduate students for the past 33 years. His current research involves studying the effects of various nutrients and compounds on longevity and life span in *Drosophila Melanogaster*. He is a member of Community Friends Meeting in Cincinnati and he has been an active member and in the Friends Association for Higher Education. Another interest of Doug's is Bioethics. He has taught Bioethics at Wilmington for over twenty years and is currently writing a textbook for use in an online Bioethics course.

Max Carter is the director of Friends Center and Quaker Studies at Guilford College. A recorded minister among Friends, he has previous teaching experience in the Ramallah Friends Schools, Earlham College, Friends' Central School, and Friends Select School. He is an adjunct professor of Quaker spirituality at Wake Forest University Divinity School. He holds an M.Min. from the Earlham School of Religion and a Ph.D. in American Religious History from Temple University. Max and his wife Jane, Associate Head of New Garden Friends School in Greensboro, lead annual volunteer work and study trips to Palestine and Israel.

Jay R. Case is Professor of History at Malone University, where he has worked since 1999. He earned a B.A. in History & Education from Taylor University in 1984 and his M.A. and Ph.D. (1995 and 1999) in American history from the University of Notre Dame. Dr. Case's main areas of scholarly interest are in American Religious History, particularly the history of American evangelicalism. He has published a book, *An Unpredictable Gospel: American Evangelicals and World Christianity, 1812-1920* from Oxford University Press, and has also published several articles on the missionary movement. He has been a member of the Jackson Friends Church in Massillon, Ohio for fifteen years.

Steve Chase is a member of the Putney Friends Meeting in Vermont, the author of *Letters To A Fellow Seeker: A Short Introduction To The Quaker Way*, and the Director of Antioch University New England's environmental studies master's concentration in Advocacy for Social Justice and Sustainability. His dissertation, *Activist Training In The Academy*, has been downloaded by over 1,000 academics and has provided the basic curriculum framework for his program and The Change Agency, an activist training organization in Australia. A long-time Quaker activist, Chase is also a local community organizer in the global Transition Town Movement and lives with his partner in Keene, New Hampshire.

'Ben' Pink Dandelion has worked for Woodbrooke Quaker Study Centre since 1992 and currently directs the work of the Centre for Postgraduate Quaker Studies which is a collaboration between Woodbrooke and the universities of Birmingham and Lancaster. He is also Professor of Quaker Studies at the University of Birmingham. He has written and edited numerous books and articles on Quaker history, theology and sociology including the new *Oxford Handbook of Quaker Studies* (with Stephen W. Angell). Ben has been a Friend since the mid 1980s and worships at Sawley Quaker Meeting in the shadow of Pendle Hill. He gave the Swarthmore Lecture at Britain Yearly Meeting in 2014.

Jeffrey Dudiak is an Associate Professor of Philosophy at The King's University College in Edmonton, Canada, specializing in Continental philosophy of religion and ethics. Among his interests is developing a philosophical reading of Quaker religious life and thought, especially as it has taken shape and evolved under the pressures of modern thought. He has served as Canadian Yearly Meeting's representative to Friends United Meeting, and is currently the clerk of the Friends Association for Higher Education.

Gary C. Farlow is Associate Professor of Physics at Wright State University, Dayton, OH. His research involves radiation effects in solids and radiation analysis applied to solids, with emphasis on electronic oxides. He also dabbles in innovative teaching methods applied to physics. He has served as assistant and recording clerk of FUM; clerk of Wilmington Yearly Meeting, Miami-Center Quarterly Meeting, Xenia Monthly Meeting, and FAHE. He is currently a member of Wilmington Yearly Meeting Permanent Board, and a Guilford College Trustee.

Laura Foote is an Assistant Professor at Malone University in Canton, Ohio. She teaches courses in communication, writing, faith and worldviews, and fine arts for the Malone Management Program in the School of Business and Leadership and is the Prior

Learning Assessment coordinator. She has a Doctorate of Education in Adult Learning from Regent University; a Bachelor's of Science in Elementary Education from Pennsylvania State University, and a Master's of Fine Arts in Communication from the University of Akron. Her research has focused on women's public speaking, Christian-faith and cognitive development in college students, service learning, and andragogy. She attends Canton First Friends Church where her husband is the Executive Pastor.

Janet Gray is an Associate Professor of Women's and Gender Studies at The College of New Jersey. Her interdisciplinary courses also serve programs in Religious Studies, Environmental Studies, Holocaust and Genocide Studies, and International Studies. Having grown up Quaker in a family that was deeply involved with the American Friends Service Committee, she is interested in the ways that Quaker educational practices correspond to and inform contemporary best practices in public higher education.

Mike Heller is a Professor of English and co-coordinator of Peace and Justice Studies at Roanoke College in Virginia. He has taught and written about the colonial American Quaker John Woolman, Mahatma Gandhi, the personal journal, autobiography, and the place of spirituality in education. He edited the essay collection, *The Tendering Presence: Essays on John Woolman*, and co-edited with Sterling Olmsted *John Woolman: A Nonviolence and Social Change Source Book*. He has written about his own spiritual journey to Quakerism in the Pendle Hill Pamphlet, *From West Point to Quakerism*. He lives with his wife in Roanoke, where they enjoy their grandchildren.

James W. Hood is Professor of English at Guilford College in Greensboro, North Carolina, where he teaches courses in Romantic and Victorian British literature, literature and ethics, American nature writing, composition, and the natural history of central North Carolina. His publications include works on Alfred Tennyson and Victorian gift books, and he regularly reviews books for *Friends Journal*. A member of Friendship Friends Meeting (North Carolina Yearly Meeting–Conservative), he has served on the Friends Association for Higher Education executive committee and as clerk of the New Garden Friends School board of trustees.

Paul Lacey, a convinced Friend, first met Friends in Philadelphia during weekend work camps while in high school. He is married, with three children, and is an emeritus professor of English at Earlham College. Paul is the literary executor for Denise Levertov, and co-edited her *Collected Poems* in 2013. He published a book of poems, *We Learn to Swim in Winter*, in the fall of 2013.

Rebecca Leuchak taught World Arts at the undergraduate and graduate levels at Roger Williams University (RI) where she founded the department of Art History. She also served as the Executive Director of Global and International Programs for the University, building a robust program of international partnerships and designing educational exchange opportunities for scholars and students. Prior to her university career, she worked at The Cloisters Museum and The Metropolitan Museum of Art in New York and at the Philadelphia Museum of Art designing educational programming and researching collections. She has returned to student life and is pursuing a doctorate in the Humanities at Salve Regina University in Newport (RI), giving her the time to research and write on education issues more broadly and the global turn in art history, specifically. She is a member of New England Yearly Meeting Permanent Board and served for many years as a trustee for The Beacon Hill Friends House in Boston and at Moses Brown School, a Quaker K-12 school in Providence (RI).

Susan McNaught is Dean of the Dallas Campus of Chemeketa Community College based in Salem Oregon. She has a Ph.D. in Post-Secondary Education from Oregon State University. She has worked extensively in developmental education at both the community college and university levels. While at George Fox University, she taught management courses in the degree-completion program and did Prior Learning Assessment. While at George Fox, she became involved with FAHE.

Julie Meadows runs *The Generous Reader*, a coaching and editing service for academic writers. She was Assistant Professor of Philosophy at Presbyterian College in Clinton, SC, from 2006 to 2012, when her position was eliminated in budget cuts. She holds an MDiv from Earlham School of Religion and a PhD in Ethics and Society from the Graduate Division of Religion at Emory University. She began her teaching career at Thornton Friends Middle School in Silver Spring, MD. She is a member of Alexandria Friends Meeting in Virginia. Julie's scholarly work explores justice, the arts, and embodiment.

Richard Miller is an Associate Professor of Philosophy at East Carolina University in Greenville, North Carolina. His primary specialty is metaphysics but with interests in many areas of philosophy. He has been active within North Carolina Yearly Meeting (Conservative) for thirty years. He has served as both the Recording Clerk and the Presiding Clerk of the Yearly Meeting. He is a recorded elder.

Mike Moyer serves as Assistant Professor of Religion and Ercil and Maxine Beane Chair of Quaker Philosophy at William Penn University in Oskaloosa, IA. He also serves as coordinator for the Clarence and Lilly Pickett Endowment for Quaker Leadership. Mike teaches a variety of religion courses at William Penn including a Quaker Values course required of all graduates and a special topics course, Of Light and Life, that introduces students to the Quaker mystical tradition. His academic interests include Quaker thought and practice, American church history, and the life and writings of C.S. Lewis.

Diego Navarro is the founder of the Academy for College Excellence (ACE), a nation-wide program for underprepared college students funded by national foundations including the NSF and the Gates Foundation. He is a Professor at Cabrillo College, where, in addition to teaching courses on social justice, he performs research on effective and accelerated approaches to basic skills education. Prior to working in higher education, Diego spent 25 years in the high-tech industry. He is a member of Santa Cruz Monthly Meeting, was the former Clerk of Pacific Yearly Meeting's Ministry and Oversight Committee, and served on the National Board of Directors of the American Friends Service Committee.

Peter V. Oliver is an Associate Professor at the University of Hartford where he has taught courses in self-awareness, educational psychology and human development to students in education and the helping professions for the past 25 years. Peter is also nationally certified as a Professional Counselor with extensive experience in mindfulness meditation and the healing arts. He received intensive foundational training in Mindfulness Based Stress Reduction through the Center for Mindfulness at the University of Massachusetts School of Medicine. Peter has also led a study abroad program to Thailand where he co-taught Buddhist approaches to healing and meditation. Peter's current research focuses on mindfulness and its impact on student achievement.

Stephen Potthoff is an Associate Professor of Religion and Philosophy at Wilmington College (Ohio), where he teaches courses in comparative religion, biblical studies, early Christianity, ethics, and dreams and world mythology. He wrote his dissertation on North African early Christian cemeteries as material expressions of the paradise martyrs experienced in the context of near-death visions. He is presently writing a book, begun while on sabbatical as the Cadbury Scholar at Pendle Hill, on dream and visionary experience as a vehicle of reconnection and healing in relationship with the natural world. He is a member of New Garden Friends Meeting in Greensboro, NC and attends the Wilmington College Campus Meeting.

Laura Rediehs is an Associate Professor of Philosophy and Coordinator of Peace Studies at St. Lawrence University in Canton, New York. She teaches courses in peace studies, philosophy of science and religion, modern philosophy, ethics, and logic. In her research, she examines how Quaker thought suggests a theory of knowledge that synthesizes science and religion. She holds a B.A. in philosophy and religion from Earlham College, and an M.A. and Ph.D. in philosophy from the University of Minnesota. She is a member of the St. Lawrence Valley Friends Meeting in Potsdam, New York, and is a member of the Friends Association for Higher Education and the Quaker Studies Research Association.

Diane Reynolds is a lecturer in English and religion at West Liberty State University and an adjunct instructor of English at Ohio University Eastern. She has had a varied career, including being an education and religion reporter for daily and weekly newspapers. As a journalist and book reviewer, her work has appeared in The Washington Post, Publisher's Weekly, the Baltimore Sun and other publications. Beyond her interest in Dietrich Bonhoeffer and his Quaker connections, she is pursuing research into why Quakers have not produced world class fiction and has a strong interest in both Jane Austen and, more broadly, the novel as genre, as well as genre and depictions of women in the Bible. She belongs to the Stillwater Monthly Meeting of Ohio Yearly Meeting, where she serves on the Ministry and Oversight and Friends House committees.

Jay Roberts is an Associate Vice President for Academic Affairs and the Director of the Center for Integrated Learning at Earlham College in Richmond, Indiana. A Teagle Pedagogy Fellow for the Great Lakes College Association, Jay also serves on the editorial board for the Journal of Experiential Education. His most recent publications include (2013) "The Campus and Community as a Learning Laboratory: Possibilities and Limitations," in *Teaching Sustainability: Perspectives from the Humanities and Social Sciences*, Texas A & M Press, and (2011) *Beyond Learning By Doing: Theoretical Currents in Experiential Education*, Routledge Press. He is currently working on a new book, *Experiential Education in the College Context: The Promises of the Live Encounter*, under contract with Routledge Press. Jay is a member of First Friends Quaker Meeting in Richmond, Indiana.

Theodore Sawruk is an Associate Professor of Architecture with the University of Hartford (CT), focusing on design, theory, and history. He has previously taught at: Hampton University, Southern Polytechnic University, University of Arkansas, and Drury University. His experience in starting new degree programs allowed him to help establish a new architecture program at Herat University in western Afghanistan. Sincerely interested in architectural educational at the elementary and secondary levels, he has received Fannie Mae Foundation and HUD: HBCU Grants to further educational outreach, community revitalization, and fair housing initiatives. Recognized nationally, he has served five consecutive terms as a grant review panelist for the National Endowment of the Arts: Arts Education Grants.

Deborah Shaw is the director of the Quaker Leadership Scholars Program at Guilford College and is the assistant director of its Friends Center. A recorded minister among Friends, she has led numerous retreats and workshops at Pendle Hill, Woodbrooke, and local meetings, and has spoken at yearly meetings and other Friends gatherings. Deborah's service to Friends includes longtime involvement with FAHE, clerking at the monthly and yearly meeting level, board work for Pendle Hill, and long service of traveling in the ministry amongst Friends as elder and spiritual support of those engaged in Truth's work.

Don Smith is an Associate Professor of Physics at Guilford College in Greensboro, North Carolina. He received a doctorate in Astrophysics from the Massachusetts Insititute of Technology and a Bachelor's in Physics from the University of Chicago. He teaches courses in physics, astronomy, history, and science fiction. His research interests involve transient sources of light in the sky, including material falling into black holes and the death throes of giant stars. He has helped to build and used space-based X-ray telescopes as well as robotic optical telescopes on mountains around the world. He has taught Scientific English in Russia for three summers, and has lived in Germany for several years. He has served Friends General Conference as director of the High School program, has served on the Executive Committee of FAHE, and is currently the co-editor of *Quaker Higher Education.*

Steve Smith grew up as a member of Iowa Yearly Meeting (Conservative). He attended Scattergood Friends School, Earlham College, and Harvard University, from which he received an M.A. and Ph.D. in Philosophy. He retired in 2008 from 40 years of teaching in the Department of Philosophy and Religious Studies at Claremont McKenna College in Claremont, California. He is a member of Claremont Monthly Meeting (Pacific Yearly Meeting), has served as presiding clerk of his monthly and quarterly meetings, and is the current Presiding Clerk of Pacific Yearly Meeting.

William Upholt is Professor Emeritus of Reconstructive Sciences at the University of Connecticut Health Center where he conducted research and taught/advised graduate students working on PhDs in Biomedical Sciences. He is active in a variety of sustainability/environmental efforts in the Hartford CT area. He serves or has served on the boards of the Interreligious Eco-Justice Network, the Hartford City Advisory Commission on the Environment, the Hartford Clean Energy Task Force, and the CT Partnership for Sustainability Education. He has participated in the annual meetings of Friends Committee on National Legislation and Quaker Earthcare Witness. Presently he is particularly interested in new economics, permaculture, and food security.

Lonnie Valentine is the Trueblood Chair of Christian Thought and Professor of Peace and Justice Studies at the Earlham School of Religion.He has taught at Earlham for 25 years working with students who have an peace studies emphasis in the M. Div. or M.A. in Religion program. He teaches at the intersection of peace studies and the theological disciplines of biblical studies, theology, church history, and spirituality. His primary scholarship interests are the Quaker Peace Testimony and pacifism. The new *Oxford Handbook of Quaker Studies* has his article on "Quakers, War, and Peacemaking" and he has several articles, including "Christian Peace Testimony," "Pacifism in the Peace Moment," and "War Tax Resistance" in the *Oxford International Encyclopedia of Peace*. He has served on the Executive Committee of the Friends Association for Higher Education and was co-chair of the Religion Peace and War group of the American Academy of Religion.

Donn Weinholtz is a Professor of Educational Leadership at the University of Hartford (CT) where he teaches graduate courses in research methods and professional ethics, as well as undergraduate courses in American Studies. He is a former dean of the University of Hartford's College of Education, Nursing and Health Professions, and is currently the Director of the Doctoral Program in Educational Leadership. He was the founding editor of Quaker Higher Education, which he now co-edits. He is also the Assistant Clerk of Friends Association of Higher Education, a member of New England Yearly Meeting's Permanent Board and a member of the Friends Committee on National Legislation General Committee.

Chapter 1

Introduction

Since 1980, Friends Association of Higher Education has been an international consortium of Quaker colleges and Quaker scholars striving to strengthen the Quaker mission in Higher Education by:

- Providing a supportive relationship and opportunities for fellowship among all who share Quaker ideals of higher education, whether on Quaker or non-Quaker campuses.

- Enhancing member's appreciation of Friends religious heritage and nurturing the individual and corporate search for Truth.

- Lending support to the Quaker ideal of integrating spiritual commitment, academic excellence, and social responsibility.

- Lending support and encouragement to scholarly research directed toward perceiving and achieving a more perfect human society.

- Helping to clarify and articulate the distinctively Quaker vision of higher education, in terms of both curriculum and teaching.

- Assisting Friends Colleges in their efforts to affirm their Quaker heritage.

- Fostering communication and cooperation among Friends' educational institutions and the various Friends constituencies to which they may be connected.[1]

---

[1] See also http://quakerfahe.com/about/

Each year, FAHE convenes its annual conference on a Quaker campus. These gatherings have been held every June since 1981 and have been hosted over the years by many Quaker colleges and universities throughout the United States, as well as the Woodbrooke Quaker Study Centre (U.K.). FAHE also coordinates an annual Quaker College Fair for high school students in the Greater Philadelphia area, and supports other Quaker college initiatives, such as Earlham School of Religion's recent creation of the Quaker College Leadership Network. During the last decade, FAHE has substantially increased its publishing activities.

Quaker Perspectives in Higher Education is composed of articles drawn from the first fourteen issues of Quaker Higher Education (QHE), FAHE's biannual, scholarly journal, which the association launched in 2007. Initiated as a vehicle for promoting communication among Quaker scholars, QHE has become a popular venue for sharing many of the finest papers and write-ups of presentations from the annual FAHE conference, products that previously too often disappeared following each conference's conclusion. It also solicits articles addressing a wide variety of topics and issues of interest to Friends. QHE is published in April and November of each year. It is emailed to all FAHE members, and is posted on the FAHE website. All issues can be accessed at : `http://quakerfahe.com`.

For this book, we have attempted to select articles that will provide readers with a good overview of some of the major areas of concern for Quaker-flavored higher education, and a taste for some of the persistent issues we find ourselves dealing with as Quaker educators, or as educators within Quaker-connected universities, colleges, seminaries, and study centers. Clearly, no issue could be dealt with comprehensively here; but we hope that the articles selected will draw readers into our ongoing discussions around important, and perennial, concerns. We believe the depth and breadth of engagement reflected in the essays of this book will stimulate Friends, and educators working in the context of Friends, and others!, to ask important questions about what we do–yet again, more thoughtfully, and with increasing spiritual sensitivity. We trust this book, through the wide variety of Quakerly voices it presents, will help readers to more effectively, and more faithfully, reflect upon, and engage in, the calling to Quaker higher education.

This book is the first in a planned series sponsored by Friends Association for Higher Education. Each volume in the series will focus on Quaker contributions to a specific academic discipline, such as history or economics, or to a broader academic area, such as the humanities or sciences. There will also be occasional volumes addressing Quaker academicians' contributions to important concerns such as peacemaking, commerce and environmental steward-ship. While numerous texts and journals have explored the lives and works of Friends who are academicians–for example Rufus Jones, Howard and Anna Brinton, Kenneth and Elise Boulding and many others–collective Quaker contributions within the various academic disciplines have been largely ignored. This series will address that gap.

Royalties from *Quaker Perspectives in Higher Education*, and all other books in the Friends Association for Higher Education series, will accrue to FAHE to support the association's ongoing publishing efforts.

Chapter 2

Environmentalism and Sustainability

Modern Quakers are steadfastly committed to caring for and preserving the natural environment. This is reflected in many Friends adopting a stewardship testimony. It is also evident in the environmental work of monthly and yearly meetings, as well as that of organizations such Quaker Earthcare Witness, Friends Committee on National Legislation and American Friends Service Committee. Quakers' concerns for the environment and sustainability are naturally reflected in the teaching and learning experiences at Friends' colleges and universities. This chapter offers snapshots of Quaker educators' environmental views and their teaching practices.

Jay Case, from Earlham College, starts the chapter proposing that , in the United Nation's Decade of Education for Sustainable Development (2005-2015), Friends should ask the question, "What does it mean to take a Quaker approach to education for sustainability?" Jay responds by offering five guiding principles for organizing educational program and collegiate responses. He suggests that Friends efforts should be comprehensive, contemplative, consensus-oriented, critical and connective. He fleshes out the implications of each of these recommendations, and reminds us that, in the face of daunting challenges :

> Education for sustainability must, in the end, be about holding things in tension, dealing with conflicting values, ambiguous goals, and multiple contexts. Rather than lamenting this state of affairs, we Friends can celebrate it and, in turn, find a certain strength in our distinctiveness that may shine a light to the rest of the world.

Gary Farlow moves the focus to his Wright State University physics classroom, pointing out that one of the earliest lessons students in his discipline learn from the theory of thermodynamic equilibrium is that the universe will eventually die and that: "You can't win... You can't break even... You can't even get out of the chain that is the game." Gary points out that this is not the best way to motivate students to tackle the challenges of promoting sustainability. However, he offers a way out of the bind, providing illustrations from engineering (applied physics) showing how highly efficient techniques for heating and lighting can be obtained. Adopting the metaphor of "fooling Mother Nature," he argues that doing so, wisely, involves knowing Mother Nature intimately; thus, carefully learning the advanced lessons of physics, chemistry, biology and geology. It also involves implementing engineering solutions sufficiently intelligent to forestall the inevitable in ways that Mother Nature won't mind.

Next, Doug Burks, a molecular biologist at Wilmington College, offers specific examples of teaching biology in ways that address the global sustainability crisis. Doug points out that, given the nature of his particular discipline, it would be easy to ignore sustainability issues; but that his religious experience as a Friend compels him to find ways to address these pressing concerns. Acknowledging that all of us carry a heavy burden of responsibility for the sustainability crisis, he shares how he has his students calculate their ecological footprints in order to bring important lessons home to the personal level. He also goes a step further, providing data from his own ecological footprint and showing how he needs to dramatically decrease his own consumption of resources in order to live sustainably. His message to the reader is apparent and compelling.

William Upholt delivers a distinctly different story, focusing on his personal transition from a full-time professor and basic science researcher at the University of Connecticut Health Science Center to a dedicated promoter of education for sustainable development. Early on, he recognized the important intersection of economic development and environmental issues. His continuing journey has been distinctly Quaker, informed by Friends and Friends' organizations; but necessarily involving a wide range of allied environmental groups. Indeed, his first sustainability lesson was conducted at Hartford (CT) Friends Meeting's First Day School using curricular materials developed by Friends in Unity with Nature (now Friends Earthcare Witness.) Bill went on to become a founding member of the Connecticut Partnership for Sustainability Education, which subsequently merged with the Connecticut Outdoor and Environmental Education Association, becoming an ongoing working group of that organization. Bill's commitment to education for sustainability development remains strong, and his efforts ongoing.

Janet Gray shares her experiences teaching an Ecofeminism course at The College of New Jersey. Wrestling with the concepts of "abundance" and "scarcity," she draws on the writings of Parker Palmer to shed light on how the "...messy, multidimensional bigness of ecofeminism makes it a dynamic resource for merging critical thinking with engaged citizenship." After two uneven semesters teaching the course–one wonderfully successful, the other not so much–her students took on the challenge of starting a garden serving as a resource for the wider community. Of course, semesters end quickly and new students do not always embrace the goals adopted by their predecessors. Janet explains how she negotiated this divide, while finding fruitful intellectual synergy in ecofeminism's intersection with deep ecology and social ecology.

Stephen Pothoff , from Wilmington College, closes the chapter with an ecospirituality narrative drawing on the dreams reported to him by students during a two-week, research trip to Costa Rica. Inspired by Thomas Berry, Stephen wondered, "...how encountering Costa Rica's extraordinarily diverse and often formidable tropical environments might activate the inner archetypal dream world of my student colleagues, most of whom had never set foot in a tropical forest." The vivid dreams that he describes and analyzes reveal the profound impact nature has on individuals when they allow themselves to become immersed in it; how alienated from nature those living in the technology-driven world have become; and how aspects of psychic/spiritual adjustment unfold. The experiences described were transformational for the participating students, as well as for Stephen, their dreamkeeper.

Quakers, Education, and the Question of Sustainability

by Jay Roberts, Earlham College

Introduction

The United Nations has declared the period 2005-2015 as the decade for Education for Sustainable Development. Clearly, within the last five years, we have seen a fast and remarkable turn toward issues of climate change and sustainability within the United States. Seemingly, everyone is thinking about it, discussing ways forward, and (maybe) willing to commit to serious action. Amidst all of this dusty stampeding however, there remains little to no talk about the role of education and schooling in either the problem or imagining potential solutions. This is curious. Surely, the cumulative experiences of sixteen to twenty years of schooling ought to have a profound influence (negatively or positively) on our relationship to the natural world? Indeed, many progressive educators have made the point that schooling is not *neutral*.

Educator and critical theorist Henry Giroux is famous for saying that "the political is pedagogical and the pedagogical is political." The seeming neutrality of the college canon was questioned in earlier decades by the rise of Women's Studies and African-American Studies, to name two of the more notable challenges. David Orr, perhaps our most noted thinker on issues of education and the environment, has noted: "It is a matter of no small consequence that the only people who have lived sustainably on the planet for any length of time could not read, or, like the Amish, do not make a fetish out of reading. My point is simply that education is no guarantee of decency, prudence, or wisdom. More of the same kind of education will only compound our problems. It is not education, but education of a certain kind, that will save us."

Whether or not one may agree that schools are part of the problem, it is worth asking ourselves as Friends: What does it mean to take a Quaker approach to education for sustainability? We believe that peace, for example, ought to become a central part of both the content and method of teaching. This is played out in many ways within Friends schools: the informality of student-teacher relationships, the unique approach to conflict resolution, the coverage of social justice topics within the curriculum, and the progressive orientation to addressing real, community-based problems. Are we in a time, now, where a similar approach ought to be taken for issues of sustainability in both K-12 and higher education?

8

I think this query ought to apply to us as individuals aligned in some fashion with the religious Society of Friends. And, importantly, I think it also ought to apply to Quaker *institutions* of learning and, in particular, higher education. Why? While it is vital that we, as individuals, work through our own leadings as it relates to being in integrity with the natural world, it is just as crucial that our public personae–our schools–also do this form of institutional "inner work." It would seem silly if we asked our students to "act peacefully" if our institutions did not attempt to do likewise in all areas within their responsibility. This explains why, at Earlham for example, we are mindful of our investments and have a committee who is charged with monitoring how our institutional values remain in integrity with the companies that we invest in.

To this end (and with apologies for the somewhat cheesy model), I offer what I have tentatively described as "The Five C's of Quaker Education for Sustainability." What follows below is, I hope, just the beginning of a deeper and more sustained look at both the role of schooling within the issue of sustainability and the voice that the Religious Society of Friends might bring to the table.

Five C's of Education for Sustainability

I see at least five areas that provide a unique and distinctly Quaker approach to the problem of education for sustainability. Any such attempt ought to be:

1. Comprehensive

2. Contemplative

3. Consensus-oriented

4. Critical

5. Connective

There are likely other areas, and good people will disagree. My point here is to begin to open up space for the conversation to take place.

First, our responses to the current environmental challenges before us (importantly, this goes beyond "climate change" to a much more broad intersection of areas of ecological justice including basic needs, quality of life standards, equity issues, etc.) must be comprehensive. That is to say, we cannot adequately address the issue by simply tacking on a required general education course, or by

9

simply signing on to the Talloise agreement (though these actions may well be good ideas to pursue). Friends have long advocated for deeper assessments of causes and effects. Indeed, such an approach forms the cornerstone of our witness for peace and stance against acts of war.

Thus, we must approach the issue of sustainability broadly and deeply by examining the ways a sustainability stance in education affects the curriculum, the co-curriculum, the mission, and the community (both inside and outside of the school). This moves us beyond education "about sustainability" to a place where sustainability becomes something that is "lived out" through all the elements of the institution. Thus, it becomes more of an ideal than a checkbox of behaviors that must be constantly re-interpreted and deliberated upon by the community as it wrestles with the tensions of what it means to "live sustainably." In many ways, this mirrors what many educational theorists have argued about democracy–that, within the realm of schooling, it ought to be viewed as an active "way of life" and not a passive birthright.

In addition to being comprehensive, a Quaker approach to education for sustainability ought to be contemplative. Environmental problems are, by definition, *human* problems. A commonality among many environmental writers and thinkers, from Arne Naes to Rachel Carson, Aldo Leopold to Vandana Shiva, is that environmental problems arise from a failure of contemplation and thoughtfulness. This can range from scientific notions of mindfulness (Leopolds "pedagogy of place" or Carson's oft-quoted caution that "before we think whether we *can* do something, we ought to think whether we *should*") to spiritual and aesthetic constructions (Thoreau's transcendentalism or Buber's "I:Thou" relationship). A Quaker approach to sustainability would amplify the importance of contemplation and thoughtfulness to both our theory and our practice. As John Ralston Saul once said:

> But is the nature of civilization 'speed'? Or is it 'consideration'? Any animal can rush around a corral four times a day. Only a human being can consciously oblige himself to go slowly in order to consider whether or not he is doing the right thing, doing it the right way, or ought to be doing something else... Speed and efficiency are not in themselves signs of intelligence or capability or correctness.

Parker Palmer also once remarked, during a speech at Earlham College, that modern colleges and universities resemble the hum and whir of "munitions factories" rather than places of contemplation and scholarship. I once heard a colleague talk of how students these days are subjected to a "brutal pace" and "bombarded with information." How fast we normalize the logics of the market and the military into the language of school! Quakers have long demonstrated the case that long and sustained focus on a particular issue yields great results, if one is only patient enough and willing to plant a seed without the benefit of witnessing it bear fruit. But, I think we can do better here, as Friends. To what extent are we (either as individuals or institutions) a shining example of simplicity, contemplation, and the virtue of slowness to the rest of the world? Thomas Merton once chided the stressed and overworked advocates for peace in the world by saying "busyness itself is a form of violence." I wonder if we have done enough to demonstrate to the world how "peace begins with me" when we seem to be as focused on production, efficiency, and speed as everyone else seems to be. It may require us to reconsider *how* we, as Friends, are orchestrating educational environments for the students in our care.

When we are busy we cannot nurture our spirits, we have a harder time being contemplative and, as a consequence, I believe our students simply "model our model." In the end, this may contribute to the objectification of the natural world. There is a difference between data, information, knowledge, and wisdom. What do we wish to promote and practice? Changing *inward* institutional culture at this level would be difficult and challenging work. While we all may agree on the surface that "less is more," how many of us, when pressed, would agree to eliminate assignments, class-time, courses, or even departments in the name of "inner-sustainability"? I believe this is, perhaps, our most important task as Quaker educators. Can we find the resolve to alter the unconscious and consumptive wheels of "progress"?

Another aspect of a Quaker approach to education for sustainability would utilize a perceived weakness to strategic advantage. As climate change becomes increasingly apparent, many talk of the need for quick and resolute action. However, fast and determined leadership is not necessarily appropriate leadership. I am reminded here of a political cartoon I recently saw that included a group of lemmings lined up to jump off a cliff. As one of the lemmings was preparing to jump, he turns around and says to the lemming behind him, "dont you just love resolute and determined leadership?" The Quaker process of consensus may not yield efficient results, but in a crisis-oriented climate, as we seem to be in now, it has distinct advantages. First, by taking the time to deliberate and examine a problem from many perspectives and listening to all voices, we may be better able to get at root causes and issues as opposed to simply dealing with the symptoms.

This is what Peter Senge calls "second loop" thinking. In single loop analysis, we move from doing to observing to reflecting and finally deciding. This is technical or action-oriented thinking and it is the predominant way most organizations operate, at least in the West. Second loop thinking involves pausing at the reflection stage and sinking deeper through the process of re-considering, re-connecting, and re-framing which leads you back to reflecting and then on to deciding and doing. The problem with single loop thinking is that it has the tendency to focus on technical solutions without more carefully examining the assumptions and ideologies that generated the problem in the first place. Quaker process, done well, brings the community down to the second loop, and ensures that possible ways forward have adequately considered both root causes and possible consequences. Second, it has the potential to bring the community together in purposeful and agreed upon action that itself is far more "sustainable" than committee recommendations, presidential declarations, and the like. This "bottom-up" approach is the hallmark of much of community activism and is well suited for the kind of culture change necessary for sustainability to become more than a label or shallow and technically driven enterprise on campuses.

Fourth, a Quaker approach to education for sustainability should have a decidedly critical orientation. I am choosing to use the term "critical" here to denote the importance of social justice related work both within the Quaker faith and as a growing area within the sustainability and environmental movements. In a well-read parable of the New Testament, Jesus tells the story of the shepherd who, when just one of his flock goes astray, leaves the rest to go and tend to his one wayward animal. Friends have often interpreted this passage as a metaphor for being attentive to those at the margins of society–the poor, the excluded, the discriminated upon, and even the perceived "villains." The current "environmental movement" (whatever that is) has often been critiqued for its elitist and privileged status, and perhaps, rightly so. Any casual observer would point out that activists tend to be white, middle to upper-class, well-educated, and located in the northern hemisphere. These folks, with their "full stomachs" and comfortable standard of living are quick, so the argument goes, to tell everyone else to stop consuming so much. Indeed, a recent highly publicized essay (now a book) by Earlham College graduate Michael Shellenberger and Ted Norhaus provocatively titled *The Death of Environmentalism* takes the movement to task for its anti-capitalistic, anti-progress, foundations.

But I think we need not throw the proverbial baby out with the bathwater. The rise of "eco-justice" and the synergies between ecological concerns and social justice concerns creates new terrain for rearticulating environmental concerns as the concerns of those from the margins. In many ways Hurricane Katrina was as much about ecology as it was about race and class. The world over, it is the destitute and the unseen who live at the ecological margins–in the floodplains, near industrial waste sites, on dry and infertile land. Quakers, with our longstanding work on behalf of those society has chosen to ignore, are well-positioned to work toward rearticulating sustainability as a social justice concern. In the words of Vandana Shiva:

> On the streets of Seattle and Cancun, in homes and farms across the world, another human future is born, a future based on inclusion, not exclusion; on nonviolence, not violence; on reclaiming the commons, not their enclosure; on freely sharing the earth's resources, not monopolizing and privatizing them.

We build this road by traveling it. Friends know this work, it only will take focus, commitment, and a willingness to re-think what education and schooling is for.

A final aspect of a Quaker approach to education for sustainability, would involve connectivity–the conscious and deliberate interplay between "faith and works." Here I am reminded of the old Quaker saw about a new attender to Quaker meeting who, after several uncomfortable minutes of silence turns to an elder to his right and says, "excuse me sir, but when does the service begin?" The elder replies, "we are worshipping now, the service comes after." The connection between faith and works is certainly part of all Christian denominations as well as many, if not all, world religions. But, Friends do place an unusually strong emphasis on "letting your life speak." George Fox himself once said that he wished "to know God experimentally." If he had the word available to him at the time, I wonder if he might have said that he wished to know God "experientially"? Experiential education, at its root, is about the connectivity between theory and practice or, in religion, between faith and works. As Friends, we learn to place great weight on our actions in the world. This is particularly true within schooling as we adhere to value statements such as "knowledge has moral consequence." This form of praxis is geared toward both personal and societal transformation.

13

Thus, education toward sustainability from a Quaker standpoint would emphasize an experiential understanding of our current and future environmental challenges. For example, to what degree are our students active participants in both problem generation and problem solution in regards to education for sustainability? Are we expecting them to merely learn about it in the classroom? What opportunities exist for student-faculty connectivity beyond the usual classroom-based research projects? In the words of German educator and founder of Outward Bound Kurt Hahn, "we must give students the freedom and the power to wreck the State. Only then will they understand the responsibilities of citizenship." Experiential connection also goes beyond education "about sustainability," enabling students to "ground truth" content against what they see, hear, and experience either on their own or in a group. It taps into the affective domain, with the understanding that true learning is not merely a cognitive exercise. When students and their teachers connect emotionally, viscerally, with nature, the marginalized, the community, each other, it becomes much more difficult to objectify and to remain aloof, cynical, and indifferent to the plights of others and our natural world. In 1976, the educational anthropologist Dorothy Lee gave a speech where she worried aloud about an overemphasis on literacy, on words (or, for our purposes on the word "sustainability" at the expense of the experience of it). She said:

> Are we paying a heavy price for literacy? Are we giving
> up our heritage of wonder, of curiosity, of questing, of
> plunging into chaos and creating life out of it? Are we
> giving up our sense of mystery, the excitement of being
> lost in ambiguity and building a world out of it? Have
> we given up this heritage for the sake of literacy, which
> gives us a label instead of experience?

A Quaker approach to education for sustainability would be constantly vigilant so we do not replace experiences with labels and that our students, together with our faculty, connect theory and practice, faith and works, that we come to know sustainability "experimentally."

Conclusion

In the end, learning about our environmental problems and their causes can be a depressing and energy-sapping process. With all the apparent "sickness" that is around, it can be easy to develop a cynical or weary attitude (which fish am I allowed to order at a

14

restaurant again?). George Fox famously reminds us all to "walk cheerfully over the earth answering that of God in everyone." Perhaps the "cheerfully" part might be a sixth "C" of Quaker education for sustainability. This can be a struggle even in good times. But the power of a faith, to me, lies in its ability to, in the words of Maxine Greene, "imagine how things might be otherwise."

Even if the end-goal of sustainability is not a fixed destination (which I do not think it is) but rather a constantly receding horizon that gives us a direction to travel, it still provides us with a sense that there is good work to be done. It is faith that allows me to go forth on that path joyfully, even in the face of so much sorrow and worry. As Friends, we seem more comfortable with the idea of holding things in tension and working with ambiguity. It is another one of our perceived weaknesses that is, to me, a great strength. Education for sustainability must, in the end, be about holding things in tension, dealing with conflicting values, ambiguous goals, and multiple contexts. Rather than lamenting this state of affairs, we Friends can celebrate it and, in turn, find a certain strength in our distinctiveness that may shine a light to the rest of the world. May we always strive to live out the questions. Wendell Berry perhaps says it best:

> It may be that when we no longer know what to do.
> We have come to our real work.
> And that when we no longer know which way to go.
> We have come to our real journey.
> The mind that is not baffled is not employed.
> The impeded stream is the one that sings.

Resources for those wishing to read further in issues of sustainability, environment, and education

Bowers, C.A. (1997). *The Culture of Denial: Why the Environmental Movement Needs A Strategy for Reforming Universities and Public Schools*. One of the more cited, sustained, criticisms of the role of education in our current environmental crisis.

Bonnett, Michael (2004). *Retrieving Nature: Education for a Post-Humanist Age*. A nice treatment of the philosophy of environmental education with a particular argument toward pulling back from post-modern and post-structural critiques of environmentalism.

Heiffetz, Ronald (1994). *Leadership Without Easy Answers*. One of the best texts (in my opinion) dealing with the topic of leadership and leadership theory. While Heiffetz does not deal with issues of sustainability directly (though he does refer to them), his notion of Adaptive Leadership is very Quaker-esque and I see it as an excellent model for environmental problem solving.

Noddings, Nel, ed. (2005) *Educating for Global Citizenship.* Noddings is a well-known philosopher of education. While this edited volume is not her best work, she deals specifically with issues of globalization and sustainability in the chapter, Place-Based Education to Preserve the Earth and Its People.

Orion Magazine. If you havent heard of it and you like (progressive) intersections between nature, culture, and society it is worth checking out (no ads!). Many prominent environmental writers are featured including Barbara Kingsolver, Wendell Berry, Terry Tempest Williams, Gary Nabhan, etc.

Orr, David (1994). *Earth in Mind: On Education, Environment, and the Human Prospect.* An environmental education classic, particularly the first chapter, What Is Education For? which can also be found on-line with a simple Google search.

Orr, David (2002). *The Nature of Design: Ecology, Culture, and Human Intention.* One of Orrs best works, in my opinion, in terms of its trans-disciplinary focus and the creativity of the ideas presented.

Capra, Fitjof (2002). *The Hidden Connections: A Science for Sustainable Living.* (see also his website: Center for Ecoliteracy) An interesting read from a world-renowned physicist as he makes the argument that in order to sustain life the principles underlying our social institutions must be consistent with the broader organization of nature.

Shiva, Vandana (2005). *Earth Democracy: Justice, Sustainability, and Peace.* Another well-known environmental writer from India. While perhaps not as rigorous as some might prefer, it is a nice treatment of the topic from a developing world perspective.

Sobel, David (2004). *Place Based Education: Connecting Classrooms and Communities.* A bit more K-12 in emphasis but, nonetheless, the best resource on this growing pedagogy which pushes beyond more traditional environmental education to incorporate service learning and curriculum integration into a holistic model for schooling. Nice on practice and specifics.

Wayne W. Au and Michael W. Apple. "Reviewing Policy: Freire, Critical Education, and the Environmental Crisis." Educational Policy 2007; 21 457-470. I havent read it yet, but Apple is well-known for his neo-Marxist and critical takes on the state of education and schooling in the U.S.

Teaching the Physics of Energy and the Sustainability Zeitgeist

by Gary C. Farlow, Wright State University

One might think that physics would be the natural place to discuss questions of energy use and sustainability in the context of modern life. This almost never happens. One wonders why.

Let's start by considering energy. Physics invented the concept of energy. It has to do with motion, or more properly with work which causes a change in the energy of motion that we call kinetic energy. We can store that kinetic energy. Lift a bucket of water and put it in a bowl with a hole in it. Let the water run out and turn a paddle wheel. The work of lifting is ultimately what turns the paddlewheel, after having been stored in the lifted water. Such observations have led us to believe that energy comes from some source: the lifting results from the work of stretching muscles, which comes from metabolism of sugars, which results from plant synthesis, which is driven by light energy, which is released by thermonuclear fusion, which comes from... You get the idea.

"But," you say, "I do work all that time, and nothing moves." BZZZT!!!! Effort is not work. That is the other thing we observe about energy: Most times, all the work does not come back in a useful form. Some of it usually gets wasted as random motion at the molecular level that we call heat. Straining against a door that does not move does no work, but the energy released in trying to stretch the muscles to move the door shows up as motion in the cellular structure of the muscles and registers as heat. So what! It gets stored as something, right? BZZZT!!!! Energy stored as random motion will never do work again. It will just spread out and, over time, uniformly warm the universe.

Well, we will just have to find some new energy and so we don't have to worry about it, right? BZZZT!!! "There is no new thing under the Sun" intones Ecclesiastes. In this case at least, Solomon was right. Things are energy, energy are things–courtesy of Einstein. (Pardon the grammar.) There is no new stuff, neither energy nor mass (Anwar notwithstanding). There are only places where energy has been stored over time. When the source of storage is gone, the usable energy is also gone. The universe will eventually die of thermodynamic equilibrium.

So let's summarize the physics view of energy: 1) You can't win. 2) You can't break even. 3) You can't even get out of the chain that is the game. This is not a way to motivate interest in a zeitgeist of sustainable, meaning repeatable, world processes; nor in the hard work of studying physics. It's more of a "Eat, drink and be merry for tomorrow you may die" conclusion. Thus, at a fundamental level, physics has little to say about the zeitgeist of sustainability and what it does have to say does not encourage engaging the discipline. Naturally, we don't make much of it.

By late in the junior year of a major in physics, however, we address less and less the cosmic questions and focus much more on the practical problems of how to fool mother nature. We discover that timescale can make a profound difference in the relevance of the zeitgeist of sustainability. This has little to do with physics and everything to do with engineering, which is applied physics. Let's consider some examples.

One of the real sustainability problems with nuclear power is not its waste products, but its heat load. Nuclear reactors are inefficient thermodynamically because they run at low temperature compared with coal or gas fired plants. It turns out that the higher the temperature a heat producing plant runs compared to its surroundings, the smaller the fraction of heat relative to work is produced from the released energy. Coal and gas fired plants run typically at 1000°C, nuclear plants are closer to 400°C. This is the origin of the big cooling towers at nuclear plants. The heat dumped into those towers is all waste. It makes no great sense to use the electricity to produce more heat in homes or offices. Rather, take that hot water and pipe it into schools, hospitals, office buildings etc., to heat them, and provide hot water. (This cooling water is not radioactive.) Some of the "planned" cities in the old Soviet Union used just such a system to heat major buildings. The electricity can now be used more profitably (in ecological terms) to run refrigerators, lights, and motors. This does not make a lot of economic sense because of the miles of pipe that would be needed, but it does make energetic sense.

One of the ways nature avoids waste heat energy is though quantum electronic processes. In these processes light is absorbed and an electron changes its energy with no heat loss. That electron can then move around and do work under the influence of electric fields, or pressure, or chemical gradients. Solar cells are an example. Photosynthesis is another (sort of). But this process can also work in reverse. About 60% of the electricity used in the US is for lighting. Light bulbs generate light by generating heat in a wire. Less than 1% of the power consumed shows up as visible light. Fluorescent lights send a small lightning bolt through a gas which changes the energy of some of the electrons in the gas. These then emit ultraviolet light, no heat, which is then absorbed by the glass shell which changes the energy of the electrons in the glass shell. These electrons then give off visible light with very little heat: You can take hold of a fluorescent bulb while it is on and not get burned. There are now LED devices that give off bright light directly if supplied a small voltage. There are two materials GaN and ZnO from which almost no waste heat is produced. A company called Lumileds is now making very bright GaN lighting that runs on milli-watts instead of 100s of watts of power. The GaN and ZnO devices are however very expensive to produce so you may not see these in the hardware store next Christmas.

The moral of the story is that sustainability means fooling mother nature. If you want to fool mother nature then you must know nature intimately. That means you must study physics and chemistry, and the complex systems of biology and geology, at a level beyond that freshman survey course you hated. It means you must get over the despair of knowing that world is going to end. Then your fooling around (engineering) is likely to be sufficiently intelligent that mother nature won't mind and the inevitable can be put off a little while longer.

A Quaker Perspective to Teaching College Biology in the Context of the Global Sustainability Crisis

by Douglas J. Burks, Wilmington College

When asked to write this article on the teaching of Biology in light of the global sustainability crisis, my first thought was, "How does a molecular biologist, rather than an ecologist, address this question?" In my classes, I am addressing topics such as glycolysis and the metabolism of glucose, how lysosomes work, how acetylation of histones change the expression of genes and other topics that likely would make your eyes glaze over with resulting snoring within a few minutes into my class. I usually don't discuss ecosystems, food chains, pollution, animal behavior, and the other topics in biology that typically deal more directly with environmental and human sustainability issues. However, because of my personal concern for humankind and the sustainability of our planet coming from my religious experience as a Friend, I do address the issue. I find the space to introduce this pressing matter.

As I think about my approach to teaching biology in light of our sustainability crisis, I think of the famous cartoon where Pogo states, "We have met the enemy and they is us." In the Gospel of John, Chapter 8, we find:

> They say unto him, Master, this woman was taken in adultery, in the very act. Now Moses in the law commanded us, that such should be stoned: but what sayest thou? This they said, tempting him, that they might have to accuse him. But Jesus stooped down, and with his finger wrote on the ground, as though he heard them not. So when they continued asking him, he lifted up himself, and said unto them, He that is without sin among you, let him first cast a stone at her. And again he stooped down, and wrote on the ground. And they which heard it, being convicted by their own conscience, went out one by one, beginning at the eldest, even unto the last: and Jesus was left alone, and the woman standing in the midst.[1]

These ideas color every thought and action in my teaching when trying to address our sustainability crisis. I tread softly, for all of us

---

[1] Bible, King James Version, Electronic Text Center, University of Virginia Library. http://etext.virginia.edu/toc/modeng/public/KjvJohn.html.

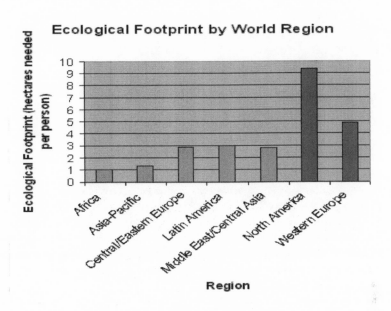

Figure 2.1: Ecological Footprint by World Region. Footprint is represented by the number of hectares needed to sustain one person at that region's standard of living (Kitzes et al., 2008).

in Western society, as illustrated in Figure 2.1, like it or not, carry a heavy burden of responsibility for creating what some are calling the sustainability crisis. Notice I say all of us. Even those who are highly aware and working hard to do little harm to the environment. It will take all of us making hard choices about our lifestyles and ways of living to solve this problem. I am always worried that when I raise the discussion of sustainability with students that I am the one with greatest number of sins and should not be casting the first stone.

I begin my discussion of sustainability with students by saying, "There is so much more I need to change in my life and habits to become a good global citizen." I then explore how that responsibility lies at two levels. Each of us has an individual responsibility to take action and society has an obligation to take action. With biology students, I don't need to go into the science and evidence for the sustainability crisis. I also don't have to discuss the evidence that new and improved technology is sufficient to solve our problems. To solve the sustainability crisis will require a change in consumption patterns and likely a decrease in population level. Their interest in science brings them to college with that knowledge. It is the idea of moral obligation and appropriate response to a moral obligation that they need to explore. This is an area that biologists are not trained to do. This makes dealing with the issue difficult.

I begin the discussion with students by introducing them to the idea of the Ecological Footprint (some students know about this but most don't). The concept of an ecological footprint was developed by Mathis Wackernagel and William Rees in 1996. The ecological footprint "accounts for the flows of energy and matter to and from any defined economy and converts these into the corresponding land/water required from nature to support these flows" (Wackernagel and Rees, 1996). One can calculate how much of the earth's resources one uses. In 2002, the total world population of humans used the equivalent of 1.2 planet Earths, a rate greater than was renewable for future generations. It is estimated that with no change in our consumption patterns that by 2050 humans will need 1.9 equivalents of planet earths to maintain the human population (Kitzes et al., 2008).

Not only can one calculate the ecological footprint for the human species as a whole, but ecological footprint models enable individuals to calculate how much they use of the earth's resources (Chambers et al., 2002). From that data one can determine what to do to lower the impact one has on the environment. It also enables someone to determine how changes in one's behavior will change one's impact. What is good about thinking about ecological footprints is that instead of focusing on what is bad (and there is plenty that is bad) it focuses on helping one to find ways to take positive actions.

There are many sites on the internet that one can go to calculate an ecological footprint and then to find steps to reduce one's footprint.[2] You should take a minute and calculate your own footprint. When I calculate mine, you see why I have trepidation in getting on a soap box and saying to students that they need to change their lifestyles. I consider myself fairly green, but it would take 6.09 planet earths for everyone on our planet to live my lifestyle. I need to decrease my use of resources by 84% to reach a sustainable average, assuming no population increase. When you further break down my footprint you see that, while my overall footprint is slightly lower than the U.S. ecological footprint, my footprint is significantly higher than the national average in the area of food consumption (Figure 2.2). As I found out in the past year, this is due to my love of beef. Current estimates are that the produc-

---

[2]One that I use with students is http://www.myfootprint.org/en/

tion of meat leads to about 5-7 billion tons of greenhouse gases a year, which is about 15%-20% of greenhouse gas production (Fiala, 2007). Beef is the worst of all meats contributing 13 times the greenhouse gases as chicken and about 6 times the amount of pork (Fiala, 2008). A single quarter pound hamburger for lunch leads to about 3.7 pound of CO2 equivalents released into the atmosphere (Fiala, 2007). By eliminating beef from my diet I can significantly decrease my impact on the environment. I have been decreasing my consumption of beef, but I doubt if I have the strength to cut it completely out.

In my discussion with students, I do discuss how I have decreased meat consumption and where I have made changes in other areas of my life. I also talk about the need to be thoughtful and that to become sustainable, it does mean making changes and sometimes making sacrifice. I encourage them to look at ways they too can make thoughtful changes. In the end, though, I also face that hard truth that sustainability is achievable only if all of us take action, for there is no easy (or even hard) technological fix that will make the problem go away. Sustainability is only possible if everyone changes their consumption patterns. We have no guarantee that this will happen. Finally, I argue that it is one of the most important moral issues facing each and everyone one of us in the world today. We need to reach out and become activists who are committed to convincing others to also take action.

I do encourage everyone to look at their ecological footprints. It is a starting point for rational personal change. Personal change is the one thing each of us has control over and something each of us can do. We need to reach out and get others and other nations to also act. In asking students to consider personal action, I in humility say that I also am working hard to change and that change is not easy.

In this short essay, I have asked you to consider three things. First, I asked you to consider and accept that our sustainability crisis will only be solved by dramatic changes in lifestyle of those who live in the Western world. Technology will play a part, but there is no magical "technological fix." Fixing our environment can only come from consuming less and looking at population control. Second, I analyzed my own impact on the environment by measuring my ecological footprint. In looking at my footprint, I see that I need to decrease my consumption of resources 6-fold to live sustainably. This is why I approach the topic with trepidation in teaching my students. It is difficult to make the argument to others that they need to sacrifice and dramatically change their lifestyles when you know that it is a message that you need to act on. Third, I gave

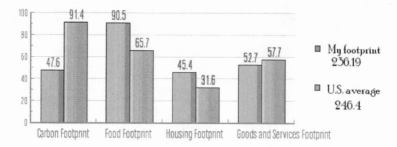

Figure 2.2: My footprint in global acres by consumption category.
http://www.myfootprint.org/en

you, the reader, some tools to analyze the impact that you have on the environment, so that you can make better decisions and more effectively take action. I also gave you some information on how food choices can make a real difference. I hope that this essay has given you some food for thought. Creating a sustainable world is a challenge that is not going away. We are at a historical crossroads for our species.

Chambers, N., Simmons, C., and Wackernagel, M. (2002). *Sharing Nature's Interest: Ecological Footprints as an Indicator of Sustainability*. Earth Scan Publications. London, England.

Fiala, N. (2007). Meeting the demand: An estimation of potential future greenhouse emissions from meat production. *Ecological Economics*, 65:412–419.

Fiala, N. (2008). How meat contributes to global warming. *Scientific American*, 300:72–75.

Kitzes, J., Wackernagel, M., Loh, J., Peller, A., Goldfinger, S., Cheng, D., and Tea, K. (2008). Shrink and share: humanity's present and future ecological footprint. *Phil. Trans. Soc. B*, 363:467–475.

Wackernagel, M. and Rees, W. (1996). *Our Ecological Footprint: Reducing Human Impact on Earth*. New Society Publishers. Gabriola Island, BC.

My Journey to Advocating For Education for Sustainable Development

by William Upholt, University of Connecticut

Before beginning to describe my journey I would like to introduce the ideas of sustainable development and education for sustainable development as understood by the UN and the academic community working in this area. Concerns about "Sustainable Development" arose in the 1980s when it became clearly recognized that there was a contradiction between the aspirations of developing countries to a standard of living similar to that of developed countries, on the one hand, and the increasing population and dwindling available natural resources of the planet. In its 1987 report *Our Common Future* the Brundtland Commission defined sustainable development as development that "meets the needs of the present without compromising the ability of future generations to meet their own need" (Brundtland Commission, 1987). The Earth Charter has also been an important document in further delineating of the concept of sustainable development.

Out of this world-wide consultation and other discussions has come the idea that sustainability is not just about the environment but is intimately interconnected with economic and social justice issues. Several visual aids are frequently used to present these ideas. One is an image of three overlapping circles representing environmental integrity, economic viability, and a just society. Only when the three concerns are balanced and fully interconnected can there be sustainability. Another model uses three concentric circles: 1) the Earth or our environment without which there would be no people or life; 2) human societies that have evolved with time as the population on Earth has grown; and 3) the global economic systems by which trade and business are conducted, systems that been formulated, in part, by human thought.

Education for sustainable development is defined by the UN as "learning to: respect, value and preserve the achievements of the past; appreciate the wonders and the peoples of the Earth; live in a world where all people have sufficient food for a healthy and productive life; assess, care for and restore the state of our Planet; create and enjoy a better, safer, more just world; and be caring citizens who exercise their rights and responsibilities locally, nationally and globally."[1]

---

[1] http://portal.unesco.org/education/en/ev.php-URL_ID=27279&URL_DO=DO_TOPIC&URL_SECTION=201.html

My parents have been an important influence in the development of my concerns for sustainability. They always emphasized our responsibility to share our well being with others less fortunate, appreciation of the Earth (through hiking and camping) and relationships between community and the earth through experiences such as picking apples and then going to a cooperative cannery to make applesauce for our family's use.

My first recollection of actively thinking about environmental issues occurred while my wife and I were living in Chicago in Hyde Park in the early 1980s. Ken Dunn, a graduate student in philosophy at the University of Chicago decided that he couldn't neglect the environmental, social, and economic concerns surrounding him and he founded a community-based nonprofit recycling program employing local youth to go through the neighborhood with an old VW bus picking up newspapers and other recyclable materials left out by the residents. The program is still directed by Dunn nearly 30 years later, and is devoted to the economic and educational revitalization of Chicago neighborhoods through recycling, urban gardening, composting, and other programs that reclaim and reuse resources.[2]

Following our move from Chicago to West Hartford, CT in 1985 we became Quakers and, through New England Yearly Meeting, I became aware of the national Friends Committee in Unity with Nature[3] and the corresponding committee of New England Yearly Meeting. My wife, Mary Lee Morrison, and I were fortunate to be able to attend a very thought-provoking workshop sponsored by the New England Yearly Meeting Committee at Farm and Wilderness Camp in Vermont with Marshall Massey as featured speaker. Around the same time I organized my first formal sustainability education work (although I was not yet aware of the term "education for sustainable development"), a spring session of Hartford Monthly Meeting's First Day School using the original Friends in Unity with Nature "Earthcare for Children" curriculum.

Subsequently, through New England Yearly Meeting I learned of the Earth Charter and became involved in some local Earth Charter events. I led programs about the Earth Charter at a local interfaith group called Earth Prayers and led a workshop at New England Yearly Meeting on aligning the Earth Charter with Quaker queries and about using it as a guide to teach about sustainability. In the summer of 2006 I accompanied Mary Lee to the 2006

---

[2] http://www.resourcecenterchicago.org/index.html

[3] currently named Quaker Earthcare Witness and whose website is: http://www.quakerearthcare.org/

International Institute on Peace Education (IIPE) on the subject "Towards a Planetary Ethic: Shared and Individual Responsibility" at the UN University for Peace (UPEACE) in Costa Rica. During our stay in Costa Rica, I became aware of the concept of "education for sustainable development" or ESD. While Mary Lee participated in the Institute, I volunteered at the Earth Charter Center for Education for Sustainable Development. There I learned about the UN Decade for Education for Sustainable Development (2005-2014) and I was also able to attend some of the IIPE workshops about the Earth Charter and its use in education. Miriam Vilela, Director of the Center, graciously accepted my offer of assistance and set me to work in the UPEACE library doing a web search to collect information about degree programs in EDS for a database.This web searching provided me with an ideal opportunity to begin to learn about the Decade and the importance of ESD.

Upon my return to home in Connecticut, I became interested in finding out more about ESD and the response to the Decade around the world, in the US and locally in Connecticut. I found that although the UN and governments of many other countries have introduced ESD programs, there has been almost no participation on the part of the US government in this movement. I did learn about the US Partnership for Education for Sustainable Development, a loosely organized NGO composed of individuals and organizations in the US concerned about ESD and working in a variety of focus areas including K-12 education, higher education, business, religion, and other sectors. In my searching for further information about education for sustainability I discovered the PhD thesis of Dr. Stephen Sterling from the University of Bath, "Whole Systems Thinking as a Basis for Paradigm Change in Education: Explorations in the Context of Sustainability", and subsequently his book *Sustainable Education* (Sterling, 2001). After reading parts of Dr. Sterling's thesis I arranged a meeting with Donn Weinholtz, a member of my Monthly Meeting and previously dean of the College of Education, Nursing and Health Professions of the University of Hartford (and editor of QHE) and explained to him my understanding of Dr. Sterling's writings and the importance of a systematic approach to educating for sustainability. Donn was quite interested in the idea and promised to look for allies with whom I might align my efforts.

Through my study of sustainability education, I became convinced that working for legislative changes, although very important, was probably insufficient to effect the changes needed to move toward a more sustainable world, which include a new consciousness and changes in values on the part of all. I also became convinced that education, particularly K-12 education, was likely the most effective way to move toward these changes. Although all types of educational approaches are important and should be pursued, K-12 education has the advantage that it has the potential to reach all of our future citizens, irrespective of their economic, cultural status or the level of education they complete. It also reaches broader aspects of our society through their parents and teachers. To follow up on this approach I began trying to identify other individuals and groups in Connecticut that might be interested in or involved in some aspect of sustainability education. While I found that there were many people concerned about global climate change and educating specifically for behavioral change around energy use and carbon emissions,there were few who were very knowledgeable about concerns about education for sustainable development. The most developed sector was higher education as several universities in Connecticut had well developed sustainability or environmental policy offices.

Later, Donn contacted me and said that the Connecticut Alliance of Concerned Educators (CACE) that had been formed in response to the No Child Left Behind Act was interested in organizing their next annual conference around the topic of sustainability education. We learned of a source of funds for planning "Community Conversations" around educational issues and Jim Malley, a professor at Central Connecticut State University and one of CACE's cofounders, took the lead in putting together a successful application for a community conversation on the topic "Education for Global Sustainability: How do we prepare our children for their roles in creating a future with a healthy environment, a strong economy, and a just society." The community conversation brought together a diverse group of stakeholders and was very successful in engaging the participants to identify their perceptions of the limitations of the present educational system and to come up with alternative approaches that they felt would benefit the students. Following the conversation, we consolidated the resulting ideas and concerns into four areas: 1) concerns of urban and low income areas, 2) advocacy, 3) educational or curricular approaches, and 4) community approaches. We invited participants from the original conversation back to a follow-up meeting to design specific plans or projects for the four areas.

Several members of the board of the Connecticut Outdoor and Environmental Educators Association (COEEA) attended the community conversation and follow-up meetings. They noted that there was substantial overlap between their concerns and ours and became actively involved in our efforts. Subsequently, combining areas 2 and 3, we formed the Connecticut Partnership for Sustainability Education (CTPSE). Our first effort at implementing our combined interests was the presentation of a panel/workshop discussion at the annual COEEA conference in March 2008. Although the workshop/panel was well-attended by an enthusiastic audience, members of the audience noted that our discussion appeared to repeat many years of similar discussions but that there had been little progress in implementing sustainability education.

In late 2008 our group received official status from the state of CT as an organization and formed a board of about 12 individuals including individuals retired from the corporate world, teachers in K-12 and higher education, and state employees from the Department of Education and the Treasurers Office. Following the 2008 conference, COEEA invited CTPSE to work with them in planning COEEA's 2009 conference on the theme "sustainability education for the 21st century." A subset of CTPSE members began actively working with COEEA on the planning committee for the conference and played a major role in identifying and inviting the keynote speaker, Debra Rowe, President of the US Partnership for Sustainability Education as well as designing a set of five 'mini-panels' on various subjects and inviting individuals as panelists, many from outside of COEEA with particularly relevant experiences pertinent to sustainability education, but not necessarily identified as "sustainability education." We also made a particular effort to advertise the conference widely among individuals involved in education, but not necessarily with a clear previous involvement in sustainability education. We planned a "VIP" session following the keynote and invited a number of individuals with policy making responsibilities to meet with Debra Rowe following her keynote. These included a number of individuals from Central Connecticut State University, the institution hosting our conference. We were quite successful in attracting a diverse group of participants from five Northeastern states that, in addition to K-12 teachers and environmental educations, included principals, heads of boards of education, heads of private schools, faculty, students and staff from higher education, particularly those in teacher education.

Now that our "big event" is past we are working to develop our organization (web site, membership, conference follow up and year goals). Directions we are considering include: working with a "green academy" in a local urban high school to help them expand their present teaching of green technology by introducing sustainability into their curriculum; working to increase awareness of sustainability education among policymakers, including members of the Education Committee of the State Legislature and individuals working for the State Department of Education; and working with COEEA as they develop a statewide environmental literacy plan. We hope that our recent conference will increase the number of individuals interested in actively working toward our vision of "a future Connecticut where everyone has the skills, perspectives, and values that guide and motivate them to seek sustainable liveli-hoods, participate in a just and democratic society, and live in an environmentally sustainable manner."

Brundtland Commission (1987). *Our Common Future.* World Com-mission on Environment and Development, Oxford University Press.

Sterling, S. (2001). *Sustainable Education.* Green Books.

Shifting to Abundance: Reflections on Environmental Education

by Janet Gray, The College of New Jersey

Spring break 2011: in my Ecofeminism course, our explorations of epistemology have begun to compete with *doing*. For this third round through the course, I've redone it to address my lingering disorientation about conflicts among different schools of ecological thought, and I'm learning a lot. The group is the biggest yet: 28 students at all levels of their college careers, with majors in all seven schools on our campus. And they're fired up. Before the break, charged with brainstorming an "eco-adventure," they sketched a plan for raising support for the campus garden. We're heading into readings on science and spirituality, and committees need forming, missions need defining, strategies need to be put into action.

FAHE's announcement of the theme for its 2009 conference, *Educating for Abundance*, came as I was first preparing to teach this course and, at the same time, reading Parker Palmer.[1] This convergence prompted me to consider "abundance" as a framework for reflecting on what the course needed to do. "Abundance" fittingly describes the trove of materials one faces in designing such a course; vast in scope and varied in perspectives, ecofeminism has the "grace of great things" that Palmer names in *The Courage to Teach* (Palmer, 1999). "Abundance" also thematically links Palmer's writing with ecofeminist thought: both urgently call for a radical change in how we organize and act on our knowledge of the world–a shift to a conception of ourselves as part of a vast fullness, a wider sufficiency.

Ecofeminism offers an interdisciplinary lens on the world, building on the precept that the abuse of nature is linked to social oppressions based on categories of othering, including gender, race, and class. The messy, multidimensional bigness of ecofeminism makes it a dynamic resource for merging critical thinking with engaged citizenship. The public college where I teach, The College of New Jersey (TCNJ), centralizes preparation for community leadership in its mission and pursues institutional imperatives to address environmental issues with both a local and a global scope. The College thus cultivates *abundance* in the sense of a wider interconnectedness. Yet to get anything done here, one must confront lacks: of funds, people, time, space, imagination–scarcities that become more

---

[1] http://www.couragerenewal.org/parker

31

daunting as state funds for higher education shrink. Whatever the college's priorities, we are beholden to the fractured priorities of our political and economic context. And, as Palmer points out, educational institutions are rooted in paradigms that produce abundance for some at the expense of scarcity for others: paradigms of social inequality and human domination over nature. If we do not intentionally resist those paradigms, we reproduce them.

At the FAHE conference, Carole Spencer, the plenary speaker, focused our attention on the contemplative practice of "the abundant life," drawing on Paul's epistles. My contact at FAHE had urged me to consider this scriptural meaning of the conference's theme as I prepared a session. I found, however, that in English translations of Jesus' teachings, variants on "abundance" most often appear in the context of social critique, referring to negative excesses: the quantity of evil that pours from the mouths of "vipers" (Matthew 12:34); the surplus gained by those who have as the have-nots are deprived (13:12); the excess from which the wealthy skim off their charity (12:44); or the material goods that do not constitute a man's life (Luke 12:15). Only in the Gospel of John does "abundance" refer to a state of grace.

In *The Promise of Paradox*, Palmer (2008) offers a way of understanding connections between these divergent scriptural meanings. Today's anxieties about the division between "haves" and "have-nots" and diminishing natural resources, he writes, have their counterpart in a state of spiritual awareness he characterizes as "the life-destroying habits of scarcity" (94-95). When we tie our sense of the good life to material consumption, fears about not having enough in the future drive the "haves" to grab and hoard more than we need–behavior that worsens the deprivation of the "have-nots." Why do we buy into the scarcity paradigm? Blaming "the greed of a few," Palmer thinks, is too easy. Our compliance reflects a failed strategy in our search for meaning: defining ourselves through possessions, only leading to more anxiety and grasping. We need to rid ourselves of the false notion of abundance that underlies this failure. True abundance, he writes, comes "to those who are willing to share apparent scarcity in a way that creates more than enough."

Palmer's discussion dovetails with detailed analysis by ecofeminist writers who argue that modernity *produced* the specter of scarcity by redefining abundance as the product of technology. The paradigm of the "good life" envisioned by the Western myth of progress depends on denying the evidence everywhere that it is actually eroding the quality of life through environmental degradation. Further, colonization built this model of abundance, draining resources and devaluing diverse worldviews, ways, and knowledge. Its continuation depends upon the existence of an exploitable elsewhere where economic, social, and environmental costs can be shifted out of the beneficiaries' sight (e.g. Diamond (1994, p. 116)).

The first two semesters I taught Ecofeminism were adventures through varied inflections of abundance and scarcity: for one class wonder, collaboration, and self-investment, and for the other, bafflement, resistance, and scattered epiphanies. The idea of starting a garden on campus originated with the Bonner Center,[2] which coordinates community engaged learning on our campus. With coaching from the Bonner staff, the nineteen students in the spring 2009 class took on the task of envisioning a garden that would be a resource for schools and community organizations in our area, as well as for TCNJ courses across the disciplines. The task required the students to find their place in a change process much larger than themselves; they struggled to take ownership of a project that would outspan their college careers. In teams, they networked and researched and left as their legacy a wiki of best practices, lesson plans, and contacts. The semester ended in elation as they shared their vision at a gathering of faculty, staff, and students.

A year later, the garden project posed new difficulties for the twelve students the Ecofeminism class. Others had created the vision of the garden, but there was still no garden. My efforts to persuade the students to think of the garden as a potential space of abundance met with tense faces. Instead of feeling like partners in a larger process, the students felt used; the Bonner Center was demanding their scarce resources, time and thought. I changed the assignment, inviting the students to find their own hands-on ways of engaging with the environment. And for most, those smaller experiences were transformative. That summer, Bonner students planted and tended a small demonstration garden and took the produce to the Trenton Area Soup Kitchen. It was a start at growing into the vision, one that my current students have embraced.

With the new syllabus, I have benefited from the current students' insights into ecofeminism's intersections with two prominent strains of environmental thought, deep ecology and social ecology. Deep ecology removes humans from the center of the universe, insisting on the oneness of all of life. For social ecologists, who focus on how environmental abuse causes and results from social injustice, the contemplative orientation of deep ecology offers privileged individuals the lofty experience of dissolving into a universal whole, but leads to environmental strategies that are callous to human suf-

---

[2]http://bonner.pages.tcnj.edu/about/

fering. Deep ecologists charge social ecologists with anthropocentrism.[3] Both critiques seem to me partially just.

Great things, Palmer writes, demand diverse viewpoints because of their "manifold mysteries"; their vastness calls on us to embrace ambiguity; they generate creative conflict that challenges our narrowness; they invoke our honesty to do justice to their truth; they become visible only to our humility; they empower us for liberation (Palmer, 1999, p. 107). The "grace of great things" thus offers an orientation toward abundance much like ecological thinking: while undermining the certainties that underwrite paradigms of dominance, it offers a framework for responding to difference and community and taking responsibility for the implications of our knowledge (Code, 2006, p. 21, 24).

Considering environmental studies in light of abundance responds to my sense that when I teach deeply, with courage, I'm tapping into my lived experience of Friends' testimonies. My experiences tell me that our religious thought can serve us as critical leverage–a tool for asking and teaching questions that challenge exploitive paradigms. Environmental studies can address the need to understand and intervene in systemic factors that hold destructive paradigms in place. Wonder and reverence may drive us to seek healing for our alienation from nature, but individual contemplative practice is no shortcut to paradigm change. And shifting to abundance is not a single cognitive or spiritual act that we can undertake once and for all; we must *do*, and choose our doing based upon cultivating in communities a shared critical understanding of the ways that *scarcity* governs our inner and outer worlds. However lofty the idea of abundance, it comes into being in the immanent, everyday structures of our lives.

---

[3] Our readings included selections on deep ecology and social ecology in Merchant (2008); Warren (1994, 1997).

Code, L. (2006). *Ecological Thinking: The Politics of Epistemic Location.* Oxford University Press.

Diamond, I. (1994). *Fertile Ground: Women, Earth and the Limits of Control.* Beacon, Boston, MA.

Merchant, C., editor (2008). *Ecology.* Humanity Books.

Palmer, P. (1999). *The Courage to Teach: Exploring the Inner Landscape of a Teachers Life.* Jossey-Bass, San Francisco.

Palmer, P. (2008). *The Promise of Paradox: A Celebration of Contradictions in the Christian Life.* Jossey-Bass, San Francisco.

Warren, K., editor (1994). *Ecological Feminism.* Routledge.

Warren, K., editor (1997). *Ecofeminism: Women, Culture, Nature.* Indiana University Press.

Dreaming Into the Rain Forest: Toward a Living Relationship with Mother Earth

by Stephen Potthoff, Wilmington College

Last summer during the 2012 FAHE meeting held at Wilmington College (Ohio), I had the honor of sharing a collection of dreams gifted to me by a class of tropical ecology students whom I accompanied on a 2011 two week research trip to Costa Rica. My reflections on these dreams and their evolving impact on me feature prominently in a book on dreams and ecospirituality I began writing last year while on sabbatical as the Cadbury Scholar at Pendle Hill. As I continue my work, I strive to include the voices of the many dreamers who have shared their dream wisdom with me. I am grateful to FAHE, Wilmington College, Pendle Hill, and my students for the inspiration they provide as I follow a deep leading to promote healing by helping my fellow human beings (re)connect in a positive, balanced, and harmonious relationship with the earth and living world.

Inspiration for this dream project sprang from an article[4] I read about conservation biologists working to preserve the Farallon island ecosystem off the California coast who reported vivid and disturbing dreams reflecting their growing concern over the demise of this singularly beautiful environment (Jones, 2010). Sitting in with my students on the pre-trip tropical ecology lectures offered by my colleague in the Biology department, I began to wonder how the global ecological crisis we were all learning about might manifest through dreams in the context of our own upcoming encounter with some of the most diverse and threatened tropical ecosystems on the planet. I also considered, to paraphrase ecotheologian Thomas Berry in *The Great Work*, how encountering Costa Rica's extraordinarily diverse and often formidable tropical environments might activate the inner archetypal dream world of my student colleagues (Berry, 1999, pp. 171-172;200), most of whom had never set foot in a tropical forest.

Volunteering to serve as the dream keeper for the trip, I invited anyone in our group who so desired to record in a community dream journal any dreams they experienced before, during, and after our tropical research adventure. Our pre-trip class review of basic dream recall enhancement techniques, combined with the early mornings and disrupted sleep schedules yielded a rich crop of dreams from students and faculty alike. Upon return I transcribed

---

[4]http://www.sfgate.com/bayarea/article/
Farallones-biologists-record-similar-dreams-3179940.php

each participant's dreams, resending them to each with a short list of questions to encourage further reflection: What was your most meaningful or significant dream? If any of your dreams featured natural imagery, or violent, disturbing elements, what feelings do you remember? What have you learned about your relationship to the natural world on this trip, and what role, if any, did dream journaling play in this process?

Some of the most common dreams students reported seemed to reveal an inner process of familiarization and adjustment to an exotically new, sometimes frightening and potentially dangerous natural and cultural environment. One student (K.) who dreamed of killing an assassin version of herself reflected: "My dreams are almost always violent, but my dreams in Costa Rica were scarier than normal. I think this is because I am terrified of insects, and had to deal with this fear on a regular basis while in Costa Rica. In my assassin dream, I think the assassins represent fear, and after I conquered my fear, I was free." From my own ecospiritual perspective, the fear K. expressed–and conquered–in her dream mirrors not only the pronounced state of disconnection many human beings in the modern world experience in relation to the natural world, but also holds out the hope that we can transcend that fear as the first step toward entering a more authentic relationship with the ecosystems that sustain and give us life. K. not only participated courageously in our close studies of fiercely protective acacia ants, but also served as our main translator on the trip, and thought nothing of placing over her shoulders a burrowing python passed around for us to hold at the La Selva dry tropical forest research station.

The obvious courage K. discovered and embraced through the dream process manifests in her appearance as the superhero Spiderman in the dream of another student I'll call J., who reported: "After holding the burrowing python for quite some time, somehow I drop it! It takes off to the corner of the mess hall at La Selva and slithers up the downspout. I remember thinking, 'What will I do now?' Then, at the blink of an eye, super-spider K. comes in like a flash and climbs the downspout like Spiderman and rescues the snake from the roof." Afterwards J. reflects that "snakes were on my mind just about every day and on every hike," but goes on to conclude that his Spiderman dream was really more about the heroism K. showed as our main translator: "My dream centered around a problem with a snake that K. solved by recapturing the snake and saving the day. K. was constantly saving the day during the trip with her exceptional Spanish speaking skills. I caught myself using her to communicate the entire trip, and it's not surprising that me using her as a crutch in my dream popped up." From the perspective of Berry (1999, pp. 171-172), K. and J. were tapping into the self-renewing, self-perpetuating energy of the hero archetype in a process that, both on a social and on a psycho-spiritual level, gave others in our group the courage to forge ahead with their own hero's journey into a new and unfamiliar land.

Archetypal animals like the snake and the frog (Narby, 1998) showed up in the dreams of another student I'll call M.: "I was doing flip turns in a really big pool. The pool was really huge. There was a snake and a frog at the bottom of the pool. I didn't think they were real until they came up and bit me. They sucked my blood on my arm and left a hickey...." Reflecting on this dream, M. emphasizes the fear she remembered: "They bit me and sucked my blood, so I was scared of them." Like her fellow students, M. seems to have experienced significant personal growth as a result of her hero's journey to Costa Rica, discovering inner resources that helped her cope with homesickness and her up close encounter with the tropics. Regarding the most valuable thing she learned about herself and her relationship to the natural world, she concluded: "I have a big appreciation for other cultures. I have grown because I have never been that far away from my family and friends and boyfriend for that long of a time, without being able to speak or see them. I also really got in touch with my nature side, yes even including spiders and snakes!"

From a Jungian archetypal perspective (Taylor, 1998), the snake is associated with birth and the passage to adulthood (as in the garden of Eden story), while the frog (as in the story of the Frog and the Prince) is associated particularly with transformation following descent into the underworld (the well from which the frog retrieves the princess's lost bauble in exchange for a kiss). M.'s own descent into the waters of the unconscious brought her closer to her "nature side", and reflects in a personal way M.'s transformed relationships to her loved ones and to the natural world.

I conclude with a final dream from a student (H.), who recorded the following before our trip: "I dreamed that my mom and I were in Costa Rica on the beach and we saw a leatherback turtle right at our feet. I hurried to get a camera as the turtle ran from us into the ocean. Then it joined five other leatherbacks in the water. I walked along the beach taking their pictures because they stayed very close to where I was." H. identified this as her most significant dream "because my mind was making everything seem more 'foreign' than it really was." Throughout our trip, H. expressed profound excitement and curiosity about the many life forms she encountered; her beautiful dream embodies the spirited wonder that students of any age can experience in direct, close encounters with the natural world. Drawing once again on the perspective of Berry (1988), whose thinking was shaped profoundly by Native American and other indigenous spiritual traditions, I cannot help but see reflected here in H's dream not only the Great Mother, but also Turtle Island, Mother Earth who gives all of us life.

This small selection of student dreams and subsequent reflections illustrates, in Thomas Berry's framework, some of the many ways we as human beings, through spontaneous dream experience, tap into archetypal psychic energies which can transform us and our relationship to the natural, living world. I thank these students and all those who have inspired me to continue my work as a teacher and healer in the classroom and beyond.

Berry, T. (1988). *The Dream of the Earth.* Sierra Club Books, San Francisco.

Berry, T. (1999). *The Great Work.* Bell Tower, New York.

Jones, C. (2010). Farallones biologists record similar dreams. *San Francisco Chronicle.*

Narby, J. (1998). *The Cosmic Serpent: DNA and the Origins of Knowledge.* Jeremy P. Tarcher/Putnam, New York, NY.

Taylor, J. (1998). *The Living Labyrinth: Exploring Universal Themes in Myths, Dreams and the Symbolism of Waking Life.* Paulist Press, Mahwah, NJ.

Chapter 3

Lessons from Quaker History

The over three-and-a-half centuries of Friends' history is a frequent source of orientation and inspiration for Quakers today, and this is at least as true for Friends in education as it is for others. The appeal to this tradition is not unproblematic; as a "progressivist tradition," one whose internal trajectory leads beyond itself (in the idea of "continuing revelation"), the authority of the Friends tradition for Friends is not assured, and in principle cannot be, even when we inevitably ground ourselves in it. In the following articles, authors tap this history, in a variety of ways, both in order to better understand it, and for what lessons it might provide us with today.

Gregory Barnes opens this section with an historical review of Quaker environmental concern, noting that, with a few limited exceptions, Quakers were not prescient in this area of social concern as they are regarded to have been in several others. According to Barnes in "Toward a Green History of American Quakerism," Friends' current involvement and leadership in the environmental movement began only when it did for others, namely, in the middle-to-late twentieth century.

In "Mary Mendenhall Hobbs and Allen Jay: Lessons for the Abundant Life Today," Max Carter reviews the lives of these two venerable late nineteenth-early twentieth Century Quaker figures who each did much to re-build the community of Friends in the south after the civil war, and to build up Friends elsewhere. Allen Jay's work as a church, school, and college builder, Quaker minister and fundraiser, is recounted against the background of Jay's reflections on, and struggles with, having been raised a Quietist

Friend but having become a Gurneyite evangelical, and his lament at the splits this division within Friends produced. Mary Mendenhall Hobbs was, like Jay, a confirmed Gurneyite, but one who also respected the "traditionalist ways" of her Quaker father. The wife and partner of the President of Guilford College, Hobbs had a deep concern for the education of women in the poor, post-war south, setting up a cooperative housing opportunity for women at Guilford (the building still bears her name) and helping to open the first public college for women in North Carolina. She participated in numerous societies devoted to social concerns, was a progressive in matters of eduction and thought, and was committed to inquiry over settled truth. Max Carter employs these histories to remind us of the importance of: cooperation within the community of Friends; the need for "tenderness" in adopting new ways that nevertheless value and respect the tradition; and, the need for solid and committed, local Quaker leaders.

"Woolman and Kelly: Faithful Lives" is a report on two presentations made by Mike Heller and Deborah Shaw, one a retreat at The Woodbrooke Quaker Study Centre in England, and a second, shorter one at the annual FAHE conference. On both occasions quotations from John Woolman and Thomas Kelly, especially addressing moments of struggle or crises, were employed to lead participants into personal explorations of the questions: How can we learn from the lives of these two inspirational Quaker figures to engage with the spirit in our own lives?; and, What does it mean to live a faithful life?

The consideration of Thomas Kelly is extended in the next essay, as Diane Reynolds explores parallels in the faith journeys of this Quaker sage and the famous, contemporaneous German theologian Dietrich Bonhoeffer in her "Thomas Kelly, Dietrich Bonhoeffer and the Search for Community." Diane Reynolds highlights the attraction that each of these thinkers demonstrated for the "Orient" as an anecdote for the crumbling "Occident," how each, ironically, "found the depth of faith they were seeking" in their experiences of the Nazi horror, and how each devoted himself to the development of an intimate, quasi-monastic pedagogical circle of students in response to his longings and aspirations. Reynolds closes by challenging us to think the implications of this for our models of Quaker higher education.

Laura S. Foote, in her "Women's Speaking Justified: Quaker Women in the Public Sphere," closes this section by briefly tracing the history of the perception of woman in Greek and Roman cultures, and the consequential demand that women be silent, through religious traditions, down into the Enlightenment culture of the nineteenth Century, to today. In light of this long and deep prohibition against women's speaking publicly, she argues that women who wished to speak had to develop apologetic strategies to justify themselves, of which she focuses upon two: bolstering (the appeal to accepted authorities who did approve of women's speaking) and transcendence (the appeal to a higher authority, often God, that trumped the lower authorities, often men, who prohibited such speaking). Laura Foote presents the ways in which certain key women Quaker figures–Margaret Fell, and the sisters Sarah and Angelina Grimke–made effective use of such strategies in their *apologia* for women's speech, and offers these as inspirational examples for women's speaking today.

Toward a Green History of American Quakerism

by Gregory A. Barnes

Nearly a century ago, Baltimore Yearly Meeting (Women's) began an epistle to its counterparts in Philadelphia Yearly Meeting
as follows:

> Friends have so frequently been in the front in some of
> the reforms in our national life that it is most grati-
> fying to find them still alive to the needs of the hours,
> with willing hearts ready to make sacrifices for the great
> moral uplift so much needed in many avenues of life.
>
> - Collected in Philadelphia Yearly Meeting (Women's
> Branch), Proceedings, 1915

Clearly, American Quakers have long taken pride in their moral
clairvoyance. With this tradition in mind, I was led to wonder
whether we have been similarly prescient about the need to preserve the environment. I decided to sample records from our forebears' earliest days in Philadelphia and to review the Quaker role
in the larger American environmental movement during succeeding
years. William Penn, at least, showed a striking environmental consciousness. He was determined to establish a green country town,
believing that country living surpassed life in the city: "Creation,"
he once wrote, "provides a direct link to its source. Understanding
and cultivating it... is the best thing we can be about" (Penn, 2003,
p. 80). His original plans for Philadelphia effectively called for a
line of contiguous arboreta stretching up the Delaware River. The
First Purchasers would be entitled to some 800 feet of river frontage,
their property to include gardens, orchards, and fields (Soderlund,
1983, p. 82).

We should not ascribe modern motives to Penn's thinking: he
saw green space as protection against plague and fire. Still, in
organizing the much reduced area he was ultimately able to claim–
1200 acres between the Delaware and Schuylkill Rivers–he showed
himself both green and orderly. He chose a grid plan, at the time
a new idea for London following its fire of 1666, and called the
north-south streets by numbers. He rejected the east-west street
names–those of settlers–chosen by his surveyor, and called them
after plants instead. The northernmost of the early streets were
named Vine and Sassafras, the southernmost Cedar. Surely only a
true environmentalist would call a street Sassafras.

His contemporaries in the Society of Friends, however–judging
from the early minutes of Philadelphia Yearly Meeting–saw nature

as little more than a source of metaphor: "wilderness" meant moral decline and "storm" a crisis. Corporate texts ignored the beauty of green, fertile, well-watered eastern America. One would not expect the colonists to rail against pollution of the air or streams, but why no references to plowing a straight furrow or tending one's garden or husbanding animals efficiently.

Throughout the 18th century, Quakers seemed to pay little attention to nature as a part of the divine order, with Woolman the occasional exception.[1] To be sure, men like the Bartrams, Humphrey Marshall, and later, William Darlington showed a strong interest in botany. Still, Benfey argues that these men made the best of limited choices: "The prevailing judgment that music, art, and drama were wicked... and unworthy of the time and attention of the God-centered man, left little room" for study of matters other than science (Benfey, 1980, p. 11).

Among Quaker institutions, perhaps only Friends Hospital (est. 1813 in Philadelphia) seemed ahead of its time environmentally, with its design that maximized the circulation of fresh air and light for the benefit of its mental patients. Otherwise, wherever we sense a Quaker awakening in conservation or environmental matters in the 18th and 19th centuries, we tend to find compelling variant explanations. A prominent land-grant college (Cornell) was founded by a Quaker, for example, but most were not. Haverford and Swarthmore developed oasis-like campuses but the model was pioneered elsewhere and the early curricula showed little emphasis on botany; even the famous arboreta of these two institutions are 20th-century phenomena. The national park system, inaugurated with Yellowstone, in 1872 and the Sierra Club (est. 1892) came into being without apparent Quaker leadership. Contemporaneous yearly meeting Books of Discipline continued to cast aspersions on outdoor activities, such as games and horse-racing.

Change began about 1915; witness the words in this epistle from Ohio Yearly Meeting:

> The story of loyalty to conviction, which brought the pioneers to the wilderness land, we believe, can never be adequately told.
>
> They came to the majestic hills and noble forests of the then Great Northwest Territory to establish the Faith of the Society of Friends, where they, their descendents

---

[1]See in particular his "Conversations on the Harmony of Mankind."

[sic] and others, might find abundant spaces for homes
. . . .[2]

By 1925 PYM (though not many other yearly meetings at that time) recanted its opposition to outdoor activities.

> The scope of those recreations which the meeting could fully sanction may have been in some respects too restricted...

> We therefore earnestly commend to our members that they choose such recreations as out-door sports and games from which the elements of chance and stakes are absent, nature study and woodcraft, gardening...(PYM, 1925, pp. 99-100)

Other meetings followed suit in the next quarter-century.

Environmental consciousness in the larger U.S. society is sometimes dated to the 1954 Scott/Helen Nearing book, *Living the Good Life* (Nearing and Nearing, 1954). But Quakers were catching up. The next year, Howard Brinton wrote:

> As people, we are obliged to cherish the earth and to protect all its resources in a spirit of humble stewardship, committed to the right sharing of these resources among people everywhere. Query: How do we exercise our respect for the balance of nature? Are we careful to avoid poisoning the land, air, and sea and to use the world's resources with care and consideration for future generations and with respect for all life? (Brinton, 1955, p. 90)

In the 1960s, Quakers began staking out an environmental position along with their enlightened compatriots. Right Sharing of World's Resources dates its beginnings to a conference at Guilford College in 1967. Greenpeace (1972) had a Quaker founder, although Quakers later withdrew out of concern for the organization's methods. In 1972, PYM's *Faith and Practice* made a straightforward environmental declaration: "Am I clear that I am the steward, not the owner of property in my care? Do I simplify my needs, making choices that balance self-sufficiency (to avoid unnecessary dependence on others) and fair sharing of resources?" (PYM, 1972, pp. 213-214)

---

[2]Ohio Yearly Meeting to Philadelphia Yearly Meeting of Friends, 1915.

To answer my research question, then: No, Quakers (excluding Penn) were not particularly prescient in environmental consciousness. But given that environmentalism has today virtually become one of our testimonies–with green buildings a new imperative–we may belatedly find ourselves in the forefront of the movement.

Benfey, T. (1980). Friends and the world of nature. *Pendle Hill Pamphlet*, 233.

Brinton, H. (1955). *Guide to Quaker Practice.* Pendle Hill.

Nearing, S. and Nearing, H. (1954). *Living the Good Life: being a practical account of a twenty-year project* . . . Social Science Institute, Harborside, ME.

Penn, W. (2003). *Some Fruits of Solitude.* Harald Press, Scottdale PA.

PYM (1925). *A Book of Christian Discipline*, Philadelphia, PA. Philadelphia Yearly Meeting, PYM.

PYM (1972). *Faith and Practice*, Philadelphia, PA. Philadelphia Yearly Meeting, PYM.

Soderlund, J. R., editor (1983). *William Penn and the Founding of Pennsylvania 1680-84: A Documentary History.* University of Pennsylvania Press, Philadelphia, PA.

Mary Mendenhall Hobbs and Allen Jay: Lessons for the Abundant Life Today

by Max Carter, Guilford College

John 10:10–"The thief comes only to steal and kill and destroy. I came that they may have life, and have it abundantly."

While this verse from John's gospel is attributed to Jesus, I will be applying it to the lives of two Friends–humble servants of the guy from Nazareth–who committed major portions of their lives to Quaker education and, significant to our location at this FAHE conference, to making sure that Friends in the South would not only be abundant, but live abundantly: Allen Jay (1831-1910) and Mary Mendenhall Hobbs (1852-1930).[1]

I have something of an affinity for both. Allen Jay lived for much of his life in my native Indiana; he raised the funds to build Bundy Hall at Earlham, where I labored as a Head Resident for four years (and met my wife, not to mention the fact that our daughter Maia was born while we were in Bundy). The meetinghouse of West Richmond Friends (incidentally, celebrating its centennial this year), where Jane and I attended and served on the ministry team, is a memorial to Allen Jay; Guilford College might not exist were it not for Jay's incredible labors directing the work of the Baltimore Assn. to Advise and Assist Friends in the Southern States following the Civil War. Many of us in this room, in fact, owe a debt of gratitude to Jay. He raised the funds to help transition the Friends School in Carolina to Guilford College in the 1880s. He raised funds for Whittier College and encouraged Pacific College, the forerunner of George Fox University. (Incidentally, while visiting Oregon and Washington in 1906, he "milked" Elbridge Stuart, a descendant of North Carolina Quakers and founder of the Carnation Dairy Company, for the funds to purchase the lot and build and furnish a meetinghouse for Friends in Seattle!)

Jay worked for four years as the treasurer of the Friends school in Providence, R.I. that is now known as the Moses Brown School. When he was called to Earlham in the 1870s to raise money for that struggling institution, there was but one building and the heating plant, both in deplorable condition. Jay reported, in his autobiography, that after touring the campus, he sat on a log behind

---

[1]This article is adapted from a plenary session at the June 2009 Friends Association for Higher Education annual meeting held at Guilford College in Greensboro, NC.

old Earlham Hall and meditated long about the seemingly hopeless task. That many of us today sit on the Earlham campus and meditate on how on earth our institutions could have the resources our friends in Richmond have is credit to Jay. He oversaw the creation of the Earlham we know now, raised funds for six new buildings (including the aforementioned Sovereign State of Bundy!), and was a tireless advocate among Friends for the college and its sometimes beleaguered faculty.

For her part, Mary Mendenhall Hobbs was an equal partner with her husband, Lewis Lyndon Hobbs, the first president of Guilford College, in shaping the character of the place. Tom Hamm, Quaker historian at Earlham College, cites her influence in his *The Transformation of American Quakerism* in maintaining the College as a "modernist island in a sea of fundamentalism" (Hamm, 1988, p.153). She assured that Guilford, the first coeducational institution in the South, would maintain a lively female presence by forming a committee to raise funds to enable girls to attend the school. In the shattered economy of the South following the war, there was little money available for education, and boys typically were the beneficiaries of what there was. Her labors resulted in the building on campus that bears her name, a cooperative residence hall for women built in 1907. She did not restrict her interest in women's education to Friends, either. Hobbs is credited with being a major influence in the founding of North Carolina's first public college for women in the 1890s.

I want more fully to introduce you to these important figures in the life of Friends in the South–indeed, in the life of Quaker education beyond this region–and make some observations about what we might draw from their lives in our own work in higher education. I'll turn first to Allen Jay.

Allen Jay

About a two-hours drive north of Greensboro, N.C., in central Virginia, is the city of Lynchburg, known most famously as the home of Jerry Falwell's Liberty University (recently thrown back into the national spotlight by Kevin Roose, a Quaker student at Brown who has authored a popular book about his "study abroad" experience at Liberty: Roose (2009)). While at Liberty this spring to deliver an academic paper, I drove five minutes from campus to see a lovely 18th century stone Quaker meetinghouse. Lynchburg was settled by Quakers in the mid-1700s and is named for John and Sarah Lynch, members of the Society. By the 1830s, there wasn't a Quaker remaining in the area, the community having packed up and left to Free states in the anti-slavery migrations that reduced the membership of Friends in the South from somewhere around 20,000 in the early 19th century to fewer than 2,000 at the close of the Civil War. The large meetinghouse was abandoned, later to be occupied by Presbyterians, in an exercise of applying their Scottish penuriousness to obtaining cheap accommodations! Ever after, it has been known as the *Quaker Memorial Presbyterian Church*. To this day, there is but a handful of Quakers in the area.

About 15 minutes drive from Guilford College, in the southern reaches of High Point, N.C. is the Allen Jay Baptist Church, in the community of Allen Jay, across the road from Allen Jay Middle School, home to a lovely stone gymnasium known as the Allen Jay Gym (and profiled, recently, in last Monday's *Greensboro News & Record*). Within a radius of only a few miles of that Baptist Church are eight flourishing Friends meetings, and the Piedmont of North Carolina is home to one of the largest–if not the largest– concentrations of Friends in North America, more than 11,000 members residing in this section of the state alone.

The striking difference between the fate of Lynchburg and that of this area is the result largely of Allen Jay's work. But he wasn't always a "local hero." As a little boy in Ohio, Jay played an integral role in his family's activities on the Underground Railroad. During the Civil War, having moved to Indiana, he steadfastly maintained his nonviolent commitment, even when Union draft officers threatened to confiscate his animals, crops, and equipment, and large numbers of fellow Hoosier Quakers suited up. (It took the intervention of Abraham Lincoln to stop the public auction of the Jays' possessions, one of many such actions of Lincoln to "spring" Quakers during the war.) As will be described soon, Allen Jay was largely responsible for the shift in post-war Carolina from Quietism to an increasingly Protestant form of worship, but he was raised in the now-lost world of traditional 19th century Quietist Quakerism.

Deeply imbued with Gurneyite evangelical Quaker theology, the Friends meetings young Allen Jay attended were still marked by a deep distrust of emotion, of "outrunning the Spirit," of "hireling" ministers, and of formal Bible study (lest it lead to formal worship and a hireling ministry). Describing the customs of that day, he noted that when a recorded elder or minister shared a vocal message in meeting, all others rose, took off their hats, turned their backs to the speaker, and bowed–and he wondered whether such respect accorded vocal ministry might prevent some of the excesses and lack of spiritual depth of more modern messages (Jay, 1908, especially chapters 2 and 13).

Jay emphasizes the sacrifices of those recorded as elders and ministers during this period. Much as the Amish still do, leaders were recognized by the community as being selected by God, assumed the spiritual burdens of the community, and "kept their day job," never receiving a penny for their labors. When Jay's own father was recorded a minister, he took out a loan to support the travels he undertook, eventually visiting all but one yearly meeting in North America, and most of their constituent monthly meetings. When Allen Jay himself was recorded a minister in 1864, he, too, traveled at his own expense and received no compensation for his labors. Again, he wondered in his autobiography whether paid pastors of the "modern" era of Friends fully appreciate the sacrifices and dedication of their forebears.

In 1868, Jay received a letter from Francis T. King, clerk of the Baltimore Association to advise and assist Friends in the Southern States, asking him to replace newly named Earlham College president Joseph Moore in directing the Association's work in North Carolina. The Baltimore Assn. was formed during the Civil War to respond to Southern Quaker sufferings and kicked into high gear at war's end to salvage and rebuild the remnant Quaker community in the South. Legend has it that God called the young farmer to this service while Jay was picking corn in Indiana, that he unhitched the horses, left the wagon standing, and headed south. The reality is a bit less romantic. Although a recorded minister in his meeting, Jay felt inadequate to the task; he was born with a hare lip and cleft palate and felt he could not effectively speak before large crowds. He had no experience as a fund raiser; he was just a farmer. Furthermore, he felt the salary offered was not sufficient for his family (Jay, 1908, chapter 17).

Nonetheless, Jay prayed about it, consulted with his wife, and let King know that if he'd throw in a milk cow to help feed the family, they would go. King agreed, and Jay spent the next decade helping rebuild the community of Friends in the South through education, agricultural innovation, fund raising, spiritual renewal, and social outreach. Notable achievements included the establishment of a "Model Farm" to teach scientific agricultural practices, *normal* schools to educate teachers, building and improving numerous meetinghouses, and establishing more than 70 schools for Friends and the recently emancipated enslaved Africans.

The spiritual work of the Baltimore Assn. was especially important, and while Jay did not subscribe to the line in James Russell Lowell's classic hymn *Once to Ev'ry Man and Nation* that "time makes ancient good uncouth," he did recognize that the latter part of the 19th century demanded a new way of doing things. He respected the Quietist tradition in which he was raised, and he admired his parents and others who represented the best of that era, but Jay also acknowledged that times had changed, and new challenges demanded new responses.

For one thing, the mid-1800s saw unprecedented changes in transportation, communication, and education. New roads, the railroad, canals, newspapers, journals, and the telegraph rapidly tore down the "hedges" of isolation built around the largely rural Quaker communities. Quaker schools, academies, and colleges were established–and increasingly admitted non-Friends, further altering the world views of Friends. Growing cooperation with non-Friends in social and religious reform movements eroded the notion of being uniquely God's "peculiar people." The world outside the sequestered, sometimes calcified, Quaker communities was encroaching, and in large part that world was evangelical.

Jay, already in his early adolescence experiencing a conversion under the ministry in his meeting, recognized that even his mother, deeply Christian as she was, could not respond to his obvious spiritual seeking. Her schooling in the tradition prevented her from vocal prayer–even in private–unless called to public ministry, and religion was not a matter readily discussed in the home for fear of too much "creaturely" activity.

When Jay's father broke with the tradition and instituted family Bible reading and worship, young Allen found it deeply edifying. He noted in his autobiography that a public Friend visiting in the Jay home expressed shock at this display of un-Quakerly "formal worship" but, bowing to hospitality, said "I suppose it will not hurt me to sit and listen to it." (Jay, 1908, p. 26)

Jay later was part of what he claimed was the first spark of the revivals that burned across Midwestern and Southern Quakerism after the Civil War. In the winter of 1859-60 in his Hoosier meeting, he engaged with others in *Bible* School, *Bible* reading, family worship, and prayer at youth social occasions, experiencing vital spiritual growth and energy.

Most famously, after Jay assumed the superintendency in 1868 of the work of the Baltimore Association, he recognized that Quaker youth were heading off to Methodist revivals, receiving the "new birth," and facing stern rebuke by their traditionalist families and meetings. If they continued to be discouraged among Friends, he reasoned, they would be lost to other denominations, and his work of rebuilding the Southern Quaker community would be in vain. Jay won their confidence, however, by speaking with parents, elders, and ministers and attending the revivals himself. In return, the young people promised that they would remain with the Friends Church. Subsequently, he convinced Springfield Friends Meeting

52

to hold a series of "general" meetings at their meeting-house, and these specially called meetings for worship and prayer were held for nearly two weeks, adding some 150 to the rolls of the meeting.

Before long, Jay was invited to speak at a series of revival meetings in High Point. He agreed to, but with the understanding that, as with the Springfield "revivals," he would speak only as the Spirit led and not from notes or suggested topics, he would not lead singing, and he would not introduce an "anxious bench" unless desired by the full community. His ministry was so effective–along with his other work for the Baltimore Association–that at the close of his work with the Baltimore Assn. in N.C., yearly meeting membership was around 8,000.

The "new methods" employed by Jay in reviving the spiritual life of the Quaker community in North Carolina led not only to a dramatic increase in membership and number of meetings, but inexorably to a more programmed form of worship and an emerging pastoral system.

Tom Hamm labels Allen Jay as one of the most important of the "renewal" Friends in the transformation of Quakerism in the latter 1800s (Hamm, 1988), but even Jay admits to being carried away to a certain extent by the fires of revival. "During the revivals of the 1870s in Western Yearly Meeting," he writes, "evangelists condemned those in opposition to "new methods." I was a member then and enjoyed the revivals but now regret those we injured in our zeal to save souls. We pressed our views too fast" (Jay, 1908, p. 119).

Jay's *Autobiography* is peppered throughout with reflections on the strengths of the old tradition and the excesses of those who swept Quietism away.

> I am often impressed with the fact of how little theology there was mixed with the preaching of those Friends compared with the hair-splitting doctrines of...today. But after 70 years, having seen the results of the ministry of that day, which directed our thoughts to the Spirit of God...comparing it with the dogmatic and superficial teaching of some today, I am ready to say our fathers' ministry produced men and women of ability and Christian character which I sometimes fear are not produced by the methods of the modern revivalist (Jay, 1908, p. 24).

As mentioned earlier, Jay helped instigate and enjoyed the revivals that brought such dramatic change to Friends in the 1860s and 70s. However, he was deeply pained by the separations that those changes brought. He admired North Carolina Yearly Meeting patriarch Nathan Hunt for preventing the Orthodox-Hicksite and Wilburite-Gurneyite splits that wracked so many other yearly meetings and lamented the sad story of the separation in the 1840s in Indiana Yearly Meeting that led to an Indiana Yearly Meeting of Anti-slavery Friends, when members of both sides shared the same opposition to slavery. A devout Gurneyite himself, he maintained a friendship with leaders of the Hicksite community in Richmond, Indiana while working for Earlham–even good-humoredly wrangling a free piano for the College out of the Hicksite-owned Starr Piano Company!

Jay was present in Western Yearly Meeting when evangelists instituted altars of prayer and hymn-singing; they condemned any who opposed these methods for saving souls. When in 1877 leading traditionalist ministers finally admitted defeat and retreated from the sessions of the yearly meeting, a revivalist (Tom Hamm believes it was the visiting holiness preacher David B. Updegraff) called on the remaining Friends to sing a rousing hymn, "See the great host advancing, Satan leading on...," so the Conservative Friends would have it ringing in their ears as they left the meeting house.

Such a history, Jay believed, was no credit to Friends. He placed blame on both sides and believed "...it is doubtful whether separations are ever beneficial in advancing the kingdom of God....Each needed the gifts of the other. Had they remained together, some of the extreme things that have been done would not have occurred" (Jay, 1908, p.101). Jay held that separations never caused more people to hear the Gospel, never enlarged the Church, and certainly did not show the world the spirit of Christ. "Has a separation ever caused the world to exclaim, Behold how these Christians love one another'?" (Jay, 1908, p.117)

Rather than such a spirit of division, Jay believed one should feel a "deep need of living Christ before the people" (Jay, 1908, p. 374) and called for leaders among Friends who were free of extreme views, who can see more than one side of a question, and who work for unity rather than "splitting hairs" and engaging in doctrinal arguments.

Mary Mendenhall Hobbs

Mary Mendenhall Hobbs lived through the Civil War at New Garden Boarding School, owing to her headmaster father's decision to remain in the South rather than see the school die. She was educated briefly at the private Quaker Howland School in New York, where she met both the holiness preacher David B. Updegraff and the progressive Hicksite reformer Susan B. Anthony. Later she was a partner with her husband, President Lewis Lyndon Hobbs, in creating a vital Guilford College out of its predecessor, New Garden Boarding School/Friends School in Carolina. Keen to see educational opportunity extended to girls in the economically devastated post-war South, she created, as mentioned before, a system of cooperative housing at the school which enabled young women to work their way towards a degree, and her communication with the State legislature is credited with helping open North Carolina's first public college for women, now the University of North Carolina-Greensboro. Active in temperance, literary, and peace circles, she was awarded an honorary doctorate by the University of North Carolina.[2]

Hobbs did not spend as much time as Allen Jay steeped in the culture of Quietist Quakerism. Born in 1852, she was barely a teenager when she witnessed the monumental changes the post-Civil War era brought to the South, and she was sent away to the North for her formal education. But still, she describes admiringly the traditionalist ways of her father, Nereus Mendenhall, who retreated into silent prayer to discern whether it would be God's will for him and his family to leave the leadership of New Garden Boarding School before the Civil War and seek an easier life in Minnesota (God and he decided to stay!). When revivalists and programmed worship won the day among Friends in the post-Civil War South, Nereus finally did go North–to teach at Haverford College, rather than stay and make a fuss.

In an essay "After the Revival," written in 1923, Mary shared her preference for appealing to conscience rather than emotion and to the "old custom" of visiting Friends who turned people to their Inward Teacher (Hobbs, 1923).

Hobbs also recognized that the silent worship so revered by her parents' generation was not speaking to the youth and, especially as growing numbers joined the Society from outside its cultural circle, to much of the membership of Friends. A confirmed Gurneyite, she promoted study of the Bible and supported a teacher-pastor model of leadership similar to that promoted by Allen Jay. Damon Hickey noted in his study of Friends in the new, post-war South that in 1897 Hobbs chaired a committee sharply critical of traditionalists' opposition to funds for evangelism (Hickey, 1997, p.123). Hobbs was also the primary author of a 1906 report encouraging a teaching

---

[2]Information gleaned from the *Papers of Mary Mendenhall Hobbs*, Friends Historical Collection, Guilford College

ministry, arguing that Quaker opposition to a "hireling" ministry was particular to its time (Hickey, 1997, p. 85). She respected those revivalists who displayed a deep, caring spirit and simple devotion.

Although Hobbs supported many of the changes that radically altered the Quaker landscape of the previous generations, she was unwilling to go as far as fundamentalist and revivalist Friends. She was one of the moderate, "renewal" Friends who sought to bring new life into the society, but opposed a more radical break with the past. She recognized the stagnation of traditionalism but felt many were going too far in breaking loose from those moorings; her chosen task was to battle for a progressive understanding of God's revelation of truth, while respecting the best that Quaker tradition had to offer (Hamm, 1988, pp. 115; 153).

Hobbs was especially critical of revivalists and dogmatists who followed a scorched earth policy of burning bridges with the past and condemning all who disagreed with their understanding of truth. In her 1923 essay "After the Revival" she wrote: "Is it not about time for Friends to seek out some more rational and enduring manner of spreading the truths which we profess...than the outworn and mediaeval methods followed in what are called revivals?" (Hobbs, 1923)

She felt that these "rushing revivals" were contrary to the basic principles of Friends and appealed too much to emotion rather than conscience. Continuing in her essay, she expressed her favor of a more "scientific," developmental approach and stated a preference, especially, for the "old custom" of visiting Friends who continually looked after the welfare of members and who turned people to their Inward Teacher.

Along with Allen Jay, Mary Mendenhall Hobbs called for a more moderate response to the great changes emanating from the revivals. With other similarly-minded Friends, she helped stave off Wesleyan and Conservative separations in North Carolina, and the yearly meeting did not experience a real separation until 1904–over the Uniform Discipline adopted by Five Years Meeting.

Interestingly, though, one of Hobbs's concerns was the potential for mischief of the *Richmond Declaration of Faith*, a statement coming out of an 1887 conference of Gurneyite yearly meetings. Allen Jay wrote approvingly in his autobiography of the outcome of the conference and expressed deep admiration for the principle author of the document, British Friend J. Bevan Braithwaite. Braithwaite enjoyed Jay's hospitality while in Richmond, wrote the declaration at the same desk where Jay later wrote his book, and gave Jay as a keepsake the pen he used in the writing.

Hobbs was not as effusive. In an essay entitled "Creeds," she says "Before we...endorse a creed, either the *Richmond Declaration* or another, we should seriously and honestly consider two things: 1) historical effects of creeds in the church; 2) why do I want a creed? –to express to the world God's saving power–or compel others to say just what I want them to say in my way....Creeds are the inevitable precursors of inquisition" (Hobbs, 1923).

To Hobbs, such assertions as the Richmond Declaration and its later use as a litmus test by many in Five Years Meeting (now Friends United Meeting) was contrary to the spirit of early Friends. She quoted approvingly from William Penn's *A Key*: "It is not opinion or speculation or notions of what is true, or assent to, or the subscription of articles or propositions...that makes a man a true believer or a true Christian; but it is a conformity of mind and practice to the will of God...." (Hobbs, 1923).

While she admitted that the *Declaration* was never intended as a creed, but as an expression of fundamental principles of the Christian faith, she traced the sorry history in the Church of the "devastations" wrought by creedal assertions and held up as a more positive example the history of collegiality in North Carolina Yearly Meeting without such statements.

A progressive in education and thought, she had "modern" views of the Bible and free inquiry. Regarding the scriptures, she supported "progressive revelation" and the German "higher criticism" in the face of intense Christian opposition. In her papers is this quote from her father, Nereus: "If we meet in the Bible anything that confuses our sense of right and wrong–is less exalted or pure than God's character should be–even after careful thought, don't bow down to it–it doesn't meet the needs of the early and more sacred revelation God has given us in our own spirit and conscience" (Hobbs, 1923).

> Don't foreclose inquiry in any direction; Truth is always to be sought after. Scripture is but one variety of authentic tradition – the whole is larger than the part. God is in all history, not merely in Jewish or Christian history....No society or people has the full, real truth, even Christendom. The spirit of Christianity has not yet fully been apprehended (Hobbs, 1923).

Conclusion

So, what might we learn from the example of these two Friends? Why are their stories even relevant for a group of educators toiling in the salt mines of a Quaker culture nearly 100 years removed from their experience?

The first lesson I draw from their lives is the importance of the "lost art" of cooperation within the community of Friends. Reading Jay's autobiography (available, by the way, in a very readable format on-line), I am amazed at the breadth of his impact on so many Quaker educational institutions: secondary schools from N.C. to R.I.; Guilford, Whittier, Earlham, Pacific, even the now-defunct Central College in Nebraska. While serving Earlham in the 1880s, he took leave to come back to N.C. to assist Jos. Moore, also an Earlham College stalwart, in transforming the boarding school into Guilford College. He did the same for other Quaker colleges while maintaining his loyalty to Earlham. His assistance to monthly meetings and yearly meetings here and abroad was also incredible. Sure, most of that was among sympathetic Gurneyite bodies, but he maintained friendly relations with those who didn't share his own envangelistic passions. He was on good terms with the Hicksites in Richmond, and he "had the back" of Elbert Russell in the Bible Dept. of Earlham, even while others were out to get Russell for his acceptance of the German school of biblical "higher criticism". He and Mary Mendenhall Hobbs were close friends and fellow workers in the common cause of strengthening Southern Friends, even if Jay cherished the pen used to write the *Richmond Declaration*, and Hobbs was less prone to idolatry!

While Hobbs didn't travel as widely as Jay, her correspondence certainly did, and her friendships ranged from M. Carey Thomas of Bryn Mawr, her old classmate at the Howland School, to Traditionalist Friends, to revival preachers. She was "practical, not ideological," in the opinion of Hickey (1997, pp. 123-127). Her social involvements also ranged widely: she was active in the WCTU (a front for women's suffrage work as well as temperance!), peace societies, anti-capital punishment work, home missions, orphanages, Indian concerns, the League of Nations, and, of course, education. She recognized the value of Quaker educational institutions in improving the life of the wider society and encouraged a new generation of Allen Jays and Joseph Moores to "go into neighborhoods, speak in meetings, visit families, and promote the general improvement of society," feeling that it should be the work of the colleges rather than the Yearly Meeting–so as not to appear to be propagandizing. It's probably worth mentioning here that while Joseph Moore was in charge of the Baltimore Assn.'s work in N.C., he was very effective in such educational endeavors throughout the state. On one occasion, following a public lecture that included such advice as standing brooms up on their handles so as not to ruin the broom straw, a woman in the audience was overheard commenting, "I cain't hardly believe Moore has a college "edgicaytion;" I could understand everything he said!" (Oral tradition in North Carolina)

In a course I taught in London on Friends in business, industry, and reform, during Guilford's study abroad program in England, I mentioned the contribution of Quaker community to Friends' success in business: not only was there a ready-made customer base, but there were trustworthy suppliers, financial advice and assistance from Quaker bankers, and the "encouragement" of disownment if one went bankrupt! One of the students commented that it's a shame our Quaker educational institutions don't support each other in the same way, aiding in mutual success and strengthening each other. Certainly Friends Council on Education and Friends Association of Higher Education are great steps in that direction, but at the local level, we tend to be discreet entities, looking out for ourselves, in many cases in competition with each other. And we certainly often don't have the time to look beyond our own campuses to engagement in the communities around us.

A second lesson I find in their example is the need for "tenderness" in introducing "new methods" or understandings, of valuing the Tradition, while recognizing the fact that, indeed, it may be time to move on. As educators, we often are privileged to have access to new ideas ahead of others–and have access to captive audiences for those thoughts. Jay and Hobbs have impressed me with their ability to stand firm in their own understandings while typically dealing gently with those whose lights have not yet led them there. And, at the same time, we, too, may have to examine whether the "new methods" that have so inspired us, that were so "cutting edge" in our past experience, have become a "Tradition" that is in need of challenging.

A third lesson I draw from these two figures is what I'll risk calling the need for "Quaker bodhisattvas." I probably don't need to explain the concept much here (or apologize for referring to a Buddhist concept!), but, in brief, a "bodhisattva" is one whose degree of enlightenment would qualify him or her to shuffle off to that Club Med of Nirvana, but who remains on earth out of compassion for others, seeking to lead them into the same experience that so benefited them.

Hobbs's family served in this way for the Southern Quaker community before the war. Her father, Nereus, was Haverford educated, an engineer and teacher, fully capable of going anywhere in the country he might have wanted and prospering. Guilford County, N.C. contemporaries of the Mendenhalls, Samuel Hill and Elbridge Amos Stuart, did just that, migrating first to the Midwest and then to the Northwest and making a boatload of money! Hill, also an engineer, created the Maryhill community and a re-creation of Stonehenge in Washington State, overlooking the Columbia River into the Oregon High Desert, and built the Columbia River Gorge scenic highway. Stuart, as stated earlier, founded the Carnation Company, making far more profit from his "contented cows" than Allen Jay ever squeezed out of his one!

But while the South was emptying of its Quaker population, and Nereus Mendenhall was serving as the boarding school's headmaster, in a dramatic gesture he and the family determined to remain in N.C. rather than leave and see the school close. This meant that they lived through the horrors and leanness of the war years–but the school remained open, because they didn't leave, the young men didn't march off to war, and Northern Friends funneled aid to the community.

Mary and her husband, progressive, well-educated–either formally (Lewis at Haverford/Mary at the Howland School in NY) or on their own–also could have moved North (as Nereus eventually did). But they remained here, in spite of the hardships and almost unimaginable work load that is evident in Mary's descriptive correspondence. They saw a deep need to be addressed, and they remained to address it.

Jay, too, could well have remained happily farming in the "High Gap" south of Lafayette, Indiana. He had a nice farm and was in a thriving community of Friends with an excellent academy - Farmers' Institute, a library and literary society that were the envy of the region, and a vibrant spiritual life. It was the community in which his wife's family lived–and where they laid to rest in the meeting's cemetery two small children. But service beckoned, first in North Carolina and later at a variety of struggling Quaker institutions. Can we learn from these Friends and educators to find ways, ourselves, to live more fully in Quaker educational community? To be, in our own ways, Quaker bodhisattvas? What would that community look like? What service might take us out of our "comfort zones"? Perhaps Allen Jay and Mary Mendenhall Hobbs can offer hints at what Spirit might lead us into today. The results, I believe, would lead not only to a more abundant life in the Quaker community and in our educational work, but in our own lives.

Hamm, T. D. (1988). *The Transformation of American Quakerism*. Indiana University Press.

Hickey, D. D. (1997). *Sojourners No More: The Quakers in the*

New South 1865-1920. North Carolina Friends Historical Society; North Carolina Yearly Meeting of Friends (FUM).

Hobbs, M. M. (1923). Ms 223. In *Mary Mendenhall Hobbs Papers.* Friends Historical Collection, Guilford College, Greensboro, N.C.

Jay, A. (1908). *The Autobiography of Allen Jay.* The John C. Winston Co., Philadelphia, PA.

Roose, K. (2009). *The Unlikely Disciple: A Sinner's Semester at America's Holiest University.* Grand Central Publishing, New York, NY.

Woolman and Kelly: Faithful Lives

by Mike Heller, Roanoke College
& Deborah Shaw, Guilford College

In designing courses or coming up with retreat themes, it seems useful to think about what we are most interested in as well as what might be of interest and useful to others. For a retreat at Woodbrooke and a workshop for the Friends Association for Higher Education annual conference, we decided to offer "Woolman and Kelly: Faithful Lives." John Woolman and Thomas Kelly are much admired for their faithful lives, even beyond the Society of Friends. We see them as models for exploring these questions:

How can we learn from John Woolman's and Thomas Kelly's lives to engage with the spirit in our own lives?

What does it mean to live a faithful life?

Embedded in these overarching queries are further questions about service, Quaker testimonies, simplicity, and how we respond to students and colleagues. We wanted to approach this experientially through worship, corporate and individual reflection, and journal writing and sharing. The beginning place for us, that we feel almost everyone can identify with, is in the struggles of our own lives. John Woolman becomes all the more inspiring when we see how he struggled to accomplish what he felt called to do and how he drew upon the inward experience of the Spirit to guide him through difficulties. Perhaps more than Woolman, Thomas Kelly went through an extremely dark time in his life, but this became a turning point after which his life's work changed and deepened. We identified the aspiration of returning to our institutions or our daily lives with a renewed sense of what it means to be faithful to our spiritual gifts. Each evening in epilogue at Woodbrooke, we emphasized with participants our daily practices as the center of how we live out a life of faith. We also made our concluding session a time of worship out of which we invited people to speak to the question "What Does It Mean to Live a Faithful Life?" As one Woodbrooke participant expressed it, we seek a practice of presence in everyday life.

The beginning questions in our retreat were "Where are you now? What brings you here?" People shared a wide range of experiences, and we felt moved by their honest sharing. One of the participants shared how she was in the beginning stages of Alzheimer's disease, and she wanted us to know that she does not do well with numbers if we asked people to count off for discussion groups. She spoke throughout the retreat with insight and gentleness that touched all of us. Toward the end of the retreat she spoke of how we are called, with childlike radiance, *to be* rather than *to do*.

We structured the retreat around stages of life. We began each session with quiet worship. In the second session "Childhood-Young Adult Journey," Mike asked people to write in their journals a brief statement on each of these questions, and then to choose one and write more: "How did your father influence your spiritual journey? How did your mother influence your spiritual journey? What was an early memory of awareness of social injustice? When did you first speak in Quaker worship? Who helped you find a song for life?" The first two questions about fathers and mothers raised such painful memories for some that it felt as if the room temperature dropped twenty degrees. We were in a kind of vortex of swirling emotions. Perhaps we should have not jumped into such questions so soon or prepared people better before asking them to write on these questions. We saw what was happening, and fortunately, Deborah threw a life-line to those who needed it. We slowly regained our footing and Mike ended up not being entirely exiled by the group.

In another session, looking at Woolman's and Kelly's lives, we talked about how we all face difficulties in life. We called this session, "Falling Apart: Life Changing Events," and used this focus as a way to recover from the turmoil of the previous session. Drawing from the spiritual journey as described in studies of myth and mysticism, we talked about how we each experience entering the dark forest and must find our way to the other side. In a passage from "A Plea for the Poor," Woolman writes that, "To labour for an establishment in divine love where the mind is disentangled from the power of darkness is the great business of man's life" (Woolman, 1989, pp. 249-50). As we talked about how we make our way through the difficult times in our lives, one participant observed that we surrender to that place, even with a smile into the dark.

In another session, from Kelly's life we focused on two letters to his wife Lael and excerpts of his writing compiled in *Sanctuary of the Soul*. In one of the letters to Lael, Kelly begins by saying "I have never had such a soul-overturning summer or period such as this." He speaks of having an "amazing series of 'openings' and experiences" amongst those struggling in 1938 Germany, "men and women who have stirred me with their Christlikeness or their simple trust or their deep insights or their intuitive flashes" (Kelly, 1997, pp. 17-18). Visiting Germany, during a period when Nazism was nearing the height of its power, Kelly was moved by seeing the human spirit in the face of oppression. This experience contributed greatly to his finding his proper path.

These passages helped us consider the theme "Our Journeys–

Way Opening." Here we asked participants to enter into "paired listening" in which they responded to the question "When was a time when you experienced the way opening with respect to a choice, a decision, a discernment?" For follow-up evening home-work (contemplation or journal writing), we asked them to think about this question: "How have you experienced spiritual accom-paniment: mentors, elders, companions?" We talked about how we come out of crises in our lives. In Woolman's *Journal*, chapter 12, there is the passage about his sickness and his dream of merging in a murky cloud with suffering humanity (Woolman, 1989, pp. 185-87). As one participant observed, Woolman was so low then, disappearing into the great mass of humanity, that he finally be-comes accessible. We talked about the great crisis in Kelly's life when he faced not being allowed to complete his dissertation at Harvard.

Friends in the retreat raised perceptive questions about how Woolman consciously shaped the life story in his *Journal*, and we talked about the implications of that conscious shaping of one's own narrative. His *Journal* gives us the portrayal of a man who has great empathy and imagination, a man who is utterly believ-able. Beyond that literary achievement, the shaping of the *Journal* also becomes an act of faith–partly as an expression of trust in the reader's ability to feel and understand and partly as an extension of ministry through the sharing of his experience with his community.

We talked about "Simplicity: What Are You Called to Do?" and drew upon quotations from Caroline Whitmire's *Plain Living: A Quaker Path to Simplicity*. We found useful Richard Gregg's quotation from a conversation he had with Gandhi in which he, Richard, was counseled to "Only give up a thing when you want some other condition so much that the thing no longer has any at-traction for you, or when it seems to interfere with that which is more greatly desired" (Whitmire, 2001, p. 25). We could see ex-amples of that course in Woolman's and Kelly's lives. We discussed the connections between Kelly's "Holy Obedience" and "Simplic-ity." One participant observed that Woolman speaks to us across the centuries as a man who made sacrifices little by little, living out of the center. And another participant observed that this sim-plicity is not in giving up or in sacrifice or in bravery, but rather in making a choice to do something else, and this becomes a spiritual maturity.

We talked about "Struggling to Be Heard" and we posed the questions: "How Has the Spirit Prospered with You? What does thankfulness have to do with the faithful life?" For homework that evening, we asked people to think about what they are doing to take care of the self.

In our shorter version of the retreat, presented as a workshop at the Friends Association for Higher Education annual conference, we examined Woolman's statement that "The true felicity of man in this life, and that which is to come, is in being inwardly united to the fountain of universal love and bliss..." (Woolman, 1989, p. 249). We asked people to write in response to "What rises up for you? How do you envision or imagine 'being united to the fountain of universal love,' as you consider your work/ministry in your college or university?" From Kelly's writing, we read out loud this passage:

> There is a way of ordering our mental life on more than one level at once. On one level we may be thinking, discussing, seeing, calculating, meeting all the demands of external affairs. But deep within, behind the scenes, at a profounder level, we may also be in prayer and adoration, song and worship and a gentle receptiveness to divine breathings. . . .
>
> Between the two levels is fruitful interplay, but ever the accent must be upon the deeper level, where the soul ever dwells in the presence of the Holy One. For the religious [person] is forever bringing all affairs of the first level down into the Light, holding them there in the Presence, re-seeing them and the whole of the world of men [and women] and things in a new and overturning way, and responding to them in spontaneous, incisive and simple ways of love and faith. Facts remain facts, when brought into the Presence in the deeper level, but their value, their significance, is wholly realigned (Kelly, 1941, pp. 35-36).

In response to these paragraphs, we asked participants to write and respond to this question: "As you listen to Thomas Kelly's words how do you imagine working/ministering in and through that fruitful interplay?"

One participant at Woodbrooke observed that Woolman and Kelly offer us two ways: in Woolman we see the steady, stone by stone submission to the cross, and in Kelly we see a glorious blossoming–the calling is to love. In the Woodbrooke retreat and the FAHE workshop, we came away strengthened in our sense that what we do in our institutions is a kind of "advanced work." We are showing students a threshold that we are beckoning them to cross.

Kelly, T. R. (1941). *A Testament of Devotion*. Harper & Row Publishers, New York, NY.

Kelly, T. R. (1997). *The Sanctuary of the Soul: Selected Writings of Thomas Kelly.* Upper Room Books, Nashville, TN.

Whitmire, C. (2001). *Plain Living: A Quaker Path to Simplicity.* Sorbin Books, Novato, CA.

Woolman, J. (1989). *The Journal and Major Essays of John Woolman.* Friends United Press, Richmond, IN.

Thomas Kelly, Dietrich Bonhoeffer and the Search for Community

by Diane Reynolds, Earlham School of Religion

Although separated by nationality and denomination, Quaker mystic Thomas Kelly and Lutheran pastor and theologian Dietrich Bonhoeffer had surprisingly similar faith journeys. Both were transformed by their encounters with the divine, and for both, their search for meaning was structured by their shared social location as Euro-centric early twentieth century white males. In their most famous writings, which were informed by their experiences of German totalitarianism, each man shared a similar quest: to find a vehicle for the Christian faith that would transcend the limitations of convention. Each came away with the conviction that developing small, cohesive "monastic" student groups was critically important to reinvigorating the church and hence society. In an era of increased isolation, in which on-line education is aggressively marketed as the answer to the cost of higher education, Bonhoeffer and Kelly's monastic models are relevant to the survival of Quaker liberal arts colleges.

Thomas Kelly was born in 1893 in southwest Ohio, to an evangelical Quaker farming family of modest means. He graduated from Wilmington College with a degree in chemistry, then attended Haverford College, where he fell under the influence of Quaker theologian Rufus Jones. This encounter led him to a master's and then a doctorate in philosophy at Hartford Theological Seminary. Because of the cost of his education, Kelly would battle "crushing debt" problems that hung "like a noose over his head" for most of his life (Kelly, 1966, p. 91). Also, until 1938, as a poor farm boy he felt a sense of intellectual inadequacy that he hoped to overcome through a PhD from Harvard. That dream crashed spectacularly when he failed his oral exams, but his deep distress over this failure led to his first great spiritual breakthrough in December, 1937.

Dietrich Bonhoeffer was born in 1906, 13 years after Kelly, to a wealthy and distinguished German family. From the age of six, he grew up in sophisticated Berlin, a far cry from rural Ohio. The sixth of eight children, Bonhoeffer lived in a grand house with a large staff of servants. Although his family suffered temporarily from troubles brought on by World War I, Bonhoeffer's entire life was cushioned by money. As the grandson of a countess and son of a prominent psychiatrist, doors opened for him to attend the best universities, where he wrote not one but two dissertations, standard at the time for those teaching in German universities, and moved in elite German and international circles (Bethge, 2000).

Bonhoeffer was ridiculed by his older brothers and met with scant support from his father when he announced his intent to pursue a pastoral career (Bosanquet, 1968, p. 32). Few in his social set saw the Lutheran church as a place for a person of talents to make a mark on the world. Thus, the young Bonhoeffer announced: "If the church is feeble, I shall reform it!" (Bosanquet, 1968, p. 45)

In 1924-25, Kelly and his young wife Lael Macy Kelly spent 15 months in Germany, primarily in Berlin, on behalf of American Friends Service Committee.[1] They participated in the founding of the Quaker German Yearly Meeting (Kelly, 1966, p. 49). When the couple returned to the U.S., Kelly accepted a teaching position at Earlham College in Indiana. Once home, he recognized that Germany had broadened his religious perspectives:

> I found there in Germany a new Quaker movement. Men in it were facing essentials in a way I never had. They were inquiring regarding the essence of religion and coming to conclusions far more daring than I had ever dreamed for myself (Kelly, 1966, p. 54).

Kelly abandoned what he called the "narrow" and "undeveloped" evangelical Quakerism of his youth and embraced a new version of Quakerism as a "mystical fellowship, which transcends the ordinary barriers of religious organizations" (Kelly, 1966, p. 54).

Bonhoeffer had a similarly transformative experience crossing the Atlantic in the opposite direction. Arriving in 1930 for a year at Union Theological Seminary in New York City, he soon abandoned his parochial religious outlook,[2] replacing nationalism and militarism with ecumenicalism and pacifism. Bonhoeffer's outlook

---

[1] Although both Bonhoeffer and Kelly were in Berlin at the same time twice—in 1924-25 and in 1938, there's no published record that they ever met. Since almost all of Bonhoeffers papers and letters have been published, any record of a meeting would be lurking among unpublished Kelly papers. Since Bonhoeffer did not become famous until well after Kelly's death, Kelly may not have particularly noticed Bonhoeffer if the two did meet. However, Bonhoeffer, from a different social class, may never have been introduced to Kelly.

[2] As a young pastor to a German church in Barcelona in 1927-28, Bonhoeffer believed that an ethic of love for family and Volk allowed a nation to defend itself against aggression. He wrote: "love for my people will sanctify murder, will sanctify war" (Bonhoeffer, 1996a, p. 618).. Also, "Strength also comes from God, and power, and victory, for God creates youth in the individual as well as in nations [Volk], and God loves youth, for God himself is eternally young and strong and victorious," he writes in his "Basic Questions of a Christian Ethic" (Bonhoeffer, 1996a, p. 373).

underwent transformation as a result his cross-cultural encounters, most notably through attending the black Abyssinian Baptist Church in Harlem and through such fellow seminarians as the
black student Frank Fisher, and the Frenchman and pacifist, Jean
Lasserre.[3]

Both Kelly and Bonhoeffer sought to enliven their faith traditions. Kelly believed that "Quakerism needed men who could make
its ministry a vital and living organism" (Kelly, 1966, p. 27). He
followed in the footsteps of Jones, who wanted to rescue Quakerism
from its growing provincialism and adherence to "narrow conventions" (Vining, 1958, p. 39). Kelly criticized contemporary Quakers
"for a cooling down, a shrinking back, a delicacy not found either
in Scripture or in their founders" (Flora, 1990).

At the same time, 1924, the youthful Bonhoeffer ruminated
on "the present calamity" and "the terrible plight" of the German Protestant church, which, bleeding membership, "concealed a
great deal that, frankly and honestly, was nothing but materialism"
(Bethge, 2000, pp. 61-62).

Casting for a solution, Kelly and Bonhoeffer both initially turned
to the "Orient" as a way to gain a new perspective on the problems
of Western Christianity. Troubled by what he termed the "narrow
exclusiveness" of much of Christianity, Kelly longed to travel to
the East (Kelly, 1966, p. 55). He wrote to Harold H. Peterson, a
Quaker living in India, of hoping to "sit at the feet of the professors
of the Orient to learn their wisdom" (Kelly, 1966, p. 60). He believed it important to discover Eastern religion first hand, writing
to another friend: "One can hardly comprehend fully the quest of
the Buddhist sitting under the Bo Tree when one is sitting under a
sugar maple in an Midwest cornfield" (Kelly, 1966, p. 81). Arriving in Hawaii, he wrote to a friend that it was, "a real opportunity
to develop the basic familiarity with Eastern philosophy which I
wanted" (Kelly, 1966, p. 84). Kelly hoped to stay on the island for
several years but an offer to teach at Haverford brought him, with
his family, to Philadelphia after only a year.

Like Kelly, Bonhoeffer also yearned to travel the Orient. In 1931,
Bonhoeffer hoped to go straight from Union Theological Seminary
to India to study Eastern religions. However, by April 1931, he
concluded it "was just too far," as he wrote in a letter to his grand-
mother (Bonhoeffer, 1996b, p. 293). Back in Germany later that
year, when the Nazis were capitalizing on the worldwide economic
crisis, he wrote a friend, "I would like to see still one more great

---

[3]Most Germans, Bonhoeffer included, had a bitter feelings towards the
French over the Versailles Treaty. Nevertheless, Lasserre became a close friend.

country in order to judge whether the solution will possibly come from there–India; for otherwise things appear to be beyond repair, the great death of Christendom seems to have arrived" (Peck, 1968). In 1932, he wrote to his friend Edward Sutz: "I can hardly think of [the Manhattan year] without experiencing a great desire to travel again, this time to the East. There must be other people on earth who have deeper knowledge and more capacity than we have..." (Peck, 1968).

In 1934, while serving as a pastor for two German congregations in London, Bonhoeffer's interest in India continued and he wrote to Gandhi, receiving a letter of invitation in return.

Looking back at Kelly and Bonhoeffer from a twenty-first century perspective, we note that both men were seeking "Orientalism," what Edward Said described as a Western mode of appropriating Asia. According to Said, since the late 18th century Orientalism has denoted a way of dominating and systemizing the Orient–"of knowing about it, teaching it, having authority about and over it" (Said, 1978, p. 3). To the West, the "Orient"–always conceived as a monolithic whole that stretches from the Middle East to the Far East and never what in reality it is, a multiplicity of diverse cultures–represented the exotic Other, which, weaker, more feminine and more mysterious, could be consumed for the benefit of European and American culture.[4]

Clearly, both Kelly and Bonhoeffer hoped to find a way to fill the "narrowness" they perceived in western society through appropriating the wisdom of the "East." This "Orient," of course, was mythic–a vessel which could be filled with whatever was required to "fulfill" Western needs. Hence, Kelly could write of wanting to experience the "absorptive attitude of the Oriental faiths" (Kelly, 1966, p. 55), whatever that might mean, and could state, confidently, without differentiating between the multiplicity of Eastern cultures or religions, that "the [Eastern] concern is to reflect in order to live the good life. Knowledge [in the "Orient"] is not abstraction" (Kelly, 1966, p. 75).

Likewise, Bonhoeffer commented on "the distant, fertile, sunny world... of India." (Peck, 1968) In such "sunny" worlds, in true Orientalist fashion, Bonhoeffer could experience his "animal existence awakened, not the kind that degrades a man, but the sort that delivers him from the stuffiness and spuriousness of a purely intellectual existence and makes him purer and happier" (Peck, 1968).

If both men sought a presence or wisdom in the "Orient" that was missing from "provincial" Christian culture, both, ironically,

---

[4]See also http://postcolonialstudies.emory.edu/orientalism/

found the depth of faith they were seeking in large part through the distorted mirror of Nazi Germany.

Thomas Kelly travelled to Germany in 1938, to assess the Quaker situation. What he witnessed shocked him. Kelly wrote to his wife:

> Until you have lived in this world of despair and fear and abysmal suffering of the soul, you can never know how serious the consequences of a chance anecdote may be, in the way of life imprisonment, beatings with clubs, family separations, death... Many a time we sat in the middle of a room and whispered (Kelly, 1966, p. 97).

He also wrote to his wife of the loss of integrity in Germany, of "a great undermining of character" as people capitulated to the regime out of fear: "Suffering of the body" he wrote, "is only the vestibule of suffering. Suffering of soul, of spirit, is terrible. Dear people, how I love them! Dear people, how they suffer!" (Kelly, 1966, pp. 99-109) He wrote too of vicarious suffering, of the desire to help people, a concept similar to Bonhoeffer's notion of *Stellvertretung*, vicarious representative action.

In Nazi Germany Kelly had his final spiritual awakening. According to Douglas Steere,[5], Kelly's 1938 German experience led him, in Kelly's own words, to be "melted down by the love of God." In the cathedral in Cologne, Kelly felt God "laying the whole congealed suffering of humanity upon his heart"–but with the divine help to bear it.

Kelly had what he described as a "very difficult" adjustment back to the United States. The security of his "park like" suburbs around Haverford seemed "a travesty." His family described him as in a "daze." His heart remained with the his friends in the "Blessed Community" in Germany, a place he deemed "vital." In contrast, his comfortable Philadelphia surrounding seemed "humdrum," the US, "pasty and artificial" (Kelly, 1966, pp. 108-109).

Bonhoeffer traveled back to Manhattan in June, 1939, where, coincidentally, Kelly's brother-in-law, Paul Macy, picked him up at the boat dock (Bonhoeffer, 1996c, p. 182). After four anguished weeks, Bonhoeffer left the refuge offered in the US to return to Germany. His heart, like Kelly's, was with the "brothers" there. Like Kelly, he was distressed at the triviality of life in the United States, writing:

> One sat for an hour and chatted, not at all stupidly, but about matters that were so utterly trivial to me,

---

[5]In the introduction to Kelly (1941)

whether a good musical education is possible in New
York, about raising children, etc. etc., and I thought,
how usefully I could spend these hours in Germany
(Bonhoeffer, 1996c, p. 222).

Paradoxically, Christ seized the hearts of both men most fully
in a nation that was doing its best to eradicate Christianity from
its midst.

After his arrest in 1943, Bonhoeffer found that "silence and the
love of life" he hoped to find in India in a prison cell in Berlin.
The "view from below" that a Nazi prison afforded became for
Bonhoeffer the "new" perspective that he was seeking.

Bonhoeffer's heart and soul had been poured into the seminary
at Finkenwalde, run by the Confessing Church, which opposed the
Nazi-run Ayran Church. In this monastic type community, Bonhe-
offer had found his life's calling (Bethge, 2000, p. 419), although he
had previously dismissed state-run seminaries as a waste of time.

At Finkenwalde, the seminarians not only studied theology, but
listened to music together, including the then-exotic Negro spiri-
tuals Bonhoeffer had brought back from Harlem, played musical
instruments, performed Shakespeare and participated in sports.

Likewise, Kelly founded a student group at Haverford after his
return from Germany in 1938 that met weekly at his home to read
devotional classics such as Augustine's Confessions and Brother
Lawrence. Following the reading, one student remembered that
"Lael Kelly would bring in the crackers and peanut butter and
laugher and jolliness prevailed." As at Bonhoeffer's seminary, the
group would listen to records, such as Kelly's recording of Gregorian
chants. A student described it as a "little religious order grounded
in seeking God and thankful for the life that resulted from the corporate search."[6] Kelly wished for his students to become "a band
of itinerant preachers like George Fox, shaking the countryside for
10 miles around." One student remembered the idea as "utterly
fantastic and repulsive to us" (Kelly, 1966, p. 120). Nevertheless, a
number of group members later became involved in larger Quaker
service organizations.

Both Bonhoeffer and Kelly, seeing the urgency of the crisis at
hand, forced themselves to jettison the superfluous and focus on the
essentials they believed would help build a better world. What was
left standing at the point of crisis was not appropriating Eastern
religions, adopting new technologies or new programs or building

---

[6]Douglas Steere, in the introduction to Kelly (1941).

new buildings , but pouring energy into developing strong support groups of spiritually and ethically discerning individuals.

Bonhoeffer, seeking community, visited monastic-type communities, including Woodbrooke in England, to find a more holistic model for preparing pastors. Likewise, Kelly, on his return from Nazi Germany, groped for community beyond the classroom, a community that would grow deeper roots. Both teachers were urgent about building small groups. Both found the most profound spiritual expression in the "ordinary and commonplace" rhythms of life (Kelly, 1966, p. 110). As Kelly put it, he came to recognize living in suburban Philadelphia was a "holy trust, out of which we must make something that is an offering to the wounds of this terrible world" (Kelly, 1966, p. 103).

While Bonhoeffer's and Kelly's monastic circles shared similarities, Kelly's model is clearly closer to the American liberal arts experience. However, both attempts at community building share commonalities:

1. Each developed largely within institutional boundaries but operated with little institutional supervision. Bonhoeffer's Finkenwalde was supported by the Confessing Church, a breakaway from the sanctioned German Christian (Nazi) Church. The Confessing Church largely left curriculum-building to Bonhoeffer. Kelly created a Haverford student group, but ran it independently.

2. Participation was self-selecting, voluntary, and only attracted a minority of students.

3. Bonhoeffer could have as easily gone to America or to India to live with Gandhi; Kelly didn't have to invite students to his home. Both were driven by a deep sense of urgency–their commitment to the group was deep.

4. Both Kelly and Bonhoeffer introduced culture and music and "fun" into the mix.

5. Both pushed their students' boundaries, Bonhoeffer through advocating pacifism in the context of a culture of young pastor trainees eager to avenge Versailles: "The majority of the students completely rejected his suggestion that conscientious objection was something a Christian should consider" (Bethge, 2000, p. 431). Kelly, as we have seen, urged his students to embrace a George Fox-like evangelism that rubbed against upper middle class American cultural norms.

The question that underlies all of this is why the experience of Nazi Germany made developing small, holistic, monastic groups seem so critical to both men. Why did such groups seem imperative, not frivolous? Why did such a seemingly tiny gesture become of primary importance to them?

One answer might be that both Kelly and Bonhoeffer, had they still been alive when the book was published, would have agreed with Frederic Jameson's contention in *The Political Unconscious* that change bubbles up to the top from below. Both men might echo John Woolman, who in his "A Plea for the Poor" writes:

> A day of outward distress is coming, and Divine love calls to prepare against it. Hearken then, O ye children who have known the light, and come forth. Leave every thing which Jesus Christ does not own. Think not his pattern too plain, too coarse for you. Think not a small portion in this life too little. But let us live in his spirit, and walk as he walked: so shall we be preserved in the greatest troubles (Woolman, 1972).

Quaker colleges already have the infrastructure and methodology to build strong spiritual/intellectual communities in a context of egalitarianism and might do well to more fully embrace that tradition, which is at the heart of Quakerism. In a world that is increasingly commodified, hurried and "cyber," some students hunger for meaningful living interactions. Both Kelly and Bonhoeffer would likely have advocated for not taking the opportunity to build human capital for granted. Instead, like Woolman, they sought, in a "pattern...plain," a way to build up that community.

Further, not only does holistic, spiritually-based community help students enter into the world in useful and transformative ways, it also offers colleges sustainability in the potential to build an alumni system that can help institutions themselves survive.

Bethge, E. (2000). *Dietrich Bonhoeffer: A Biography.* Fortress Press, Minneapolis, MN.

Bonhoeffer, D. (1996a). *Works in English, vol. 10.* Fortress, Minneapolis, MN.

Bonhoeffer, D. (1996b). *Works in English, vol. 11.* Fortress, Minneapolis, MN.

Bonhoeffer, D. (1996c). *Works in English, vol. 15.* Fortress, Minneapolis, MN.

Bosanquet, M. (1968). *The Life and Death of Dietrich Bonhoeffer.* Harper and Row, New York, NY.

Flora, J. (1990). Searching for an adequate life: The devotional theology of thomas r. kelly. *Spirituality Today*, 42(1).

Kelly, R. M. (1966). *Thomas Kelly: A Biography.* Harper & Row, New York, NY.

Kelly, T. R. (1941). *A Testament of Devotion.* Harper & Row Publishers, New York, NY.

Peck, W. J. (1968). The significance of bonhoeffer's interest in india. *Harvard Theological Review*, 61:431–50.

Said, E. (1978). *Orientalism.* Random House, New York, NY.

Vining, E. G. (1958). *Friend of Life: the Biography of Rufus M. Jones.* J. B. Lippincott Company, Philadelphia, PA.

Woolman, J. (1972). *A Plea for the Poor.* The Citadel Press.

Women's Speaking Justified:
Quaker Women in the Public Sphere

by Laura S. Foote, Malone University

Who are the most famous public speakers in history? Familiar names that come to mind might include Martin Luther King Jr., John F. Kennedy, Winston Churchill, or even Adolf Hitler. An Internet search on "famous public speakers throughout history" lists similar familiar names, like Abraham Lincoln, Mohandas Gandhi, or Malcolm X. One noteworthy aspect of this list is that it is primarily male. People are most familiar with the speeches of men. In the list of the top 100 speeches in *American Rhetoric*[1], the top 20 includes the name of one woman, and overall there are 19 women in the top 100.

This list does not imply a lack of women's rhetoric–women have been speaking and writing throughout history. Rather, women's rhetoric has not been viewed as valuable or noteworthy. Virginia Woolf has been quoted as saying "For most of history, *Anonymous* has been a woman."[2] Historically, cultural injunctions required women to remain silent and to operate within the private and domestic spheres of home and family (Stallybrass, 1986) or their virtue was called into question. For millennia women were "closed out of the rhetorical tradition, a tradition of vocal, virile, public–and therefore privileged men" (Glenn, 1997, p. 1). Consequently, if women wanted to publish, they often did so under male pseudonyms. If women dared to write or speak publicly, their rhetoric was not published or archived, as it was deemed neither appropriate nor significant.

In spite of these injunctions against women publishing and speaking publicly, women throughout history have demonstrated moral courage by speaking up and speaking out. They developed creative and effective strategies to justify speaking publicly. In particular, several Quaker women have had a noteworthy impact on women's rhetoric and women's public speaking. The following essay addresses the following aspects of women's rhetoric: (a) women's apologia, (b) the influence of Quaker women on public rhetoric, and (c) implications for women speaking today.

Women's Apologia

Apologia is a rhetorical category of public speaking designed to defend one's positions, opinions, or actions. For example, Chris-

---

[1]http://www.americanrhetoric.com/top100speechesall.html
[2]http://www.brainyquote.com/quotes/authors/v/virginia_woolf.html

tian apologetics is the defense of Christian theology and doctrines. Moreover, Ware and Linkugel (1973) proposed that apologia is the speech of self-defense used in response to "an attack upon a person's character, upon his worth as a human being" (Ware and Linkugel, 1973, p. 274). Speakers using apologetic rhetoric may use *justificatory speech* as a means of defending themselves when moral character has been questioned, as has been the case for women speaking publicly throughout much of history.

The rhetorical posture of justification is comprised of two strategies: *bolstering* and *transcendence* (Ware and Linkugel, 1973). Bolstering reinforces the existence of the beliefs and values and sentiments of the audience. Transcendence connects a viewpoint, value, or sentiment to a larger, noble concept that the audience can accept but has not previously associated with that viewpoint, value, or sentiment. The use of bolstering and transcendence has been a primary strategy used by women throughout different eras to justify speaking and writing publicly. Women used justificatory speech to establish their credibility to speak publicly, thus, in essence, asking the audiences for understanding and approval of their rhetorical situation.

The necessity of using these strategies was prompted by the misogynist social taboos that called women's virtue and piety into question if they spoke out publicly, particularly if their speaking challenged patriarchal and or hegemonic norms. These norms can be traced back to misogynous Greek and Roman philosophies and practices that influenced Western intellectual traditions and the misuse of the Christian scripture to silence women.

Misogyny and Women's Rhetoric

In ancient Greece and Rome, women were considered subordinate to men in every way; they were not educated formally and not given citizenship. They were considered little better than chattel. They were considered to be a curse and the source of evil (Cunningham and Hamilton, 2000, p. 75). Influential thinkers in the succeeding eras echoed the Greek and Roman belief that women were inferior to men intellectually, morally, emotionally, and physically. Cunningham and Hamilton (2000) explained that Greek hostility toward women "was repeated for many generations by Greeks, Romans, Jews, Arabs, and Europeans, shaping politicians, artists, educators, architects, generals, and entrepreneurs" (p. 78). These views were perpetuated rhetorically through the "classical" education of men via the study of classical rhetoric. Rhetoric, as established by the Greeks, was one of the cultural cornerstones of the intellectual system for centuries.

The influence of Greek and Roman views about women also leavened Jewish rabbinical tradition and the early Christian church. Jewish rabbinical leaders over the centuries had incorporated Greek hostility toward women by teaching that women were more prone to sin and considered possessions to be used (Cunningham and Hamilton, 2000). "Jewish women were marginalized from the worship of God. They couldn't participate in many of the most important rituals. They were segregated into a separate court...even though this was not God's original design for the tabernacle" (p. 105). This is in contrast to the Judeo-Christian tradition established in the Genesis account of creation where "man and woman are shown to have a shared origin, a shared destiny, a shared tragedy, a shared hope" (p. 93). The early Christian church in many ways reflected the Jewish tradition that birthed it, particularly concerning women speaking publicly.

In contrast to traditional Jewish views of his time, The Apostle Paul commended numerous women to ministry which included public speaking: Priscilla, Euodia, Synthyche, Lydia, Phoebe, and Junia were released into leadership positions in the early church. Additionally, the Gospel accounts reveal that the risen Jesus commissioned women to preach and fulfill the requirements of apostle (Cunningham and Hamilton, 2000, pp. 24-26). In spite of Paul's account and apparent approval of women in leadership, his words in I Corinthians and I Timothy have been misused and misinterpreted to marginalize women's voices since he wrote them:

- Let the women keep silent in the Churches; for they are not permitted to speak, but let them subject themselves, just as the Law also says. And if they desire to learn anything, let them ask their own husbands at home; for it is improper for a woman to speak in Church. (I Cor. 14:34, NASB)

- Let a woman quietly receive instruction with entire submissiveness. But I do not allow a woman to teach or exercise authority over a man, but to remain quiet. (I Tim. 2:11)

In spite of the common historical misapplication of the scripture, men and women throughout successive eras have challenged the application of this scripture to all women, at all times, and all places.

These strong cultural, social, and religious injunctions restricted women's roles and inhibited them from speaking or writing publicly for many centuries. Consequently, women throughout different eras

78

have had to (a) establish their ethos to speak publicly as women, and (b) to find a way to make their arguments palatable to mixed audiences in spite of the challenge their rhetoric might level against patriarchal, political, or cultural ideologies of their day. That is, they specifically utilized forms of women's apologia, characterized by the strategies of bolstering and transcendence indicative of justificatory speech. I will illustrate this technique through the example of women speakers in the Society of Friends.

Quaker Women Speaking

Women throughout every era have demonstrated great ingenuity in addressing injunctions against their rhetoric. Some of the best examples have been Quaker women. The Quaker movement is a Protestant movement, birthed in the seventeenth century and characterized by its egalitarian views. Quakers, or "The Society of Friends," emphasized the right of each person, male or female, to listen to the "inner light" or leading of the Holy Spirit.

Consequently, Quaker women were active members of the congregation and many travelled extensively to preach the gospel: "Especially in the early years, a large number–possibly the majority–of travelling Quaker preachers were women" (MacLean, 2013). Quaker women were arrested, beaten (Ann Coleman, Mary Tompkins, Alice Ambrose), and even martyred (e.g., Mary Barrett Dye) because they refused to stop preaching.

Margaret Fell

One of the best known Quaker speakers is Margret Fell (1614-1702), wife of George Fox, the founding father of Quakerism. Fell was a gifted speaker and writer who had a skillful command of scripture. In particular, she is famous for her arguments against misinterpreting Paul's words; she spoke out rigorously in favor of women speaking publicly, especially Christian women. Her knowledge of scripture and argumentation skills made her a powerful advocate in defense of women's right to speak publicly. Fell relied on bolstering and transcendence to make her case. She bolstered her arguments by appealing to the cultural value placed upon Christian scripture by relying on biblical themes. Similarly, she relied on transcendence by referring to the importance of obeying God and the guidance of The Holy Spirit rather than the laws and traditions of men.

Fell (1666) outlined her arguments in her essay *Women's Speaking Justified, Proved, and Allowed by the Scriptures.* She bolstered her arguments by relying on the Bible to disprove prevailing false perceptions about women based on the misapplication of Christian scripture. First, she cited Genesis–explaining that when God created man and woman He created them equally in His image: "God joins them together in his own image, and makes no such distinction and differences as men do" (Fell, 1666, p. 753). Her argument transcended the cultural belief that women were inferior by demonstrating their equality as proven by the Genesis account.

Next, she explained that silencing women was the devil's scheme: "if the seed of the women speak not, the seed of the serpent speaks . . . those that speak against the woman and her seeds speaking, speak out of the enmity of the old serpent's seed" (p. 753). That is, she accused those who would silence women as being in league with Satan: "All this opposing and gain saying of women's speaking hath risen out of the bottomless pit and the spirit of darkness that has spoken for these many hundred years together in this night of apostasy" (p. 756). Thus, women's speaking transcends cultural prohibitions because if women don't speak out, the devil will.

Fell addressed Paul's exhortation for women to remain silent by explaining the cultural context in which Paul delivered that message. She argued that specific scriptures can only be interpreted in the light of the whole scripture. Bible verses must not be taken out of the context in which they were written. She explained that the Corinthian church (made up of men and women) was in confusion over the use of the gifts of the Holy Spirit, and Paul was writing because he was concerned about the disorder and chaos. She pointed out that both men and women (not simply women) were commanded to be quiet, if there was confusion or disorder. Moreover, the women who were to save their questions for their husbands at home were Jewish and Gentile women who had not yet converted to Christianity. That is, these women were under the Law and had not been liberated in Christ. Fell inferred that these unconverted women were causing confusion and strife, not the Christian women who had received the Holy Spirit and the gifts of the Holy Spirit. She suggested that perhaps these women were attempting to introduce heretical teachings associated with the pagan religions of that day. This would have been true of women in Ephesus also, famous for its worship of the goddess Artemis (Diana), where Timothy was the pastor. Additionally, Fell pointed out that Paul allowed women to pray and prophesy; that is, Paul allowed women to speak for God. Fell reminded her readers that according to Joel 2 "handmaids would prophesy. . . [and asked] are not handmaids women?" (p. 759). Similarly, she referenced the book of Acts when "the Spirit of the Lord was poured forth upon daughters as well as sons" (p. 758), who were all speaking in many languages and glorifying God. Fell argued that the "True Church" was made up of men and women compelled to speak by the power of the Holy Spirit.

Furthermore, Fell bolstered her arguments by citing precedents of women speaking, as cited in the Bible. She listed Mary Magdalene, Mary (the mother of Jesus), and Joanna whom Jesus commissioned as the first apostles because he told them to go and tell others about his resurrection. They were commissioned by Jesus to speak publicly about what they had witnessed. Fell also lists Priscilla, Hannah, Elizabeth, the daughters of Phillip, Hulda, Miriam, and Esther–women in the Bible who spoke publicly by the authority of God.

By explaining that Jesus and the Apostle Paul allowed women to speak, she also bolstered her argument by appealing to the importance of the authority given to these men in scripture. Not only did women in the Bible speak with God's blessing, but also these same women have been cited by famous men throughout history. Undergirding her argument with examples of men who supported women speaking allowed Fell to appeal to hegemonic gender norms of her time, a means of bolstering. Consequently, Fell bolstered her own credibility and justified her own public speaking. Bizzell and Herzberg (2001) explained Fell's strategy:

> Fell did not justify her own speaking merely on the grounds that she was possessed by God, prophesying in the grip of a holy vision.[3] Many Protestant women adopted the posture of prophet to justify their public speaking, but this was an inherently humble role, implying that the women herself did not speak but that God spoke through her, and that she would subside when the divine spirit left her. Fell, in contrast, behaved like a full-scale leader of the Society of Friends throughout her life. She was never silent on any controversy within the Society. (p. 751)

Fell relied on bolstering by using the Bible itself as the source of her arguments, and she skillfully demonstrated the strategy of transcendence indicative of the justificatory stance of women's apologia.

---

[3]This argument had been made by Christian women previously, especially religious women, such as Hildegard of Bingen and Teresa of Avilla, in convents who wrote about their mystical experiences with the Lord.

Women and the Enlightenment

During the nineteenth century, Enlightenment philosophies had taken root and the separation of the public and private spheres influenced ideas about women's roles in society (Hoffecker, 2007; Pearcy, 2005). The public sphere belonged to reason, logic, and scientific discovery; it was the world of rational, educated men. The private world was reserved for domestic and spiritual pursuits; it was better suited for women because of their highly "emotional" and "irrational" natures. This directly influenced views about women's roles in public: they were to be seen but not heard.

Religious institutions reinforced the misinterpreted biblical injunctions that had successfully silenced women and demanded they demonstrate piety and submission. This manifested in strong social sanctions meant to keep women from speaking, especially to mixed audiences of men and women, or "promiscuous" audiences (Zaeske, 1995). Although originally signifying mixed audiences, the term "promiscuous" came to represent a term that cast doubt on a woman's femininity, chastity, and virtue. The idea of the promiscuous audience reinforced "early nineteenth century conceptions of woman's sphere and became a puissant weapon in the hands of traditionalists secular and religious alike–who sought to keep women off the platform and out of the public arena" (p. 191). No woman wanted to be identified as promiscuous.

The threat of having one's virtue called into question silenced women: "At the time piety was considered a preeminent feminine virtue; few women dared to risk appearing un-Christian by speaking to mixed audiences" (Zaeske, 1995, p. 197). At that time the ideology of "true womanhood" reinforced the belief that women were irrational and seductive and should be silent. Welter (1966) defined the ideology of virtuous womanhood as "the cult of true womanhood" or "the cult of domesticity." MacHaffee (1982) explained:

> The word "cult" is used to indicate that this was an almost sacred ideal to which many people were devoted. The ideal American woman was described as submissive, morally pure, and pious. She found power and happiness at home in the role of wife and mother. The cult of true womanhood permeated American culture even in remote corners of the frontier. (p. 93)

In other words, women who ventured out of their assigned private spheres of house and family to speak publicly risked harsh social consequences. Consequently, the challenge for women who felt compelled to speak out was to prove it was virtuous and in accordance with moral authority to do so.

The Grimkes

This was the rhetorical situation in which Sarah and Angelina Grimke found themselves during the early 1800's. The Grimke sisters grew up in the Southern United States; their father was an influential judge and slave owner. As young women, Sarah and Angelina moved to the North and became abolitionists. They attracted much attention not only because they were southerners speaking out against slavery, but also because they were women who dared to breech social conventions by speaking to mixed audiences. They traveled all over America, speaking out against the injustices of slavery.

Initially, they spoke to women's groups. However, they spoke so effectively that men came to hear them as well. With increased fame came increased risk, because male hecklers followed and threatened them. Sometimes violence broke out, and the sisters found it harder to find places to speak. Consequently, they received harsh criticism not only from men but from women also. Sarah and Angelina also became role models for generations of women who followed because of their skill in taking on arguments in defense of women's right to speak publicly.

The rhetorical situation demanded that the sisters devise a strategy of defense; they did so through justificatory speech in defense of women speaking publicly. The sisters used similar strategies of bolstering and transcendence. A comparison of Sarah's rhetoric in "Letters on the Equality of the Sexes and the Condition of Women" (Grimke, 1666) and Angelina's rhetoric in "An Appeal to Christian Women in the South"[4] reveals that both sisters were well educated, intelligent, and had a good theological grasp of biblical texts.

Like women rhetors before them, both women relied heavily on transcendence via the use of biblical themes. They indicated their desire to obey the New Testament and the teachings of Jesus above the traditions of men. Citing the Bible bolstered their argument by appealing to the cultural and religious norms that placed value on the Christian scriptures, and it bolstered their credibility as moral, pious women who desired to live virtuously before God.

Sarah Grimke explained that women were to depend on God for truth and instruction. She directly challenged hegemonic gender views about women. She explained that men and women were

---

[4]http://utc.iath.virginia.edu/abolitn/abesaegat.html

"CREATED EQUAL; they are both moral and accountable beings, and whatever is right for man to do, is right for woman" (Grimke, 1666, p. 1051). Insisting that God did not make distinctions between the sexes in terms of intellect and morality, she challenged male-biased interpretations of scripture as a means of silencing and subordinating women unjustly. She reminded her audience that Jesus required all, men and women, to shine before men, and defends her obedience:

> I follow him through all his precepts, and find him giving the same directions to women as to men, never even referring to the distinction now so strenuously insisted upon between masculine and feminine virtues: this is one of the anti-Christian "traditions of men" which are taught instead of the "commandments of God" (Grimke, 1666, pp. 1050-1051).

Sarah argued that the doctrine of silence imposed upon women only was an "antichristian" doctrine damaging to a woman's moral being and destructive to her soul. Bizzell & Herzberg (2001) explained her arguments against the hypocrisy of men's perceptions of womanhood:

> She denounces men's insistence on seeing women always as sexual beings and argues that women's eloquence arises not from sex but from spiritual and mental powers that they share equally with men and that they must be allowed to exercise (p. 1048).

Thus, Sarah confronted the hypocrisy of applying biblical truths to women and not to men.

In contrast to Sarah, Angelina took an indirect approach by appealing to women's beliefs about their own abilities to speak up and make a difference. Like her sister, Angelina used biblical themes and demonstrated her familiarity with Bible history, texts, and interpretations. Angelina urged women to speak to their fathers, husbands, brothers, and those within their sphere of influence, i.e., their homes. By doing so, she affirmed the hegemonic gender norm of a woman's place in the home.

She skillfully developed her argument against slavery by asking her southern sisters to first pray, then read, then speak, and finally to act. She told them to search the scriptures for themselves and allow God to speak directly to them before they spoke to others. In this way, Angelina does not directly attack the views of men; she simply addresses women from a moral stance, asserting that speaking out against slavery is a Christian and virtuous act of righteousness, approved by God.

Angelina developed her arguments in the letter by explaining that women should care for the slaves, be patient with them, teach them to read, and intervene on their behalf. She appealed to women's nurturing side, which further bolstered her argument by affirming the piety and virtue of godly womanhood. In other words, she indirectly offered a contrast between virtue and ignorance–the virtuous, kind woman in contrast to the ignorant and/or cruel male.

Sarah and Angelina both used similar arguments and bolstered those arguments by appealing to biblical themes and hegemonic gender norms, and demonstrating their own virtue and piety and their desire to be godly women, wives, and daughters. Both Grimkes bolstered their arguments by appealing to male authority: they both listed the males in the Bible and in church history who sanctioned and allowed women to speak. They bolstered their arguments by demonstrating that wise men not only allowed women to speak, but stood up against unrighteousness and injustice. Both used transcendence by calling women to obedience to God over man. They wanted women to speak up for righteousness and truth and against injustice and oppression because God had called them to obey Him rather than the traditions of men. These Quaker women demonstrated brilliance and invention when crafting their arguments in favor of women speaking publicly.

Down to Today

During this time other social movements were germinating as well. Many in the women's suffrage movement began as abolitionists, e.g., Cady Stanton and Lucretia Mott. The Quaker and Methodist denominations both produced and released women into leadership and speaking ministries. As a result many social agencies aiding orphans, the poor, and the sick were started by women from these denominational backgrounds. Some of the names of women speaking powerfully in that era include: Mary Bosanquet, Sarah Crosby, Sarah Mallet, Phoebe Palmer, Jarena Lee, and Catherine Booth. All of these women made an indelible mark on society because they dared breech conventions that would silence them and instead spoke out for the Lord and His cause.

These women learned from women before them and utilized the same kinds of arguments representative of women's apologia. Because of these feminist forerunners, women secured the right to vote, and a greater acceptance of women's public speaking took root in

America by the twentieth century. This is still not the case in some areas of the world today.

Does this have any relevance for women speaking today? Is women's apologia still needed? Do women still need to justify speaking publicly to mixed audiences? Although most do not think immediately of women when they are asked to think of a famous public speaker, most would not argue that women should not be allowed to speak. However, there is still ambivalence, some confusion, and even some hostility that exists on the subject of women speaking in the Church. Some denominations have lifted restrictions; some still have them. A letter asking well-known female Christian speakers about their public speaking policies revealed that each one had formed a defense of her right to speak publicly, using strategies of bolstering and transcendence that echoed female rhetors in previous eras (Foote, 2003).

If one does a simple Internet search on women speaking in the church today, there are numerous web sites condemning the practice and justifying keeping women silent. Many of these reflect the same misconceptions and misuse of scripture that has been evident since the Apostle Paul wrote to the Corinthians and to Timothy. However, there are also others that defend women speaking in the church, and books have been published by godly men defending such practices (Cunningham and Hamilton, 2000; Grady, 2006).

Women in every era have demonstrated wisdom, skill, intelligence, and creativity when approaching and overcoming hegemonic gender norms. In particular, women's apologia gives women a historical well from which to draw strategies to bolster and transcend sexist ideologies and gender norms that compel them to remain silent when they know they must speak. Quaker women, such as Margret Fell and the Grimke sisters, have given women good examples of how to rise above cultural, social, and religious barriers to speak in obedience to God rather than be silenced by traditions of men. Young women today who want to speak can learn from women before them who have spoken. Perhaps in the future, when asked to think of influential and famous public speakers, more women's names will make that list.

Cunningham, L. and Hamilton, D. (2000). *Why not women? A fresh look at scripture on women in missions, ministry, and leadership*. Youth With A Mission Publishing, Seattle, WA.

Fell, M. (1666). Womens speaking justified, proved, and allowed by the scriptures. In Bizzell, P. and Herzberg, B., editors, *The*

rhetorical tradition: Readings from classical times to the present,
pages 753–760. Bedford/St. Martin's, 2nd edition.

Foote, L. (2003). A history of womens apologia: The necessity of
using the justificative posture. Master's thesis, The University of
Akron, Akron, OH.

Glenn, C. (1997). *Rhetoric retold: Regendering the tradition from
antiquity through the renaissance.* Southern Illinois University
Press, Carbondale, IL.

Grady, L. (2006). *Ten lies the church tells women.* Charisma House,
Lake Mary, FL.

Grimke, S. (1666). Letters on the equality of the sexes and the
condition of woman, letters iii, iv, and xiv. In Bizzell, P. and
Herzberg, B., editors, *The rhetorical tradition: Readings from
classical times to the present*, pages 1050–1060. Bedford/St. Martin's, 2nd edition.

Hoffecker, A. (2007). *Revolutions in worldview: Understanding the
flow of Western thought.* P&R Publishing, Philipsburg, NJ.

MacHaffee, B. J. (1982). *Her story: Women in Christian tradition.*
Fortress Press, Philadelphia, PA.

Pearcy, N. (2005). *Total truth: Liberating Christianity from its
cultural captivity.* Crossway Books, Wheaton, IL. Study guide
edition.

Stallybrass, P. (1986). Patriarchal territories: The body enclosed.
In Ferguson, M., Quilligan, M., and Vickers, N., editors, *Rewrit-
ing the renaissance*, pages 123–144. University of Chicago Press,
Chicago, IL.

Ware, B. L. and Linkugel, W. A. (1973). They spoke in defense
of themselves: On the generic criticism of apologia. *Quarterly
Journal of Speech*, 59(3):273–275.

Welter, B. (1966). The cult of true womanhood: 18201860. *American Quarterly*, 18(2):1521–174.

Zaeske, S. (1995). The "promiscuous audience" controversy and
the emergence of the early womens rights movement. *Quarterly
Journal of Speech*, 81:191–207.

Chapter 4

Quaker Scholarship

Among the concerns of scholars who participate in the Friends Association for Higher Education is a commitment to inquiring how being a Friend, or a "Friendly" non-Quaker, contributes to the way in which we go about pursuing our academic work, and the impact of this orientation upon our scholarship. In this section of the book are essays that ask these questions, and begin to answer them, around the more general topics of academic writing styles and scholarly detachment, as well as the attempt to think in a Quakerly manner about the specific fields of anthropology, English, art, and philosophy.

In her essay "'In this World, but not of This World': An Unprogrammed Friend and Anthropologist Reflects on Fieldwork among Evangelical Friends," Abigail Adams wrestles with how, as a young anthropologist, she had attempted to negotiate the tensions between researcher and researched, between science and faith, between developed and developing cultures, between liberal and Evangelical Friends with their divergent theological and political sensibilities. While her experience as a Ph.D. researcher in Guatemala serves as the backdrop for this discussion, the challenges it touches upon are faced by most of us who conduct research among those with whom we are in community.

The next three articles on "Plaining the Academy," making up a set, address the issue of how to bring the traditional Quaker testimony of "simplicity" (formerly "plainness") to bear upon the practice of academic writing. In the first of these, "Plain Art: The Un-embellished Ideal of Quaker and Academic Writing," Pink Dandelion outlines Peter Collins' thesis that "plaining" (which "points towards inward spirituality even whilst its emphasis is the outward reduction of superfluity") runs through the history of Quakerism.

He suggests out of this discussion that the Quaker "plaining" tendencies toward "integrity and fit for use" fit well with "the economy and directness of style of academic prose" (provided that it can avoid the excesses that can infect academic writing) and that Quaker academic thinking in its creative and artistic drive to create new ways of thinking about the world can be described as "plain art." Laura Redieh's joins the conversation with her "'Plain Style' Academic Writing: Not Just for Quakers?" Redieh's helpfully asks whether "plainness" and "simplicity" should be taken as synonyms, and across an examination of the ideas of dialectic, rhetoric, jargon, and equivocation, suggests that what "plainness" should be taken to mean in Quaker academic writing, indeed, in any academic writing, depends to some degree upon the purposes and intended audience of any given piece of writing. Mike Heller rounds out this discussion of "Plaining the Academy" by investigating–in dialogue with John Woolman among others, and thinking writing in relation to the Quaker experience of speaking in meeting–how plainness might be understood in relation to honesty and clarity, i.e., as a faithfully artful, outward expression of an inner, spiritual ethos, or in terms of his title, a matter of "Taking the Meeting with Us."

Steve Smith, in his "Scholarly Detachment and Quaker Spirituality," provides an analysis of the idea of scholarly detachment as it is traditionally understood (that is, as a species of Platonic abstraction, or as the indifference of empty theorizing), and offers an alternative vision that he associates with wisdom: that is, with the ability to attend to the larger context and meaning of the topic under investigation. Steve challenges scholars, across his proposal to understand "detachment" as "non-attachment," to consider how their work can be both academically rigorous, and at once heart-led, that is, spiritually aware and communally responsible.

In his "John Keats and Ethical Practice," James Hood provides an interpretation of Keat's three 1819 odes–"Ode to Psyche"; "Ode on Melancholy: and "To Autumn"–across an examination of their relationship to Keat's personal biographical concerns as these related to the poet's parallel movement toward what Hood calls "ethical practice." Ethical practice, in both writing and reading, is presented here as the negotiation of a mid-space between pure aesthetic enjoyment, on the one hand, and didactic morality on the other, a space of choice between competing goods. Hood evocatively suggests that Keat's trajectory, across these poems, from ego centered concerns toward attentiveness to the human and natural "other," articulated in the poet's ideas of "negative capability" and "disinterestedness," resonate with the experience of Quaker meeting.

"As Quakers we know that the silence of expectant waiting which lies at the heart of our spiritual practice is a very powerful force." In her "The Art of Silence: Exploration of an Artistic Medium" Rebecca Leuchak explores the self-conscious use of silence in the musical, visual, and performance arts emerging over the recent centuries. Sometimes as a way of experimenting with Asian, North American, or medieval spiritual practices, sometimes as meditative preparation for artistic creation, sometimes as an exploration of the unconscious, or of the tabula rasa of being, sometimes as artistic, social, or political critique, and sometimes as a deeply positive, spirit-led search for the transcendent–the use of "silence" abounds in recent Western art. Leuchak's essay challenges us to consider our own attachment to silence in light of its plurality of possible meanings.

A second set of three articles bring together three philosophers who discuss the intersection of their discipline with their Quaker faith, reflections generated out of a Friends Association for Higher Education session on this topic that attracted thirty participants. In her "Where Quakerism and Philosophy Meet: The Ethical Ideal of Respect," Laura Rediehs examines her identity as Quaker, and identity as philosopher, and ponders the resonances (while confessing the frequent dissonances) these evoke in her. Philosophy as the "love of wisdom" provides her with a first indication of such a convergence: being a lover in pursuit of not only the knowledge of what is, but in developing a sensitivity "to the play of the light of goodness upon the world." She suggests "respect" as a candidate for the core principle of Quakers in philosophy. Richard Miller shares his experience of doing philosophy in a Quaker context in his essay: "Broadening Philosophy's Appeal." Miller bemoans as largely destructive the tendency among most current academic philosophy toward professionalization, specialization, and insularity, seeking instead to draw philosophy back to the questions of vital concern to everyone, and to discourses that are open to all. He proffers the pragmatic philosophy of C. I. Lewis as a helpful way toward this end, and finds encouragement in the resonances he has discovered for these concerns among other Quaker philosophers. Finally, in an essay entitled "Philoi sophias: Quakerism and the Vocation to Philosophy," Jeffrey Dudiak strives to articulate the relationship between his Quakerism and his philosophizing by (despite the dangers!) adopting the designation "Quaker philosopher" over the less integrative possibility: "Quaker who is also a philosopher." For Dudiak, the concern here is not one of content, but of "taking up philosophizing in a Quakerly manner," where one's faith stance is non-incidental to both the "what" and the "how" of one's every activity, where one's "confession" radically effects one's "profession" (in the sense of vocation).

"In this World, but not of This World": An Unprogrammed Friend and Anthropologist Reflects on Fieldwork among Evangelical Friends

by Abigail Adams, Central Connecticut State University

In 1990, as Guatemalans prepared for elections that would transfer power from a civilian to a civilian for the first time in nearly forty years, I spoke with a U.S. nurse who worked in that country's east. Although she could not vote in this election, she favored one "candidate": former dictator General Efrain Rios Montt. The Constitution prohibited him, a coup leader, from holding executive office. Furthermore, Rios Montt, an evangelical Christian and former military dictator (1982 to 1983) is associated with the worst of Guatemala's genocidal violence. With the eyes of the seer, she was describing the "spiritual warfare" in Guatemala that she sensed all around her, supernatural forces of evil that were battling the Christian faithful.

She was a missionary, I was an anthropologist. She was discussing spiritual warfare, I was conducting social science. She sought to live "in this world but not of this world," I worked as a lobbyist. She was a born-again evangelical Christian, I was a member of a theologically liberal faith.

I took notes, noting how fellow anthropologists would "eat up" this material on U.S. missionaries involved in conflict regions subject to U.S. policy. Anthropologists regard missionaries as intolerant of non-Christian, non-Western ways of life, and as handmaidens of imperialism. I was beginning doctoral research in cultural anthropology, a fragile process I hoped would eventually land me a coveted job in academia. This interview seemed to be going well.

She was Quaker. So was I.

A month's work later, I moved to another fieldsite.

I now revisit that decision, as well as hopes for continuing research with the evangelical Friends of eastern Guatemala. FAHE provides me a wonderful opportunity for discernment; I am considering the following queries: What happens to Friends and scholarship when Friends research and produce scholarly work on other Friends? What happens to the researcher's faith and relationship with her faith community? How do we handle potential conflicts between our Quaker loyalties and uncomfortable research material? How does one's research benefit from the potential insider's insight?

Anthropologists describe these queries as cultural reflexivity, the two-pronged dilemma that all researchers working with another culture learn about their own culture–and cannot shed their enculturation and social statuses when entering the field. Cultural research becomes more complex when one's subject is culturally "close to home." Many anthropologists address this challenge by choosing a "foreign" fieldsite first, and later, a "home"-sited inquiry. The initial cross-cultural stretch gives the researcher the distance to review one's "home" with more perspective. My faith and identity find their primary home among Quakers, an ancestral home with conflicting housemates–in part, the same conflict over proselytizing that anthropologists and missionaries have.

The Friends mission was a rich site for my dissertation's exploration of the claim that counterinsurgent Guatemala was undergoing an "evangelical boom." The Evangelical Friends Alliance missionaries in eastern Guatemala welcomed me warmly, when I asked to visit them in a pre-research fieldtrip. From California, their churches founded one of Guatemala's five original Protestant denominations in 1903, a few years after the United States won the Spanish-American war. The missionaries built their headquarters in Chiquimula, a regional center in Guatemala's rugged east. They initially had little success converting either the Ch'orti' Maya people or the Spanish- speaking Ladino majority of the region. Then, with the invitation of the U.S.-owned United Fruit Company (UFCo), they held services among banana workers in rooms provided by the Company. UFCo was a key player in the 1954 U.S.-sponsored coup in Guatemala that ended democracy, began over 36 years of military rule, civil war and bloody counterinsurgency.

Rios Montt, whom the Guatemalan Friends supported, was one of those military dictators. The Guatemalan Friends, in fact, sponsored one of his first public appearances since his fall from power. In 1988, Rios Montt visited the headquarters of the Chiquimula-based denomination, taught Sunday School and raised funds for their radio station campaign.

I was fascinated–and honestly, angered–by their seeming distance from the Friends historical peace testimony and advocacy for Native Americans. However, the picture was much more complex. The U.S. Friends had worked for decades in this region, often times with the poorest of the poor. The U.S. missionary featured in the opening of this essay had, with her husband, helped a group of Ch'orti' Maya people secure a settlement in Guatemala's northern regions. They had carried out this longterm work in social justice, even though the mission and home churches regarded such projects as tangential to evangelism and church building. The Friends churches had finally began to grow in the 1970s, tripling in the number of congregations by the time I arrived in 1990. Nevertheless, after nearly a century, this was not a booming evangelical field by any account, serving at most 30,000 attenders.

I faced many conflicts of interests. Besides the longstanding friction between missionaries and anthropologists, I felt strongly opposed to any support for Rios Montt, based on my experience of having worked as for three years a journalist in the region during the 1980s wars. But many other anthropologists have overcome obstacles such as these.

The deal breaker was my loyalty to Friends, all Friends of our wider fellowship. Involved with unprogrammed Quakers since high school and a graduate of Haverford College, the first meeting I joined (Monteverde, Costa Rica) was affiliated with the Friends World Committee for Consultation. I knew about pastored and evangelical Friends, and cared about our diverse ways of being Friends in an increasingly globalized world.

I made the right decision to move my doctoral work. At that point, I was vulnerable, a proto-anthropologist undertaking the project that would serve as the basis for my career for several years. Despite the famed holism of anthropology, I had to be single-minded. My dissertation committee would not have been sympathetic to any diversionary audiences or sets of concerns.

I also felt vulnerable about discussing my faith in both the field and write-up. In the field, I felt dishonest because I was not the born-again Christian the Guatemalans assumed all Friends were. In the write-up, author reflexivity would be obligatory. Ethnographers freely shared reflections about their privileged or marginalized racial, ethnic, class, sexual or gender subject positions. But those practicing Christian faiths, even universalist, rational versions, were still in the closet as near as I could tell, perhaps because of Christianity's infamy of imperialistic ethnocentrism, and the perceived impasse between science and religion.

So I moved to the Verapaz, in northern Guatemala and another historic Protestant denomination, the Nazarenes. Results? Research in the Verapaz plunged me into discussion about my faith. Few interviews, few friendships, moved far before I answered the question, "What do you believe?" Following William Christian in his study of Spanish pilgrims, I introduced my faith to my readers; I would say that in difficult times, like most Guatemalans, I turn to friends for help. Failing that, unlike most Guatemalans, I turn inwards rather than toward divine figures. Nevertheless, I found that I was open to the validity of practices directed towards divine beingsand that I was willing to immerse myself in hours of worship quite different from that which I choose to sustain myself. I am ready for the "return home with perspective" to the eastern Guatemalan Friends.

Plain Art: The Un-embellished Ideal of Quaker and Academic Writing

by Pink Dandelion, Woodbrooke Study Center

Within the sociology of British Quakerism, there is a debate between those who see narrative threads of Quakerism running throughout the history of Quakerism, such as Gay Pilgrim, and those who see the twentieth century and the birth of Liberal Quakerism as significantly different to the degree that it represents a wholly new form of Quakerism. Peter Collins has claimed that one of the threads running through the history of Quakerism is the tendency to "the plain" and to what he calls "plaining" (Collins, 1996, 2001, 2008). This article attempts to outline his theory of the plain whilst allowing for the shifts Liberal Quakerism introduced as a precursor to thinking about how far academic writing can be considered plain in Quaker terms (or, as the companion articles ask, how far Quaker academic writing can be considered plain).

The impulse to the plain as a consequence of spiritual transformation came very early in the history of Friends. We find a distinctive set of behaviours readily identifying Quakers from "the world" almost from the beginning. The following quotation, written by one of two cousins appointed to police plainness amongst the homes of the members, is from the 1680s, and depicts well the main concerns.

> As to our own clothing, we had but little to alter, having both of us been pretty plain in our garb, yet some things we did change to greater simplicity. But my dear cousin, being naturally of a very exact and nice fancy, had things in more curious order as regards household furniture than I had: and therefore as a testimony against such superfluities and that spirit which led into it, he altered or exchanged, as I did, several articles that were too fine . . . Our fine veneered and garnished cases of drawers, tables, stands, cabinets, escritoires, &c., we put away, or exchanged for decent plain ones of solid wood, without superfluous garnishing or ornamental work; our wain-scots or woodwork we had painted of one plain colour; our large mouldings or finishings of panelling, & c., our swelling chimney-pieces, curiously twisted banisters, we took down and replaced with useful plain woodwork, & c.; our curtains, with valences, drapery and fringes that we thought too fine, we put

away or cut off; our large looking-glasses with decorated frames we sold, or made them into smaller ones; and our closets that were laid out with many little curious or nice things were done away. (Braithwaite, 1919, p. 507)

"Plain" is the key word here: Collins (1996) suggests that Quakers "plained" their lives and their Meeting Houses and that "plaining" acted as the creation of a symbolic order vis a vis the apostate church they defined themselves against. Plaining points towards inward spirituality even whilst its emphasis is the outward reduction of superfluity. Collins suggests that theologically it points to the hidden, to God, only to be revealed once the outward is removed (Collins, 1996, p. 285). Fox issued this advice on dress in 1688:

Away with your skimming-dish hats, and your unnecessary buttons on the tops of your sleeves, shoulders, backs and behind on your coats and cloaks. And away with your long slit yokes on the skirts of your waistcoat; and short sleeves, and pinching your shoulders so as you cannot make use of your arms, and your short black aprons and some having none. And away with your visors, whereby you are not distinguished. From bad women, and bare necks, and needless flying scarves like rollers on your back. (Braithwaite, 1912, p. 511)

Superfluity is contrasted with necessity.

Collins, in his work, places Quaker plain style within the broader context of Christian plain style and the important work by Peter Auksi. Auksi outlines the ideology of plain style:

If the devotee of Christian plainness in artistic expression has one central premise, it is this: the more lowly, artless, ineloquent, unadorned, and 'earthen' the outward vessel or covering garment of its style is, the more God-given and divinely persuasive appears the excellency of the matter to be conveyed or covered. (Auksi, 1995, p. 91)

The plain represents purity, a necessary but unadorned veil to cover the divine. As Collins writes "plain is to grand as spirit is to Flesh" (Collins, 2001, p. 127).

In other words, as Collins and I have written elsewhere (Collins and Dandelion, 2006), the holy is "wrapped" by the codes and rules of the group to enforce cohesion and to protect the means to, and expression of, experience, always central in the Quaker polity:

"The plain is rarely artless, it is generally a construction, a more or less conscious means of eschewing establishment" (Collins, 2001, p. 129). However, in plain style, a theological impulse is present too: "The Preacher is pressed to conceal his art and artifice and any mode of artistic expression, plain or not, as representing a formal technical skill" (Collins, 2001, p. 129). Plain is about minimalizing the world behind which or within which the holy operates. Plain is thus about constructing the un-embellished to protect and express the pure, both in terms of the human elect and the spiritual outworkings of transformation and providence.

In the eighteenth century, the plain was increasingly central as a measure of authenticity and the Quaker organization saw its transgression as one form of spiritual delinquency (Marietta, 2007). Quaker houses were plain and unadorned. The only picture found in British Quaker homes in the eighteenth century was the ground plan of Ackworth School, plain in its aesthetic and its affect. The battle over "the hedge" (between Quakers and the world) and its trimming after the 1850s included a battle over whether "plain" could be inhabited without outward expression. The debates in London Yearly Meeting over ending compulsory plain dress and speech were couched in terms of the ability to maintain "simplicity" inwardly. As a result, British Quakerism moved from the collective formality to individualistic choice, a shift mirrored in other parts of the Quaker world.

Testimony no longer functions as an automatic consequence to spiritual experience as it did for seventeenth century Friends, or as a rule of life in the way that it did in the eighteenth century. Testimony rather has become a set of values which are interpreted individually (Jung, 2006, pp. 32-56). Testimony as a necessary corporate category has become smaller as less is collectively agreed on as vital and also as the corporate experience reduces more and more to what happens at Meeting, with the home life outside of the control of the Meeting. Friends choose what is and is not plain for them. As Collins notes:

> After the mid-nineteenth century, what had been implicit was necessarily made explicit: the centrality of 'the plain' to Quaker faith and practice gave rise to the associated process, that is, plaining. Plaining is a learned and cognitive tendency to classify the world in terms of the distinction plain/not-plain. Quakers, as they mature, become more or less conscious of practicing such discrimination. I remember a long conversation between Friends after one Meeting for Worship in 2003

which was explicitly about the pros and cons of various cars. I have time here only to note that the comments could only be understood in the context of the Quaker tendency to plain. The fact that each Friend involved in the conversation preferred a different car in no way weakens my argument: plaining is a process which enables Quakers to justify the choices they make. For instance, a commodity which might seem far from plain to one Friend can be justified as plain in terms of its good safety record, because of the savings it will generate in the long run or because of the employment its manufacture provides. The criteria used to define the plain or not-plain are neither fixed nor essential. There is nothing necessary about, or inherent in, those things which are perceived to be plain. Things are constructed as plain by Friends. (Collins, 2008, p. 44)

Collins claims the "simplicity" of the debates of the 1850s, and the term more commonly used by Friends today, as an extension of plainness, as do Quakers:

The heart of Quaker ethics is summed up in the word simplicity. Simplicity is forgetfulness of self and remembrance of our humble status as waiting servants of God. Outwardly, simplicity is shunning superfluities of dress, speech, behaviours and possessions, which tend to obscure our vision of reality (BYM, 1995, 20.27)

This extract makes it clear the bicycle is to be preferred to the Volvo.

Returning to a more essential view of the plain as unadorned, constructed or conscious or not, what then are we to make of the genre of academic writing? In the early Quaker terms of plain, plainness is not about accessibility or consumption, indeed it plays against popular culture, separating itself off. It is anti-popular, anti-consumption. The ivory towers of academia fit with the sectarian perspective of the early Friends. Rather, it is about integrity and being fit for use without adornment. Good academic writing is surely within these parameters. The economy and directness of style of academic prose, its exactitude, and pedantry is wholly in line with George Fox's desire to avoid carnal and loose talk (Bauman, 1983). A reference list, as below, is surely an epitome of plain. Maybe the plain style of academic text attracts Quakers to the academy.

Where academic writing may fail in its inherent plainness is where the author seeks to overplay their wisdom and where the writing becomes adorned with personal aggrandizement. This may be a danger related to the growing trend within the social sciences to use the first person, where the role of analyst can become enmeshed with a more self- reflective style. As a Quaker studying Quakers, my doctoral supervisors were very keen I distance myself from my daily devotional affiliation. I wrote my thesis referring to myself as "this researcher" to deliberately differentiate my role as researcher from my life as Quaker. This may be academically less fashionable now but it served to help me remember who I was, to know where I was, and to remember my place, part of the intentions and impulses underpinning Quaker plain.

I believe strongly that academic thinking is highly creative, artistic: we are artists in our desire and ability to create new ways of thinking about the world. Our writing is plain art.

Auksi, P. (1995). *Christian Plain Style: the evolution of a spiritual ideal.* McGill-Queens University Press, Montreal and Kingston.

Bauman, R. (1983). *Let Your Words be Few: symbolism of speaking and silence amongst seventeenth-century Quakers.* Cambridge University Press, Cambridge.

Braithwaite, W. C. (1912). *The Beginnings of Quakerism.* Macmillan, London.

Braithwaite, W. C. (1919). *The Second Period of Quakerism.* Macmillan, London.

BYM (1995). *Quaker Faith and Practice: the book of Christian discipline in the Yearly Meeting of the Religious Society of Friends (Quakers) in Britain,* London. Britain Yearly Meeting.

Collins, P. and Dandelion, P. (2006). Wrapped attention: revelation and concealment in nonconformism. In Arweck, E. and Keenan, W., editors, *Materialising Religion,* pages 45–61. Ashgate, Aldershot.

Collins, P. J. (1996). "plaining": the social and cognitive practice of symbolisation in the religious society of friends (quakers). *Journal of Contemporary Religion,* 11:277–88.

Collins, P. J. (2001). Quaker plaining as critical aesthetic. *Quaker Studies,* 5:121–39.

Collins, P. J. (2008). The problem of quaker identity. In Dandelion, P. and Collins, P., editors, *The Quaker Condition: the sociology of a liberal religion*, pages 38–52. Cambridge Scholars Publishing, Newcastle.

Jung, J. (2006). *Ham Sokhon's Pacifism and the Reunification of Korea: a Quaker theology of peace*. Edwin Mellen, Lampeter.

Marietta, J. D. (2007). *The Reformation of American Quakerism, 1748-83*. University of Pennsylvania Press, Philadelphia.

"Plain Style" Academic Writing: Not Just for Quakers?

by Laura Rediehs, St. Lawrence University

Some academic writing is not "plain" by any definition of "plainness." The lack of plainness is often unintentional. Sometimes authors are themselves genuinely confused about what they are writing about. Other times, authors do not think to give proper attention to their writing style. They are aware of what they are trying to say, but may fail to notice that they have not in fact expressed themselves very clearly.

The problem of obscure writing may remain unchecked in the academic world because academic readers are unusually tolerant of difficult writing–they take such pride in their advanced reading and interpretive skills that they are often willing to spend a long time decoding a difficult text. Then, wanting to receive credit for all of this effort, they may decide to publish their interpretation: thus, difficult writing can get more attention and citation than clear writing. The net effect is that obscurity can actually be rewarded in the academic world.

Some academic writers even eschew plainness intentionally. A skilled writer with good ideas can learn to obfuscate just enough to be taken seriously. A writer aiming to persuade may employ logical fallacies in place of good argument since logical fallacies, even though somewhat deceptive, often have an immediate emotional effect, whereas good arguments require thought and effort and often provoke critical inquiry rather than immediate acceptance. At a more extreme level, since language use can be a mark of group identity, sometimes the intent of a piece of writing is not so much to communicate as to show (or show off) group identity and reinforce boundaries of exclusion.

The question of plainness in academic writing is a return to the ancient debate between the sophists and the philosophers. Is the point of writing rhetorical–to employ the art of persuasion for the sake of gaining power? Or is the point of writing dialectical–to exchange ideas in a sincere quest for truth or greater understanding? While some disparage the term "rhetoric," allowing it only its negative connotations, others argue that all writing is rhetorical, and that even dialectic is one form of rhetoric. We can have noble, truth-conducive reasons for wanting to persuade, and even for wanting to gain power. What I mean to question is morally-problematic uses of rhetoric and power: those uses that not only undermine truth but also deploy power for unjust purposes. Intentional attempts to obfuscate serve dubious power purposes. The Quakerly value of plain speaking is more aligned with the dialectical quest for wisdom.

But what is plainness? Because Quakers now use the term "simplicity" more than the term "plainness" to express a similar concept, at first it is tempting to think of plainness as equivalent to simplicity. But in a recent academic writing workshop I attended, the person leading this workshop, Jeanne Barker-Nunn, offered the following rule of thumb for academic writing: express simple ideas simply, and express complex ideas complexly. Too many writers, she pointed out, are inclined to try to express simple ideas complexly in order to sound sophisticated. But the reverse problem happens too: sometimes writers suffer writer's block because they are attempting the impossible task of expressing complex ideas simply. It is of course still possible to express complex ideas clearly. In fact, clarity is especially crucial for the task of expressing complex ideas, if we really want our writing to be understood. Aligning "plainness" with "clarity" (instead of "simplicity") is helpful, but we need to do even more to specify what counts as appropriate plainness: we need to consider the purposes of writing and the audiences for different kinds of writing. What are we trying to communicate, to whom, and why?

While academics sometimes write for nonacademic audiences, even within academic writing there are different audiences and different purposes. Scholarly books, for example, usually have wider academic audiences than journal articles, and serve different purposes. We write journal articles to share specific ideas and get feedback from highly specialized scholarly communities. We write scholarly monographs to collect our now well-tested ideas, put them together into a larger framework, and share those ideas with a wider educated audience who may benefit from reading about and learning the latest advances in our field. We write textbooks to share the latest and most well-tested thinking with students. Plainness takes different forms for these different audiences and purposes.

Words can be magical sometimes. There are times when the right string of words can spark helpful new understanding in the one who reads or hears those words. How do we find that magical sequence of words? The same string of words can evoke amazed insight in one person but blank confusion in another. Not everyone, even in the academic world, is a skilled listener or a skilled reader. Perhaps, as Thomas à Kempis said about reading the Bible (and Quakers like to repeat): one has to be in the spirit in which the words were written in order to understand them correctly. We know from our teaching that sometimes the problem is that our students just are not ready to understand a given idea. They may need to learn other things before this new idea can find a meaningful place in their system of thought. We need to remember this in our writing as well. Different audiences require different rhetorical strategies, and so "plainness" may look different for different audiences.

For example, let us consider the jargon dilemma: Which is plainer: using more words and less jargon, or using fewer words and more jargon? Jargon is often an abbreviated way to express an important and recurring complex idea. In its brevity, it is simpler, but it is only "plainer" to someone "in the know." To someone else not familiar with the term, or who has not struggled to understand and integrate the complex idea the term is meant to express, such jargon is not "plain" at all. It is mysterious and obscure. To someone not "in the know," jargon hides the detail and complexity of the thought it is trying to express.

But if we are clear about what we are trying to communicate, to whom, and why, we can make appropriate adjustments in our use of jargon. For a more specialized audience, the use of one's discipline's jargon is appropriately "plain" because it keeps one's writing clear and focused. But for a less specialized audience, avoiding or minimizing jargon is often "plainer" and clearer. Or sometimes (especially in writing intended to instruct) the correct balance is to introduce some of the jargon to the reader by clearly defining it first.

Jargon can closely resemble another use of language that is more problematic and runs counter to plainness: the logical fallacy known as "equivocation." Equivocation may look like jargon because it uses compact phrasing that can hide deeper meaning to one who is not "in the know." But in equivocation, the word or phrase does not have a stable meaning throughout the piece of writing: it changes meaning in subtle ways. Sometimes equivocation is unintended: the writer has not paused to think about what he or she really means by a rich or contested term or concept such as "objectivity," "justice," or even "God." Other times equivocation can be intentional: a way of hiding a weakness in argument, or a way of persuading people to accept a course of action that may not in fact be in their best interest. Political uses of terms such as "freedom," "security," or "the American way of life," are often used equivocally.

In conclusion, plain style cannot be determined by examining a text alone, but needs to take into account the rhetorical positioning of the text. Those who wish to express themselves plainly need to be clear about what they are trying to communicate, to whom, and why, and then need to adjust their use of language accordingly. While the use of jargon does not necessarily run counter to plainness, equivocation does, and should be avoided. These basic principles of rhetorical sensitivity are appropriate not just for Quaker academics, but arguably for all writers.

Taking the Meeting with Us

by Mike Heller, Roanoke College

> . . . the Quaker method of conducting business meet-
> ings is also applicable to the conducting of our indi-
> vidual lives, inwardly. (Kelly, 1941, writing of John
> Woolman, p. 118)

A Friend in our Monthly Meeting, Bob Fetter, tells the story of
his Aunt Eliza Rakestraw who was much admired for her ability to
be centered and speak well in many situations.

"How do you prepare so well for every situation?" someone asked
Eliza.

"We take the meeting with us," she replied.

When Bob told this story, he added, "And we take the meeting away with us." Eliza Rakestraw's statement speaks to me of
the centered presence I often wish for. This summer on my way
to Woodbrooke, I was stuck in a snail-paced security line at the
Amsterdam airport, when I heard the "last call" for my flight. I
was sweaty and tired and my frustration rose. When an attendant
directed me to the wrong gate, I was ready to vent my anger on the
nearest airline representative. I did not feel like a good Quaker. In
many faculty meetings my agitation gets the best of me. At such
times, I don't feel like a good Quaker. It is not always easy to
walk through a room gracefully, or even to stand in a security line
peacefully. In a related way, in my writing I often feel I fall short
of my self-image as the plain Quaker. Eliza Rakestraw's statement
that "We take the meeting with us" expresses a way of being centered in the spirit, supported by one's community, and living one's
testimonies–including simplicity and plainness–wherever one might
be. I don't consciously set out to write in a plain style, but if I did,
what would I be emphasizing? I'd be setting out to create a particular voice, a disposition, an identity, situating myself, and I would
be seeking a relationship with an intended or imagined audience.

What elements of style would I draw upon? There are features
in early Quaker writings that we might agree comprise a Quaker
plain style. Early Quakers sought in their journals to write of their
experimental knowledge of the spirit, often excluding other topics
which today we wish they had written of–they practiced a narrative
economy; they drew upon a diction of discernment and leadings of
the spirit; they used passive structures to signal their surrender to
the felt-spirit within; some writings use repetition to capture the
chant of vocal ministry. On some level, plainness it seems is not

artless but artful. Quaker writers, such as John Woolman, revised their writings, using syntactical choices and word choices as they sought to express accurately their experiences and ideas.

Is revision toward plainness a departure from spirit-led expression? The tension between artifice and artlessness is connected with other tensions or paradoxes of Quaker faith and practice. Richard Bauman, in *Let Your Words be Few* (Bauman, 1983), describes the paradox of worshipping in silence in order to find words to speak. The opposition of silence and speaking dramatizes the tension between the spirit and the flesh. Collins (2001) expresses the paradox in terms of inward spiritual reality and outward material reality: "...To be artful... is to deny the Light Within" (127), and later he writes that "The plain style... emphasizes spirit above 'flesh' (the material world)"; he follows a Marxist argument that, in a consumer culture, art trivializes and triumphs over reality; and the plain style might "bring to mind a reality over and above that suggested by commodification and consumerism" (132). I feel something of these tensions when I choose between a linear argument and an associative line of thinking, or when I choose between personal narrative and formal persuasion. For a long time, I sensed that Quaker worship was counter to my own creative impulse. Now I am not so sure. Writers like Alice Walker make me question my assumptions. She expands the definition of Art (with a capital A). In her essay "In Search of Our Mothers' Gardens" (Walker, 1983), Walker speaks of "the Black woman's" spirituality which helped her grandmothers and mother survive; she writes of a spirituality "which is the basis of Art," a spirituality which these women knew as reality (233, 237). The plain style, for Quakers, had the purpose of recovering the inward reality–a reality which transcends the market place. When early Quakers sought simplicity, they did so to live within that spiritual reality.

From classical rhetoric, how we conceive of ethos and style is suggestive for a consideration of Quaker plainness. Aristotle and others classified style as high, middle, or low. High style was called grand or ornate; the low style was the plain style. Rhetoricians wrote of the virtues of style, which include "appropriateness," "clarity," "purity," and "impressiveness" (Aristotle, 1982; Demetrius, 1973). "Purity" can be seen as a verbal representation, another kind of construct. How we conceive of ethos is relevant to how one shapes his or her identity, as it is evoked through speaking and writing. Northrop Frye, in *The Anatomy of Criticism* (Frye, 2006), writes that ethos is primarily concerned with social values, which he calls "moral values," including "sincerity, economy, subtlety, simplicity..." (22). In classical rhetoric, ethos is determined by the

107

impression which one creates of being trustworthy, having wisdom, and good will. Collins writes that both the grand style and the plain style are influenced by the author's disposition (130). "Clarity" seems to me a high priority in academic writing. In *Spiritual Autobiography in Early America*, Daniel Shea argues that Woolman saw the essence of his rhetorical task in terms of making clear to others what he had seen: "The literary art of Woolman's *Journal* consists largely in the author's essential act of clarification" (Shea, 1968, p. 65). This observation interestingly equates Woolman's desire for clarity with the essence of his art. Note in the following quotation from Woolman's *Journal*, his interest in "purity" and "clearness":

> My heart hath often been deeply affected under a feeling I have had that the standard of pure righteousness is not lifted up to the people by us, as a Society, in that clearness which it might have been had we been so faithful to the teachings of Christ as we ought to have been (Woolman, 1971, pp. 153- 54).

Accuracy to one's observations is also an expression of honesty (Barbour and Frost, 1988, pp. 41-42), a Quaker testimony and a contributing factor to one's persuasive ethos. Plainness, then, is useful. It is evocative and it creates access. Access is inward and outward: the writer goes inward for discovery, invention, creation, and heart-felt guidance; and then he or she goes outward to make writing understandable to readers. Plainness is a marker of group identity. The writer who chooses to use obscure or convoluted sentences is also asserting an identity.

Vocal ministry is a spiritual practice. In vocal ministry, one focuses on watching how words arise within, being sensitive to an inward spiritual guide, listening to others, shaping a message, and making a statement. In worship I make choices about when to speak and how to speak. In worship I return to George Fox's question, "What canst thou say?" Preparing to speak in worship, sitting with one's inward words, is part of the spiritual practice. We can see this at the end of Woolman's *Journal* chapter 5, describing the Yearly Meeting of 1758, where he did not speak through several sessions. He writes that "The case of slavekeeping lay heavy upon me," and when he does finally speak, he tells us that he said "nothing is more precious than the mind of Truth inwardly manifested" (Woolman, 1971, p 92). Woolman's spiritual practice of waiting upon the spirit not only allows him to "save up" his thoughts but also to deepen his understanding of what needs to be said. It is easy to imagine that this discipline carried over into his writing, although, as J. William Frost points out, the kinds of expression in Woolman's essays and *Journal* represent different modes of thought (Barbour and Frost, 1988).

My experience with vocal ministry has been shaping my writing and teaching. I have been experimenting with ways to use narrative, scene, and dialogue–trying to be guided by my heart and my sense of inward leadings. In worship, we are composing and we are being composed. In worship, as I am moved to speak, I think about shaping what I can say, with some sense of clarity and emphasis–but it is not always easy to walk through a room gracefully. I have written about how with journal writing students can center down and can value their inward lives (without an overt spiritual focus), and how asking students to share small writings about their experiences parallels sharing a message in worship (Heller, 2004). In discussions, I have been experimenting with having students pause after each person speaks, and not rush in to speak next, so that we can listen and consider what to say next. If style is a matter of choice, and choice makes speaking and writing more art than artless, what do we say to the objection that in worship one surrenders to the motion of the spirit? Should individuals revise inwardly in worship? This need must vary with individuals. I am also drawn to following my initial impulse and speaking spontaneously. There was a place in previous times for chanting and sing-song, a seemingly "automatic" expression, or more recently for the spontaneous in vocal ministry. In academic writing, as well, there is a place in the composing process for free writing, automatic writing, and letting go–whether or not such writing must be shaped and revised later to reach an audience. Whether revision happens inwardly (before speaking or writing), artfulness is involved in moving a piece of writing from private communication, meaningful to the writer alone, to public communication, meaningful to others.

I want to work more in the direction of writing from the heart and trying to write with integrity, which means owning or standing by the meaning expressed. Rebecca Mays quotes or paraphrases Isaac Penington saying that we must be careful "not to profess what we do not possess." Speaking of Woolman, Kelly writes, "He yielded to the Center and his life became simple. . . . These become our tasks. Life from the Center is a heaven-directed life" (Kelly, 1941, p. 117, 123). Now I see that writing has a good deal to do with temperament. What am I cut out for? I make hundreds of choices each day and watch my courage and cowardice, confidence and fears, obscurity and light.

Aristotle (1982). *The "Art" of Rhetoric.* Harvard University Press, Cambridge, MA.

Barbour, H. and Frost, J. W. (1988). *The Quakers.* Greenwood Press, New York, NY.

Bauman, R. (1983). *Let Your Words be Few: Symbolism of Speaking and Silence among Seventeenth-Century Quakers.* Cambridge University Press, Cambridge.

Collins, P. (2001). Quaker plaining as critical aesthetic. *Quaker Studies*, 5:121–39.

Demetrius (1973). On style. In Roberts, R., editor, *Aristotle: The Poetics; "Longinus": On The Sublime; Demetrius: On Style.* Harvard University Press, Cambridge, MA.

Frye, N. (2006). *The Anatomy of Criticism: Four Essays.* University of Toronto Press, Toronto.

Heller, M. (2004). 'wait to be gathered': The classroom as spiritual place. In Dalke, A. and Dixson, B., editors, *Minding the Light: Essays on Friendly Pedagogy*, pages 27–49. Peter Lang, New York, NY.

Kelly, T. R. (1941). *A Testament of Devotion.* Harper & Row Publishers, New York, NY.

Shea, D. B. (1968). *Spiritual Autobiography in Early America.* Princeton University Press, Princeton, NJ.

Walker, A. (1983). In search of our mothers' gardens. In *In Search of Our Mothers' Gardens: Womanist Prose.* Harvest/Harcourt, San Diego, CA.

Woolman, J. (1971). *The Journal and Major Essays of John Woolman.* Friends United Press, Richmond, IN.

Scholarly Detachment and Quaker Spirituality

by Steve Smith, Claremont McKenna College

> The Lord... opened it to me how that people and profes-
> sors... fed upon words, and fed one another with words,
> but trampled upon the life... and they lived in their airy
> notions...
> – George Fox[1]

In December 1972, at the annual conference of the Eastern Division of the American Philosophical Association held in Boston,
Massachusetts, I delivered my first professional philosophical paper. As a recent Ph.D. who had little confidence in his academic
standing, I had approached this event with great fear and trembling. My anxieties proved to be well grounded. While my paper
contained (I still believe) a modest but useful insight into a central
dilemma in ethical theory, my relative inexperience and ignorance
were exploited mercilessly by my critics, leaving me in a state of
humiliation and shame that lingered long after the event. It felt to
me as if I had blundered into a professional philosophers' version
of Hobbes' state of nature–a state of war in which each is enemy to
all. My first and only appearance before an audience of the Eastern
Division of the APA had proved to be, in Hobbes' pungent phrase,
"solitary, poor, nasty, brutish and short." Fast-forward more than
sixteen years, to June 1989. Again I am delivering a paper to an
academic audience, this time during my first visit to the conference
of the Friends Association for Higher Education, held that year
at Swarthmore College near Philadelphia, Pennsylvania. Again I
had approached my presentation with fear and trembling. After
all, the topic of my paper was controversial–a veritable minefield of
potentially explosive observations about sensitive issues in gender
politics. Yet my actual experience was worlds apart from my unhappy encounter at Boston. Here were highly educated, competent
academics whose underlying attitudes toward one another–and toward me–were respectful and kind, whose predominate interest lay
not in destroying what little credibility I might have had, but in
discerning the truth together in a loving community.

As we of FAHE know well, scholarship and spirituality are not
intrinsically at odds with one another. At the philosophers' convention, the toxic environment was not a result of too much intellect
and learning, but too little heart–a lack of openness, vulnerability

---

[1] *Journal*, Nickalls ed. p. 19

and kindness. There (as is all too often true in academic environments) highly trained intellects used their well-honed skills as weapons. Though pockets of trust and comfort between ideological allies could be found here and there, the overall emotional landscape was anarchic, a shifting scene of guerrilla warfare, of overweening posturing, of frontal attacks and brilliant counterattacks. For many on the sidelines, the appeal of the convention lay precisely in the ringside seat that it afforded to view these mind-battles. The convention was not unlike an academic coliseum (or a vast video game) in which star combatants triumphed or were destroyed, while others applauded or muttered in stunned disbelief.

When academic discourse is divorced from the heart, the outcome is not always intellectual warfare, to be sure. Sometimes the salient symptoms of this separation are not hostility and attack–but indifference and empty theorizing. At the college where I have taught for nearly 40 years, a recent colloquium on just war theory was held over an elegant dinner. The presentations were erudite and witty, the ensuing dialogue salted with urbane bon mots and self-indulgent laughter. The actual reality of war–its soul-destroying viciousness, its role in the death of numberless innocents, the blighting of life prospects for generations, the lingering, unresolved hatreds–none of those bleak realities appeared in that dinnertime performance. The audience–mostly students, with a smattering of faculty–walked away from the event well satisfied with the fine food, wine, and sparkling intellectual banter that they had enjoyed.

Such an event would be unthinkable at a Quaker gathering. And the reason is not simply that Quakers from a very early date adopted a principle of opposition to "all bloody principles and practices."[2] The more fundamental reason is that this opposition arose from a profound spiritual experience that, in the words of George Fox, "took away the occasion of all war."[3] When Fox uttered these words, he was not voicing a conceptual proposition arrived at through theological ruminations; rather, he was testifying to an unshakable conviction that had taken possession of him body and soul, arising from "the power of the Lord" flooding into his life. When pressed again to become a soldier, he declared that he "was dead to it."[4] Standing in the Light, Fox's whole being affirmed love, connectedness, joy–and repudiated violence and death.

As the example of Fox and early Friends makes clear, Quaker

---

[2] From the 1651 Declaration, drafted by George Fox and eleven other Quaker men.

[3] *Journal*, p. 65.

[4] *Ibid.*, p. 67

spirituality at its best is an embodied spirituality, in which the conventional divisions of mind and body, intellect and feeling, sacred and secular are overcome in favor of an undivided life of wholeness and integrity. William Penn, writing of George Fox in prayer, gives us a glimpse of this state: "the most awful, living, reverent frame I ever felt or beheld."[5] Indeed (as we all know) the very name "Quaker" testifies to this powerful unity of Spirit and body in the Light. Shall we view such moments as so exalted and rare that they are essentially irrelevant to our daily lives? While we cannot expect to live in a constant state of religious ecstasy, still, as Friends we are called to cultivate a growing awareness of Spirit, and to manifest that awareness in our behavior. To cite just one example: the Advices and Queries of my own Yearly Meeting include the following challenging question: "Do I live in thankful awareness of God's constant presence in my life?"[6]

If in fact I lived "in thankful awareness of God's constant presence in my life," what would be the implications for my career as an academic, scholar and teacher? At the very least, I would not use a scholarly presentation as an opportunity to shame and humiliate others, nor would I treat war as a topic of idle intellectual entertainment. These conclusions are easy; more challenging are the implications for the conduct of rigorous academic scholarship, in which personal values and spiritual orientation are commonly regarded as irrelevant to the topic under discussion.

It is difficult to imagine the study of fine points in, say, linguistics, botanical research or quantum mechanics as an occasion for spiritual ecstasy–difficult, but not impossible. Indeed, the finest researchers and scholars often approach their work with what amounts to spiritual appreciation and religious zeal. This observation suggests an important distinction for our purposes, between matter and manner, the "what" of scholarly work and the "how". One would not normally expect tenets of religious belief to enter explicitly into the subject matter of quantum mechanics. (Though precisely this seems to have been true of Albert Einstein, who famously declared that "God does not play dice with the universe!") One may hope, however, that when they engage in the study of botany, or linguistics, or quantum mechanics, scholars and academics do so as whole persons, open to the vastness of the world they are exploring, the wonder of unanswered questions, the humanity of their fellow researchers and students, and perhaps also the potential benefits of

---

[5] Journal, xliv.

[6] *Faith and Practice: A Guide to Quaker Discipline in the Experience of Pacific Yearly Meeting of the Religious Society of Friends* (2001), Query on Spiritual Life, p. 48.

their work for the easing of suffering and promotion of peace and justice.

When we speak of "scholarly detachment," we may mean one of two very different things. Detachment is commonly understood to be a species of abstraction, in which irrelevancies are stripped away, leaving a simplified, purified subject for scrutiny. This model is implicitly Platonic–a divorce of the mind from the messy, muddy realities of everyday life–including especially the body, emotions and personal state of the scholar. It is well to remember that the word "academic" derives from Plato's own Academy, established during his lifetime and continuously operating thereafter for approximately 900 years. Despite many efforts to dislodge it, the Platonic model of scholarly detachment remains entrenched in many parts of today's Academy. Through Socrates in the early Platonic dialogue Phaedo, Plato puts this view very plainly: "If we are ever to have pure knowledge of anything, we must get rid of the body and contemplate things by themselves with the soul itself."[7]

Platonism is the locus classicus of what may be called "dualistic detachment" – detachment by separation and exclusion. In this view, true knowledge and wisdom can be achieved only by rising above and even scorning that which is transitory, imperfect and incomplete. It is this model that was at work in the American Philosophical Association Convention in Boston in 1972, and in the elegant dinner discussion of just war theory described above. Because we continue to exist in each moment as embodied beings, subject to a thousand "slings and arrows of outrageous fortune," dualistic detachment is inherently dishonest, a shared pretense that denies what is manifestly true. Its root emotion is fear: fear of loss of control, fear of the intrusion of unwanted elements, fear of fully experiencing the messages of one's own body and feelings.

It is possible to focus one's attention without disregarding larger realities, however; even as the scope of attention narrows, the scope of awareness may remain broad. We may, for example, address technical issues in mathematics, or chemistry, or history, while remaining aware of a broader background of meaning, seeing "out of the corner of our eye," as it were, the humanity of our students and fellow scholars, the condition of our body and its emotional state, even the wider reality of the human condition. Indeed, one part of what we call wisdom is the ability, even while giving attention to a specific topic, to keep in view the larger context and meaning of that topic. These observations suggest another model of detachment, what may be called non-dualistic detachment–or per-

---

[7] *Phaedo*, 67 (Tredennick translation).

haps better, non-attachment. Whereas the root condition of dualistic detachment is fear and a desire to exclude, the root condition of non-attachment–a broader, more generous model of intellectual activity–is an inclusive openness and loving acceptance.

In religious practice, non-attachment is found wherever spirituality entails not hierarchy, separation and rejection, but equality, inclusion and compassion. In Christianity, the guiding metaphor for this compassionate breadth of vision is the Crucifixion. As the story is told in the Gospels, Jesus released attachment to his own desires and bodily needs ("not what I want, but what you want"–Matthew 26:39) and was, even as he was cruelly treated, open to the suffering of others. His spiritual awareness did not protect him from his own suffering; we are given to understand that in the "Passion of Christ," Jesus fully experiences the worst that a human being can endure–yet his primary attention remains fixed upon the redeeming power of Love. His spiritual awareness does not exclude his rational mind, but engages it in the service of an encompassing compassion for all of creation.

In Buddhism, a similar message is conveyed through the archetypal image of the lotus flower. The pristine, exquisite beauty of the lotus exists not in another time and place, above all inferior things–but here and now, immersed in filth and disorder, "at home in the muddy water." The spiritual life, a life of integrity, entails not divorce from this life, but openness to it and awareness of our intimate interconnections with "the ten thousand things."

While expressions of Quaker spirituality have sometimes tended toward the otherworldly, on balance Quakerism contrasts significantly with dominant strands of Catholic and Protestant Christianity through its insistence upon a spirituality centered in this life, this time and space. Its distinctive fusion of mysticism and activism, its insistence upon an experiential basis for religious conviction, its testimony of equality and its non-dogmatic inclusiveness–these key features of Quakerism repudiate dualistic detachment, and thus by implication the academic scholarship that perpetuates such dichotomous thinking.

So...what does it mean, what can it mean, to be both deeply grounded in Quaker spirituality, yet also a successful scholar and teacher? I cannot recommend my own example to others. I have largely opted out of the professional academic scene. Many years ago I dropped my membership in the American Philosophical Association. I do not read professional philosophical journals, and I rarely take part in scholarly professional exchanges. Though I draw upon philosophical and religious traditions, my own writing tends toward the personal and confessional, and is often intended (as is true here) for a primarily Quaker audience. I do not, however, dismiss the activities of my fellow Quaker scholars who have remained active in the Academy. There are numerous models in our own recent history of Quaker researchers, scholars and teachers who successfully integrate impeccable scholarship with Quaker spirituality, including active engagement in the world. My own personal favorites include such giants as Rufus Jones, Thomas Kelly, Henry Cadbury, and Howard Brinton. As contemporary models of successful integration of spirituality, scholarship and activism, I would include the plenary speakers chosen for the 2008 FAHE Conference: Jocelyn Bell Burnell, John Punshon, and Satish Kumar.

In all honesty, however, I believe that the challenge of spiritual wholeness is never fully met. We are always on the road toward (or away from) integrity; we never fully arrive. The pressures that the Academy puts upon us to withdraw, deny and ignore, to cling to our privileged position and preserve our comforts at the expense of others, are indeed very difficult to resist. To maintain the unity of one's life as a Friend in the face of these pressures takes courage, persistence and practice. The Friends Association for Higher Education serves an absolutely indispensible function in this cause. I am profoundly grateful to FAHE, although I know that even here we are not always on unambiguously solid ground, that even at FAHE it is possible to forget the insights of our faith and drift away from wholeness. And so I leave us with a query: if George Fox were to appear among us, magically informed of the contemporary world and of Friends' place in it; if he attended this conference and listened to our presentations and discussions, what would he do? Would he sit back in quiet satisfaction at our continuing faithfulness to the original insights of early Friends? Or would he stand up among us, brashly interrupting, denouncing and declaiming, calling us back from our "airy notions" to live more fully in the Light? If (as I suspect) the second scenario is more probable than the first, where–*specifically*–do we imagine that he would lodge his sharpest protests? What in ourselves might we look at honestly and keenly? How may we find our own way to walk cheerfully through the Academy, answering that of God in everyone?

John Keats and Ethical Practice

by James W. Hood, Guilford College

Introduction

John Keats's "Ode to Psyche" first appeared in a lengthy journal-letter he wrote to his brother and sister-in-law between February 14 and May 3, 1819. Introducing the poem, Keats emphasizes the unusual care he has taken composing it and the happy consequence that ensued. "Psyche" is "the first and the only [poem]," he says, "with which I have taken even moderate pains." Others have been "for the most part dash'd of[f] . . . in a hurry," but "Psyche" "reads the more richly for it and will I hope encourage me to write other thing[s] in even a more peacable [sic] and healthy spirit" (Keats, 1970, 253).

Keenly conscious (as ever) of his ongoing development as a writer, here Keats both celebrates his progress and longs for something more, casting his desire predictably in the language of health and peacefulness, ideals that eluded him for most of his life and especially in that most productive poetic year of 1819 as he struggled with falling passionately in love, the lack of money, and the twin specters of his brother Tom's recent death and a creeping sensation that his own might follow shortly. A similar tension inheres to "Ode to Psyche" itself: ostensibly it praises an insufficiently celebrated goddess, but a subtle countercurrent in the poem ends up focusing attention on the writer himself. Though he adopts a modest pose at the outset, calling his poem "these tuneless numbers" (1), in the concluding verses the poet/speaker trumpets his own ability:

> So let me be thy choir, and make a moan
> > Upon the midnight hours;
> Thy voice, thy lute, thy pipe, thy incense sweet
> > From swinged censer teeming;
> Thy shrine, thy grove, thy oracle, thy heat
> > Of pale-mouth'd prophet dreaming.

> Yes, I will be thy priest, and build a fane
>   In some untrodden region of my mind,
>   .....
> And in the midst of this wide quietness
> A rosy sanctuary will I dress
> With the wreath'd trellis of a working brain,
>   With buds, and bells, and stars without a name,
> With all the gardener Fancy e'er could feign,..
>   (44-51; 58-62)

These lines may place Psyche at the center of interest, but the thudding repetition of "thy . . . thy . . . thy" underscores the "my" and "I" that reference the sub-textual star of the poem.[1] Much as Keats may wish to be writing here in "a more peacable and healthy spirit" of openness to the other, his writer's ego remains, in Iris Murdoch's formulation, "fat [and] relentless," the chief "enemy" of the "moral life" (Murdoch, 1970, 51).[2]

Yet even as the ego impedes, here we can also see Keats straining toward something finer, practicing that turning of one's attention away from the voracious self. His struggle in this and other late poems dovetails potently with the "practice" that lives at the core of Quaker engagement with the world, that ongoing attempt to become centered, to live in the life of the Spirit. Keats said very little in his writings about faith of the traditional Christian variety except to question it, but his letters and poems reveal a young person (he died at 25) deeply engaged in considerations about how to become better–as a friend, a sibling, a lover, and, above all, a writer. It is that striving to which I want to attend here, considering a progression of poems where Keats engages in what I will call "ethical practice," a divestment of the ego and a deepening regard for the claims of the other. There's something heartening about watching Keats practice getting better as a poet and a person because it reminds me that the spiritual/ethical journey is not about, to paraphrase Emily Dickinson, getting to heaven at last, but going all along.

Following theorists like John Guillory and Geoffrey Harpham, I want to draw a clear distinction between the ethical and morality, a difference that gets flattened out in ordinary usage. Fundamentally,

---

[1] Watkins (1995) suggests that "While the poem purports to be about Psyche... it actually focuses on the male poet's imagination" (99) and that the poem operates according to a "Sadeian logic" that insists on "the absolute domination of femininity by masculinity" and "of pleasure as domination" (101).

[2] Understanding the term "psyche" to refer to the self, the title of the ode might be read as "Ode to Self."

I'm defining morality as a prescriptive determination between right or wrong and the ethical as the presentation of a choice between competing goods. Morals are an algorithm, a plug and play device, if you will; the ethical is a situation, the fleeting moment or realm one inhabits prior to making a decision. A matter is considered ethical when it presents us with a genuine dilemma, any outcome of which will produce positives and negatives. Sophie's choice, in the William Styron novel by that name (Styron, 1979), presents a classic and horrifying example: the Nazis force her to select which of her two children they will spare, and if she refuses to choose they will kill both. When we enter the domain of the ethical, things get much more complex, just like they do in a tragedy like *Othello*. But by entering that realm, whether in actual situations or compelling fictions, we practice development of the *ethos* or character critical to fuller humanity.

Ethical practice, disinterestedness, and negative capability

In an essay entitled "The Ethical Practice of Modernity: The Example of Reading," Guillory (2000) argues that the act of reading attentively can be an ethical practice, an action that occupies a certain domain or space on a continuum midway between simple, pleasurable aesthetic enjoyment and didactic morality. For this to occur, however, a certain reorientation of current reading practices must take place. He begins by distinguishing between "professional reading" and "lay reading." The former is a kind of "work" that is a "disciplinary activity" governed by rules; it is "vigilant" in that it is "wary" of pleasure, and it is a "communal practice" (31). The latter is "practiced at the site of leisure," has very different conventions from that of professional reading, is a "solitary" practice by and large, and is mainly "motivated by the experience of pleasure" (32). This discrepancy has caused, according to Guillory, a cultural bifurcation, a split between the professors and the masses in which the highly sophisticated and professional interpretive technique utilized in the academy has inoculated them with the fantasy that such reading will have a far greater moral/political impact upon the world than is practicable and, at the same time, has relegated the reading of ordinary mortals to "the level of immediate consumption" (33). What we need, Guillory wants to argue, is an intermediate practice of reading between "the poles of entertainment" and "vigilant professionalism" (34), one that incorporates both the aesthetic pleasures of reading for fun and the moral awareness derived from reading with keen diligence. He calls for a kind of reading that falls within "the domain of the ethical" (34).

119

Clearly distinguishing the ethical from morality, Guillory asks us to imagine a continuum that places morality, where one chooses between absolute right or wrong, at one end of the spectrum and the aesthetic, where one chooses between various objects of beauty, at the other. The ethical, he suggest, occupies the "terrain" in between these two poles as the space in which one considers the choice between competing goods (38). If we think of reading as a domain in which we can experience both pleasure and moral instruction, and also as one in which we choose between competing goods–Do I read a Wendell Berry essay, a novel by Margaret Atwood, or a play by Eve Ensler today?–I think we begin to understand what Guillory has in mind.

Guillory calls for (though not expressly) a healing of the fracture between lay and professional reading, the goal of which would be care or improvement of the self. Time and time again, Keats's letters attest to a similar amelioratory goal, mainly with respect to his own practice of writing. For Keats, writing can be an ethical practice in a sense similar to Guillory's reading practice, and to view his 1819 odes as exercises in the development of such a practice aids us in understanding their complex movement between deep, often desperate ego-involvement and its opposite–what Keats called "negative capability."

The concept of "negative capability" Keats broaches in a December 1817 letter to his brothers has been the subject of considerable attention. Keats was influenced greatly by William Hazlitt's ideas about "the Natural Disinterestedness of the Human Mind" (Bate, 1963, 256), about which he read in Hazlitt's books or heard in his *Lectures on the English Poets* in London. Hazlitt emphasized the writerly capacity Shakespeare exhibited for identification with the other, with real or imagined persons outside himself, noting that "The striking peculiarity of Shakespeare's mind was its generic quality, its power of communication with all other minds . . . . He was the least of an egoist that it was possible to be. He was nothing in himself; but he was all that others were, or that they would become" (Hazlitt, 1849, 55-56).

Keats utilizes Hazlitt's word "disinterestedness" in various letters, most particularly noting how uncommon a feature it has been of human experience. "Very few men," he writes in the same journal letter to his brother and sister-in-law composed in the spring of 1819, "have ever arrived at a complete disinterestedness of Mind: very few have been influenced by a pure desire of the benefit of others–in the greater part of the Benefactors of & to Humanity some meretricious motive has sullied their greatness–some melodramatic scenery has facinated [sic] them . . . ." (Keats, 1970, 229).

However confident this sounds, the letter is rife with rhetorical fits and starts here, the self-questioning that constitutes his 1819 mindset. Most poignantly, perhaps, he characterizes himself as "young writing at random–straining at particles of light in the midst of a great darkness" (Keats, 1970, 230).

Ethical practice in "Melancholy" and "To Autumn"

The personal "great darkness" Keats lived within during 1819 certainly informed his writing of the "Ode on Melancholy." We can see him "straining at particles of light" in this poem, however, wishing to engage more fully in writing as ethical practice by presenting neither a simple moral pronouncement nor a merely sensuous celebration of things beautiful but a more complex articulation of competing goods. Some of that complexity introduces itself through the preposition "on" Keats chooses as the fulcrum of the title. This is not a poem written "to" melancholy, in praise or derision, but one that balances itself upon melancholy's mysterious vagaries.[3]

The poem counsels engagement with, not retreat from, "the melancholy fit" that falls "Sudden from heaven like a weeping cloud." Neither escape into the aesthetic realm for aesthetics' sake–figured, perhaps, in the poem's initial imagery of forgetfulness and suicide– nor stiff and outright rejection of melancholy will suffice. The necessary embrace of melancholy and its productive "wakeful anguish" comes only through movement toward the natural or human other:

---

[3]Keats actually moved back and forth between different title possibilities with different prepositional configurations: from "On Melancholy" to "Ode, to Melancholy" to "Ode on Melancholy" (see Keats (1978, 374n)), struggling to get the balance just right.

But when the melancholy fit shall fall . . . . .
Then glut thy sorrow on a morning rose,
  Or on the rainbow of the salt sand-wave,
  Or on the wealth of globed peonies;
Or if thy mistress some rich anger shows,
  Emprison her soft hand, and let her rave,
  And feed deep, deep upon her peerless eyes.
                                    (11; 15-20)

"Melancholy" situates itself in the space between Chatterton-esque Romanticized suicide and the "Thou shalt not" of the moralist. In its final stanza, the poem imagines Melancholy as a goddess, dwelling with Beauty, enshrined "in the very temple of Delight." Two striking images that point toward the paradox of competing goods help constitute this poem as an engagement with ethical practice. The first is of Melancholy abiding next to Pleasure, "Turning to poison while the bee-mouth sips." This remarkable image from the natural world juxtaposes honey and poison, two productions of the same bee body, one necessary for sustenance, the other for protection, both distilled from the beauty of flowers. It captures the paradox of good and bad deriving from the same source, in a puzzling and complex figure. The second image is that of a "strenuous tongue / ...burst[ing] Joy's grape against his palate fine," one that encodes the friction of strength and gustatory thrill against the hollowness of loss. He or she truly sees Melancholy who knows viscerally the paradox of gaining and losing in the same moment, who understands the delight of consuming something delicious but knows the potency of its taste depends upon its ephemerality.

If "Ode to Psyche" undercuts its intentions towards the ethical through a display of ego involvement, signified grammatically through the significant use of the first person, and a moralistic certainty, "Ode on Melancholy" moves much further toward a focus on the other and competing goods. It operates in the grammatical realm of the second person, addressing the reader as its object of interest. When we come to the last of the odes Keats composed in 1819, "To Autumn" written in September, we move into a second person address not to a reader but to a definitively separate entity (a season) and find ourselves with a poem that even more deeply engages the claims of the natural and human other even as it does not eliminate Keats's own deeply personal concerns about death and poetic fame. Here, the great cycles of the natural world embrace and subsume ego. From the writer's standpoint, "To Autumn" achieves even more fully the kind of disinterestedness or negative capability Keats desires, the capacity of the writer, absenting him or herself momentarily from the vicious grip of ego, to fashion a space into which readers may enter imaginatively through the process of identification. Its rich imagery of the natural world and complex allusion both to Keats's personal situation and the broader political milieu invite the reader into relationship with that which lies beyond the borders of the self.

"To Autumn" manifests a kind of conspiration, a breathing together of Keats's personal concerns with the larger social and political ones of the very particular moment in 1819 when he composed the poem. His own worries about death and poetic fame abide within the poem's imagery of autumn as a time of transition and ending, of ripeness and its passing, and in the figure of music that dominates the third stanza. The poem cautions autumn, and by extension its own writer, not to fret over the "songs of spring" because it "hast [its] music too." Individual anxieties take second seat to the rich imagistic celebration of the other's "mists and mellow fruitfulness," its bending, budding, swelling, plumping, and o'er-brimming.

As Vincent Newey (1995) has helped us see, "To Autumn" also engages–albeit to a limited extent–with the politics of its historical moment, nodding toward the recent Peterloo Massacre through its imagery of "Conspiring," bees as workers, and "clammy cells" that may evoke imprisonment suffered under the notorious Six Acts (186). The final stanza's imagery of small and vulnerable beings singing–gnats, "full-grown lambs," hedge-crickets, a red-breast, and "gathering swallows"–coupled with its admonishment that "thou hast thy music too," suggests a revolutionary, if subtle, reminder to all the dispossessed to bleat out the voice that must be heard. "To Autumn," therefore, focuses its energies outward from the poetic ego toward a celebration of the other of nature (the season of autumn) and the other of the politically disenfranchised even as it remains cognizant of Keats's own personal needs and fears. It articulates concerns of the I and the not-I, both of which are goods, like the competing goods it further underscores of fruition and departure.

Conclusion: reading as ethical practice

Geoffrey Harpham (1995) argues that the purpose of ethical discourse lies not in solving problems but in structuring them: "Articulating perplexity, rather than guiding, is what ethics is all about" (395). Just such a structuring of the dilemmas of loss, poetic and political voice, melancholy, and death characterizes Keats's odes. Like a photograph, "To Autumn" suspends opposing forces in a snapshot image that reads in different directions. An encounter with Keats's poems, therefore, seems capable of directing a reader toward an apprehension of competing goods, of differing and equally worthy principles.[4]

The second mechanism by which the act of reading might lead to a positive development of the self inheres to the way reading structurally negotiates an encounter with the claims of an other. In the same mode as negative capability (for a writer) requires a suppression of the ego in order to make space for the imaginative creation of other beings, the act of reading challenges us to suspend self-concern in a moment of powerful engagement with the not-I, whether human, animate, or inanimate.[5] Any child who has ever been "lost in a book" knows this. On the simplest level, the imaginative operation of identification with a character takes one out of one's self, placing the claims of that other—a mere, fictive creation of linguistic signs—ahead of the self's needs.[6]

Reading Keats's "Ode on Melancholy" or "To Autumn" with attention to his biography, we may recognize the struggling Keats himself as an other worthy of our attention, identifying with his fears, frustrations, and desire to let the music made right now suffice. Alternately, reading "To Autumn" we meet the infinity of natural cycles, of the seasons, life, and death in such a way that the needs of the fat, relentless ego may subside momentarily.

Silvia Benso (2000) has argued that the crisis of environmental destruction we now face demands a new ethic toward "things," the animate and inanimate world beyond the contours of our bodies. Keats's personification of autumn, anthropocentric as it might be, may broach a proto-environmentalism we would do well to acknowledge.[7] More generally, however, we can note that Keats's 1819 odes

---

[4]Harpham goes on to discuss, in very general terms, the relationship between the ethical and narrative structure itself, positing narrative as "a representational structure that negotiates the relation... of is and ought" (403). Narrative moves from an initial position of what is but ought not to be to a final position of an "inevitable condition that is and truly ought-to-be" (403). He suggests, therefore, that the impulse toward the ethical, deeply concerned with the question of what ought to be, may be fundamental to narrative itself.

[5]Emmanuel Levinas (1969) has probably theorized most powerfully the manner in which the encounter with an other (in particular, the apprehension of the other's face) constitutes an ethical imperative. For Levinas, the recognition, through an encounter with the other's face, of the "infinity" beyond the self annihilates the self's former "totality" and thereby creates an imperative to recognize the demands of that other upon the self.

[6]More specifically, in reading we move toward what Richard Rorty calls "solidarity" with others, a recognition that those beyond the ken of our own cultural or personal knowledge can be seen as "one of us" (Rorty, 1989, p. 190).

[7]Jonathan Bate (1991) has argued persuasively for Wordsworth's place in

constitute the layered archaeological evidence of a writer developing a greater capacity for disinterestedness through which he shapes a lyrical space wherein a reader encounters the claims of the not-I in a powerful way. Such writing and reading do constitute ethical practices, the ends of which, one hopes, might be a deeper understanding of the claims of others, both beings human and things natural, and a concomitant development of responsible partnership therewith. And isn't it just this sort of practice, a surrender of self into the abiding Light of that absolute Other, that our meeting for worship requires of us, and that I, for one, continue to find so difficult and so deeply illuminating?

Bate, J. (1991). *Romantic Ecology: Wordsworth and the Environmental Tradition*. Routledge, London.

Bate, W. J. (1963). *John Keats*. Belknap Press of Harvard, Cambridge, MA.

Benso, S. (2000). *The Face of Things: A Different Side of Ethics*. State University of New York Press, Albany.

Guillory, J. (2000). The ethical practice of modernity: The example of reading. In Garber, M., Hanssen, B., and Walkowitz, R. L., editors, *The Turn to Ethics*, pages 29–46. Routledge, New York and London.

Harpham, G. (1995). Ethics. In Lentricchia, F. and McLaughlin, T., editors, *Critical Terms for Literary Study*, pages 387–405. University of Chicago Press, Chicago and London.

Hazlitt, W. (1849). Lecture iii: On shakespeare and milton. In *Lectures on the English Poets. 3rd ed*, pages 52–81. John Wiley, New York and London.

Keats, J. (1970). Letters of john keats. In Gittings, R., editor, *Letters of John Keats*. Oxford University Press, Oxford and New York.

Keats, J. (1978). The poems of john keats. In Stillinger, J., editor, *The Poems of John Keats*. Harvard University Press, Cambridge, MA.

Levinas, E. (1969). *Totality and Infinity: An Essay on Exteriority*. Duquense University Press, Pittsburgh, PA.

---

the development of the environmental tradition.

Murdoch, I. (1970). *The Sovereignty of Good*. Routledge, London and New York.

Newey, V. (1995). Keats, history, and the poets. In Roe, N., editor, *Keats and History*, pages 165–193. Cambridge University Press, Cambridge.

Rorty, R. (1989). *Contingency, irony and solidarity*. Cambridge University Press, Cambridge.

Styron, W. (1979). *Sophie's Choice*. Random House, New York, NY.

Watkins, D. P. (1995). History, self, and gender in 'ode to psyche.'. In Roe, N., editor, *Keats and History*, pages 88–106. Cambridge University Press, Cambridge.

The Art of Silence: Exploration of an Artistic Medium

by Rebecca Leuchak, Roger Williams University

Much silence makes a powerful noise.
                                    – African proverb

As Quakers we know that the silence of expectant waiting which lies at the heart of our spiritual practice is a very powerful force. We share that knowledge with many other faith traditions where silence plays a crucial role in bridging the realms of the human and the divine. In the everyday world beyond religious practices, the absence of sound or rather the absence of speech has always had a deeply powerful and complex communicative effect. Silence in a secular context delivers a wide variety of messages. It is appreciated as an expression of timidity ("Cat got your tongue?"), embarrassment, alienation, complicity, censorship, hostility, strength, resistance and protest, approval, awe, devotion ("Silent night, holy night, all is calm, all is quiet."), empathy and love. Silence is experienced sometimes as a positive thing and at other times as a negative.

Looking back over the past century, the use of silence as an artistic medium is one way that modern artists have challenged the conventional boundaries of art, although historically speaking, silence has always held a key place in the arts. Perhaps the touchstone example of avant-garde use of silence as a medium for the making of art is John Cage's 1952 composition entitled "4'33"," to be performed by any instrument or combination of instruments that is NOT played for that exact period of time. Music, Cage's artistic art form, has always involved sound making. That is what we think of first when we think of musical compositions. And yet silence has always been an integral part of the overall composition of any musical work. Prior to the twentieth century, those passages of a musical composition which were the "rests" were important only in their relation to the greater overall context of sound making. They help to construct the melodic and rhythmic shape of the musical phrase. At mid-century Cage challenged this assumption of the musical composition by creating a work composed entirely of "rests." The resulting work "4'33", is a precisely timed stretch of silence that is "performed" by a musician who walks on-stage and sits with instrument, not playing for an audience who themselves participate in the creation of the concert by not hearing any

Figure 4.1: Edgar Degas, "Dancer Stretching at the Barre," c. 1877-1880, Pastel on ivory laid paper, 12.5 x 9.4 in., Art Institute of Chicago, Mr. and Mrs. Martin A. Ryerson Collection

sounds from the performer. The only auditory experience is that of the ambient environment, the random noises of the concert hall: the cough, the shift of bodies in chairs, or the whir of the air conditioner.[8]

Visual artists have also taken the medium of silence as the focus of their work. In two-dimensional art, whether paintings, drawings, or watercolors, "silence" may be interpreted as restraint from mark making. As with musical "rests," "white" space or the back "ground" has always been exploited as a definite element of composition among traditional, academically trained visual artists. In fact, it has had a long and respected place in the compositions of

---

[8]https://www.youtube.com/watch?v=HypmW4Yd7SY

Figure 4.2: Paul Cezanne, "Still Life with Jug and Fruit," no date.

painters and graphic artists since the first making of marks on two-dimensional surface in the Pre-historic caves of southern France and northern Spain. Especially in Asian graphic media, the economy of line in relation to space has always held the most important, the most highly revered, aesthetic value. The blank space of the canvas, the scroll, the page, is the silence of the visual composition. Watercolor and pastels are particularly conducive to the priority of the blank ground as important compositional element. In the work of the Impressionists at the end of the nineteenth century–and in particular some of the pastels of Degas (e.g. "Dancer Stretching at the Barre," shown in Figure 4.1, the oil painted views of Mont Sainte-Victoire and still life paintings by Cezanne, as shown in Figure 4.2)–there is an equal weaving of blank space with passages of colored wash or colorful dab of brush or crayon.

It is in the modernists' self-conscious confrontation with convention, that this tradition of integrated interchange of blank space with mark making is problematized. In Western art movements, increasing interest during the mid-twentieth century in those spaces between the marks was largely attributable to artists' investigations of Asian aesthetics. Their interest and experimentation with the "silence" of the image were often prompted by exploration of spiritual practices of much earlier medieval mysticism and Native

Figure 4.3: Exquisite Corpse. Web site: http://www.equisitecorpse.com

American ritual practices to some extent, but most often in East Asia and notably Zen Buddhism.

The tradition of meditative preparation for creation of works of art was adopted by a number of avant-garde artists of the 1950s and 60s. One thinks here of Jackson Pollack's action painting, where the silence of the unprimed canvas laid across the floor is the record of a flurry of "noisy" gestures in splattered, dribbled, dripped "vocalization." Or the work of Robert Motherwell, which presents the blank white of the background surface as if it were deep space, or Cy Twombley, with his delicate flurries and scrumbles of faint and barely discernible marks on vast stretches of primed canvas.

But there is another deep process at work in some artists' use of silence in their creative work. This arose with the western development of an understanding of consciousness and the subconscious. With the emerging field of psychoanalysis in the early twentieth century, the previously prevailing notion that creativity was expressed in linear, active expression of conscious thoughts in permanent, concrete media with discernible sensuous effect was undermined. The world of unconscious mind at work in all aspects of human activity, or most importantly inactivity, became the source of fascination and a generative stimulus to artists of the Surrealist movement. Taking us back to a "tabula rasa" of being, artists experimented in the 1920s and 1930s with accident as a creative process by exploring "automatic drawing," a free association of mind to mark making, working in playful collaboration to create "exquisite corpses" or "cadavres exquis" (see Figure 4.3), and inventing ways to allow

Figure 4.4: Marina Abramović's, "The Artist is Present," `http://www.youtube.com/watch?v=Ts66t9muFfQ`

chance to form a work of art. What is not intentionally thought, not said, not made became important for the first time in the West.

This movement toward negation of the previously positivist aura around art-making resulted in a number of confrontational positions, with political sub-texts, especially in the work by the Dadaists in Europe following World War I. These artists' challenge of the status quo was particularly impressive in live performances which shocked and outraged the average theater goer. Decades later, out of the theatrical exploration of the subconscious as fertile field for creativity, in multi-media events dubbed "Happenings" in the 1950s and 60s emerged a new artistic form called "time-based art" or "performance art." This melding of the sensual effects of visual, auditory, and kinetic activity evolved in the mid-twentieth century from actually quite a bit older developments of the revolutionary Dada experimentation, and even harks back to Alfred Jarrry's Ubu Roi first performed in Paris in 1896.[9]

While the visual artists and the newly emergent performance artists of the second half of the twentieth century were fascinated with the negation of tradition-bound artistic media with their very concrete tools of the maker setting up expectations for observable

---

[9]`http://www.kimcohen.com/artmusictheoryassets/artmusictheorytexts/kaprow_recent.pdf`

recording of the conscious artistic process, there was a positive influx of ideas and new ways of approaching these very same issues. Increasingly in mid-twentieth century Europe and the Americas, those seeking new creative stimuli were looking to Asia and the religious traditions that dealt with meditation for a spirit-led exploration of the inner psyche. The art making there, particularly in calligraphy, connected deeply centered meditation with the impulse to make marks–brushstrokes of black ink on the blank field of white rice paper created out of a deep calm and centering of the spirit.

So the new direction of the arts, derived from the emergent psychological science's new conception of consciousness and subconsciousness, joined with a keen interest in the medieval mystic, Native American, and Asian spiritual practices of meditation and striving toward the transcendent.

Artists could also engage the medium of silence as a political tool. From a negative motivation, an anti-art stance, to make a critical statement about traditional art forms as symptoms of the ills of society. The most recent work of Marina Abramović's, "The Artist is Present" at the Museum of Modern Art in New York in 2010, continues her concern with the female body as site of politicized inequalities. In this performance piece she silently sat at a table in the main atrium of the Museum. Visitors were encouraged to sit silently across from the artist for a duration of their choosing, becoming participants in the artwork, as depicted in Figure 4.4.

In her commitment to the duration of the performance, the artist suppressed all physical needs, thus enacting the kind of controls over her very body that society has exerted in more institutionalized ways in its treatment of women.

Artists at the same time engaged in the medium of silence for the deeply positive, spirit-led search for transcendence beyond the conventions of secular art making. In this last approach, artists may use silence in a poetic, metaphorical or mystical way. An example is the recent time-based phenomenological work of Bill Viola. One early video piece of 1979 is his "The Reflecting Pool."[10] The film, which is seven minutes long, concentrates our attention by virtue of the absence of any voiced narration. A still frame from this piece is shown in Figure 4.5.

The only sounds in this fixed-frame film are the ambient ones of nature: the bird calls and wind in the trees of the surrounding forest, interrupted at one point by the faraway whine of one lone plane engine. As a result of the recorded stillness, the viewer becomes observant of the silent figure who enters the scene and jumps

---

[10]http://www.youtube.com/watch?v=D_urrt8XOl8

Figure 4.5: Bill Viola, *The Reflecting Pool.* Color, mono sound; 7:00 minutes. Video still/Photo: Kira Perov

and then attention is drawn to minute shifts of surface tension and reflection of a limpid body of water. Both Cage's composition and Viola's film work are meditations on the transience of this world, much influenced by both artists' interest in the philosophic traditions and meditative practices of Taoism and Buddhism. Their use of silence paradoxically speaks volumes about the transcendent.

Since the close of the twentieth century, contemporary artists continue to explore and build upon these two pioneering trends of the artistic use of silence: on the one hand used as a form of protest against the traditions of art making itself or as activist statement about pressing social issues, and on the other hand celebrating the mystical power of silence to intimate the ineffable. Much more needs to be said about these most recent developments in artistic use of silence, but that must wait for a future installment.

Where Quakerism and Philosophy Meet: The Ethical Ideal of Respect?

by Laura Rediehs, St. Lawrence University

The Friends Association for Higher Education (FAHE) exists to provide "opportunities for fellowship among all who share Quaker ideals of higher education, whether on Quaker or non- Quaker campuses." As a Quaker at a non-Quaker college, I have found the annual FAHE conferences immensely valuable in providing a context for me to periodically reconsider and re-calibrate my Quaker identity and my academic identity.

My academic field is philosophy, and over the years I have met other Quaker philosophers at FAHE conferences. I began to notice how important it was for me to check in with the other Quaker philosophers I knew at each conference, and I began to fantasize about the possibility of bringing all of us together for a discussion about whether and how we each try to integrate our Quakerness and our philosophical identities in our work and our lives, and so I finally proposed the Quaker Philosophy Roundtable as a session for the 2007 FAHE conference. I wrote to all of the Quaker philosophers I had met and asked them to participate, and as I learned of other Quaker philosophers, I invited them to come as well. I had originally expected about eight of us to participate, but there were about thirty who attended.

At the Quaker Philosophy Roundtable discussion, we began with introductions grounded in two of our guiding queries: "How do you see your primary identity? Quaker? Philosopher? Quaker-Philosopher?" and, "Do you ever find your Quaker identity in conflict with your academic-philosophy identity?" Not everyone present was an academic philosopher, but all were interested in the possibilities inherent in connecting Quakerism and philosophy.

Different Quakers who are also philosophers offered different ways of responding to these queries. In my own life, I find both of these terms individually to be very meaningful and important to me. I also find that combining these terms reveals powerful resonances and creates serious dissonances, and both the resonances and dissonances help explain why I find a life as a Quaker and a philosopher to be so endlessly interesting.

Calling myself Quaker expresses my connection to a distinctive subculture I experience as *home*–a community that speaks a language I recognize as my own "native language." This is a community of seekers who perceive and experience their lives and the world in spiritual terms, and who have deeply internalized the habit of looking for "that of God" in everyone. In calling myself Quaker, I feel connected to a historical tradition and set of practices that I find tremendously inspiring.

Calling myself a philosopher connects me to a somewhat different world and set of traditions and practices. The word "philosophy" means "love of wisdom," and in Plato's *Republic*, Socrates at one point notes, only half-jokingly, that this means that philosophers are first of all lovers. His definition of wisdom is difficult to grasp. He can only explain it with images. Goodness is like the sun, he says, shining upon the earth giving light and warmth. Wisdom is a special kind of knowledge–of seeing not just what is, but also noticing how it is illuminated by the "sun" of goodness shining down on it all. In my quest to live up to this ideal about what philosophy is: to be a lover–a lover of wisdom–to seek not just to know what is, but also to be sensitive to the play of the light of goodness upon the world, I feel a profound convergence between my Quaker identity and my philosopher identity.

But there are ways that these two worlds I inhabit do not always harmonize. There are a lot of academic philosophers today who scoff at idealistic notions of wisdom. Some people in academic philosophy today are very hostile towards religion. Some academic philosophers, in the name of intellectual rigor, can behave contemptuously towards students or colleagues. And so one aspect of my attraction towards thinking of myself as a Quaker philosopher is my desire to hold the world of academic philosophy to what I regard as Quakerly standards of openness and respect.

Just as Quakerism is non-creedal, academic philosophy today tends in its own way to be non-dogmatic–focused on teaching methods of critical inquiry instead of imparting a single "definitive" subject-matter, as such. And so it is not inappropriate to hold philosophy to a high standard of openness: an openness that is not dismissive of religious thought or the idealistic quest for wisdom. And dialectic (a primary method characterizing philosophical inquiry), i.e., dialogue across different points of view in quest of greater understanding, needs to be grounded in principles of engaged respect for it to be effective. And so it is also not inappropriate to hold philosophy to high standards of respect. At the ideal level, the resonances between Quakerism and philosophy emerge again.

During the Quaker Philosophy Roundtable, someone asked if there were any specific philosophical teachings that Quaker philosophers would especially want to advocate. Would Quaker philosophers, for example, tend to argue against ethical relativism since Quakers tend to take ethics seriously? These questions sparked a lively debate. "Who gets to say what counts as moral absolutes?"

someone asked. "As soon as one person defines a moral absolute, someone else will disagree with it."

I found myself stepping in with what felt like a radical suggestion: "What about a supreme principle of respect?" I asked. "Is that a moral absolute that Quakers, anyway, do tend to believe–that everyone is worthy of respect: that there is that of God within everyone?"

In the pause that followed, I added one more question, "And if so, is this something that Quaker philosophers are especially well-prepared to argue for in our wider culture today?" Here I was trying to connect back to another of the guiding queries of our discussion: "How do we, as Quaker philosophers, see ourselves as 'scholars for peace, justice, and sustainability'?" Do the concepts of peace, justice, and sustainability imply an absolute ethical standard at least of respect towards all other people and towards the natural world?

In reply, someone perceptively pointed out that a lot hinges on how one defines "respect," and I wholeheartedly agreed. While the group seemed hesitant to fully accept, much less endorse my suggestion (and I was not at all surprised or troubled about this), I also do not remember that anyone directly argued against my suggestion either.

In the Quaker world, Friends on the whole do take respect very seriously without much need for further definition. But this is very much not true in the wider world–a world that keeps encouraging people to draw enemy lines. And so the wider world may benefit from an explication of the concept of "respect" in non-religious language, and in fact this is one of my own current writing projects–I am working on a book about respect. I see this as a kind of exercise in translation, undertaken from my full identity as Quaker philosopher–using the tools of conceptual analysis from philosophy to help translate this widely held ethical view within Quakerism into more secular language.

Too many people today vastly misunderstand religious language, and there is a great need for skilled "translators." Philosophers tend to be well-trained in the skill of translation across conceptual systems–perhaps Quaker philosophers especially so because of how the faith of Quakers is grounded much more in experience than in the particular linguistic clothing of creeds and other statements of belief. Because of this, Quakers tend to be well aware of the limits of language, and therefore also tend to develop the capacity to be flexible in their use of language.

From my Quaker identity, I find myself concerned about how radically people can misunderstand each other, how afraid they are to engage in real dialogue with each other, and how much they then can hurt each other by drawing enemy lines and writing each other off. From my philosophical identity, I want to teach the benefits and skills of engaging in dialogue across different points of view, often teaching these skills by using the analogy of translation. I tell my students that one of the advantages of studying philosophy is that it helps you to become multi-lingual within your native language. Even when others are not skilled in this kind of translation, if you are, you can help facilitate dialogue by honoring the other's use of language and taking on the burden of translation. In my writing, I try to find meaningful "translation" projects to take on in order to open up lines of communication between traditions of thought that might benefit from each other's influence.

There are, of course, other possibilities as well for how to integrate one's Quaker identity with one's academic identity. I am very glad to see other Quaker philosophers engaging these questions, and I hope that those in other academic disciplines might find it meaningful as well to consider how their Quaker identities are related to their academic interests and pursuits.

Broadening Philosophy's Appeal

by Richard Miller, Eastern Carolina University

Philosophers aren't used to being the center of attention these days. It is rare for new books by philosophers to get reviewed in any outlet that caters to the general reader, even those like the *Atlantic* or the *New York Review of Books* that aim at a well-educated audience. To write philosophy today is to write for fellow specialists. Even within philosophy epistemologists don't usually read papers published in ethics and ethicists don't read papers in metaphysics. So it was quite a surprise when our Philosopher's Roundtable drew over thirty academics few of whom were professional philosophers. What drew so many to come to hear what we might have to say?

Upon reflection I don't think I should have been surprised at all. A century ago, William James spoke of the inherent interest of philosophy to people of all kinds: "Let a controversy begin in a smoking-room anywhere, about free-will or God's omniscience, or good and evil, and see how every one in the place pricks up his ears. Philosophy's results concern us all most vitally" (James, 1991, p. 6). Great themes like the relationship between justice and equality, the existence and nature of God, the reality or the illusion of human freedom and the scope and limits of human knowledge will always draw.

Professional philosophers have gotten used to thinking of philosophy as something that is naturally and properly conducted among specialists in a language that only specialists can understand. This bothers me. The great philosophers of history did not write only for other philosophers, they sought to address a much wider audience. Our retreat to the ivory tower strikes me as tragic not noble. When I raise this issue with most philosophers they seem untroubled by the fact that these days we speak and write only for each other. The usual response seems to be: the general public simply lacks the training, the patience and frankly the intelligence to follow the details of our arguments or to see how they ultimately connect with what they say they are interested in. For years I have listened to such responses and they continue to strike me as patronizing and false.

It would be one-sided to suggest that all is wrong with professional philosophy. In my opinion much is right about it too. The articles published in professional journals may be full of jargon and technical detail that make them inaccessible to the general reader, but they are also models of clarity and rigor for those of us whose training enables us to read them. Nevertheless, I continue to feel that most of the clarity and rigor is wasted in chasing down details that are too far removed from the perennial issues that should be philosophy's ultimate concern. In other words I have a sense that the discussions lose the forest for the trees. In the process of becoming specialists we have lost sight of the purpose of philosophy.

Going to FAHE provided me with a new opportunity. I could raise these concerns, as well as my suggestions for how to approach philosophical problems in a different way, and see if Quaker philosophers would be more open. What I found was that other Quaker philosophers do see philosophy as a discipline which should properly speak to a wider audience and are like me troubled by our inability to consistently address that audience. They do not take the elitist attitude that I find so distressing in other professional philosophers. In my talk I tried to share with them my analysis of why philosophy retreated to the ivory tower and how we could do philosophy in a more accessible, more relevant way.

I shared with them the inspiration I found in the work of the last great American pragmatist, C. I. Lewis. In Lewis's conceptualistic pragmatism I find a way of articulating the philosophical enterprise that preserves the clarity and rigor that professional philosophy has attained while at the same time keeping it closer to its roots in real human concerns. Lewis tried to convince philosophers that they should stop attempting to prove that their views about justice, knowledge, freedom etc. were the one and only necessarily correct and final word on the subject. Instead we should recognize that there are in fact many possible ways to think about justice, knowledge, beauty, truth, God, freedom and the soul. It simply makes no sense, he argues, to think that one concept is "correct" and the others are false or wrong. Concepts are tools. They are more or less useful but it makes no sense to call them true or false. To argue for one concept of justice is ultimately to try to persuade others to use our concept of justice, to think with it, to see the world with it. It is wrong-headed to try to refute another concept of justice. The other concept can't literally be false but it might not work very well. We should focus our attention on how concepts help us solve our problems. To argue for one theory of justice over another is to try to persuade others that we will live together more harmoniously if we think of justice in this way rather than in that way.

In addition to stressing persuasion over intellectual coercion, Lewis also stressed creativity. Instead of thinking of philosophers as searchers looking for a fixed and immutable truth about justice or knowledge we should see our function as that of engineers designing new and improved intellectual tools for human beings to use in their lives under continually new and changing conditions. Fidelity to old ways of looking at problems is not necessarily a virtue. We should be on the lookout for new ways to think and philosophy at its best offers genuinely new and creative solutions to problems both old and new.

The reactions of the other Quaker philosophers to these ideas encouraged me. I had gotten used to very negative reactions from other philosophers. Some are dismissive because they see nothing wrong with the way philosophy is done in our ivory tower. Others find the idea of making philosophy accessible to the general reader naïve. The other Quaker philosophers were not dismissive. They took the problem and the suggested solution seriously and tried to examine it critically to see if it would stand up. We had a lively discussion of Lewis's ideas and what they mean for philosophy at this time. I welcome the opportunity to sharpen my own understanding by taking account of all the points that were raised there.

In the roundtable many of us shared what it meant to us to be both Quakers and philosophers. Some of the themes I had raised in my talk on pragmatism rose again in the roundtable. There was a general sense that we were opening a discussion that was potentially very rich, but for which there was far too little time to explore during this brief conference. Since then, several of us have remained in regular contact where we continue this and other philosophical discussions. I feel hopeful that something really valuable is beginning to emerge out of last summer's FAHE sessions, but that it is emerging slowly in fits and starts. Each of us is quite busy with typical academic duties in teaching, research and administration and so the time to continue these discussions is sometimes hard to find. Despite this, six months later the discussion has not died out, but rather deepens and becomes more meaningful.

James, W. (1991). *Pragmatism: A New Name for Some Old Ways of Thinking*. Prometheus Books, Amherst, NY.

Philoi sophias [Friends of wisdom]: Quakerism and the Vocation to Philosophy

by Jeffrey Dudiak, The King's University College

As a lifelong Friend, and a philosopher by inclination and profession, and one who has long had, moreover, a sense that my Quakerism has been an integral, formative (if often tacit) influence upon the fact and the manner of my philosophizing, I find myself–at this awkward moment of mid-life crisis (taking stock of what I have done so far, and what is left to me to do, God willing, for the next quarter of a century)–seeking to more deliberately understand the relationship between my confession and my profession. I have, for a few years now, been moving into a stage where I am increasingly understanding myself and my calling to be that of a "Quaker philosopher"–without knowing quite what that would mean, and without a community of other Quakers in philosophy with whom to work this out. Imagine my delight, then, when–as the pleasantest of interruptions to my largely solitary musings–I was invited by Laura Rediehs to participate in a "philosophers' roundtable" at FAHE. After forty(-six) years in the wilderness, was I crossing the Jordan at long last?

And a delight it was, as we scurried to expand the circle to accommodate a surprising number of Quakers teaching and otherwise engaged in philosophy, and others with sufficient interest in the philosophical enterprise to show up too. But even as we were introducing ourselves the question arose as to whether we think of ourselves as "Quaker philosophers", or, alternatively, "Quakers who are also philosophers," and while we had little time to explore this, my suspicion is that we would have been far from unanimous in our approaches to the question. Leave it to philosophers to fret over who they are even before the introductions are complete! And yet, delving into this would, I think, teach us a lot about how we conceive of both our religious commitments and philosophy itself. I seek here, therefore, to explore this issue a little–in only a preliminary and suggestive way, granted–as a question of existential importance to myself as I attempt to carve out my post-mid-life identity, but perhaps also one with implications both for other philosophers and for those of other disciplines and professions as well, since the question might structurally reverberate with the question as to whether we might better think ourselves Quaker psychologists, or Quaker biologists, or Quaker business-(wo)men, or even Quaker prison reformers, etc., or whether it is rather a matter of our being Quakers (who happen to be, additionally, or incidentally, or tangentially) engaged in some or other vocation.

What is at stake here, and why might some of us, at least, be hesitant to claim the term "Quaker philosopher"? There are indeed reasons to be wary. First, there is the rightful fear of the arrogance of thinking oneself a (self-appointed, no less) representative of a movement, representing Quakers in the philosophical world, or speaking "as a philosopher" to one's fellow Quakers, as if claiming this descriptor conferred some status. And there is the related concern of whether the adjective "Quaker" attached to something like "philosopher" does not imply an official title, a formal approval from the body thereby invoked, in the manner that "Catholic theologian" means more than a Catholic who is a theologian, but a theologian vetted and approved by Catholicism. If that is the meaning, then none of us should make this claim, because "Quakerism" (even if there were an unified society who could speak for "Quakerism" per se), as a "religious" society, is not in a position to certify any "philosophy" (in the technical sense) over another (just as Quakerism would be wise not to officially advocate for one school of psychology over another, or one political party over another). Another part of the apprehension around adopting the title, this time more from the side of philosophy than Quakerism, is that as specifically "Quaker" philosophers we then become, or are perceived to become, parochial and prejudiced in our approach to philosophy, which is particularly troubling where there is an expectation of neutrality, as is clearly the case for many schools of philosophy. We must not allow our religious conclusions to function as a starting point for our philosophical reflections; rather we must first, as philosophers, examine these assertions themselves by recourse to some or other non-sectarian standards. Even for those like myself, who are convinced that the Enlightenment's "prejudice against prejudice" (in H. G. Gadamer's phrase) is precisely that, and who do not feel the need to philosophically exorcise the particular but to engage it, do not hope to translate this incredulity towards theoretical neutrality into an alibi for uncritical assertion. As "philosophers" we hope to proceed on an equal footing with our professional colleagues, without any claims to special access to the truth, even if we feel at liberty to proceed confessionally in our meetings.

And yet, for me at least, and perhaps for others for whom the relationship between faith and philosophizing is non-incidental, the term Quaker philosopher–if considered solely for the purposes of self-understanding, and not as the adoption of a title–retains a certain descriptive force. Quakerism is not simply one among a number of aspects that together define us, one that we foreground at certain times but that falls away behind the horizon when we are engaged in others, but is a root qualification, one in terms of which we have been (re)constituted as the people we are, and that therefore radically rather than incidentally affects (or even effects) all of our other engagements. The question, it seems to me, suggested by the terminological distinction in question here, is whether or not one's Quakerism comprehensively impacts upon one's vocation, such that the vocational activity could not be the activity that it is if the Quakerism of the practitioner were lacking. This is clearly not a claim that one must be a Quaker to engage in philosophy, or that the results achieved would be restricted to Quakers, but that our Quakerism is non-incidental to both the what and the how of our engagement in it. Philosophy is, on this model, undertaken a specialized calling within the more general task shared by us all: to "translate" our Quaker spirituality into our worldly activities, or "to bring our Quakerism to life."

But what more precisely is this relationship between Quakerism and philosophy that tempts me to adopt "Quaker philosopher" as a descriptor? By this I do not mean that Quakerism becomes the focus, or the subject matter, of philosophizing (though this would not be excluded), in the manner that a "Quaker historian" (qua historian of Quakerism) studies the history of the Quakers, but without necessarily being a Quaker. Nor do I mean by this that we begin by allowing Quaker presuppositions to either govern the choice of subject matter or delimit, doctrinally or ethically, the possible outcomes of our work, for instance, that we would be attracted to and promote certain philosophers who say things that seem to us to resonate with Quaker teachings and experience, or that we would attempt to make a philosophical case for pacifism (although neither of these would be excluded either). Rather, I think it would mean something closer to taking up the task of philosophizing in a Quakerly manner, being a Quaker in our whole person even while engaged fully in the philosophical task (while "being a whole man to" philosophy, as J. J. Gurney might put it), such that who we are cannot but thoroughgoingly affect both what we do, and how we do it. A "Quaker philosopher" here would then be one who philosophizes in a Friendly manner, rather than one who is concerned with a particular disciplinary focus. Quakerism here would qualify our philosophizing adverbially.

Without pretending to, or seeking, any status official or otherwise thereby, with I hope seemly humility, and while welcoming dissent, for myself the term "Quaker philosopher" (over against the "less integrated" Quaker who is a philosopher) signals a vocation in philosophy motivated and framed by commitments that are self-consciously Quaker, or, again, deliberately engaging in philosophy in a Quakerly manner, such that philosophizing itself becomes a way in which we expresses the love of God and neighbor that our Quakerism (in its various forms and diverse articulations) is itself an attempt to faithfully embody. Or, to adopt and adapt a phrase from the Jewish philosopher Emmanuel Levinas, a Quaker philosopher recognizes that before it is the love of wisdom, philosophy is "the wisdom of love in the service of love," and the Quaker philosopher (on the model I am suggesting here) brings the Quaker sensibilities that frame his or her approach to philosophy into his or her vocation as its very heart.

Chapter 5

College and University Governance

Although no two Quaker colleges practice governance identically, Friends' approaches stand in stark contrast to methods generally encountered throughout higher education. Friends' spiritual commitments to equality, community and seeking divine truth require time-consuming searches for consensus, absent the convenient mechanism of voting. The prototype for this approach is the Quaker meeting for business, an ideal more easily imagined than implemented. The essays in this chapter address maintaining a Quaker college ethos in the face of declining numbers of Quaker students, faculty and staff; the merits and limitations of applying Quaker decision-making within a college governance framework; the governance tensions that often exist between Quaker colleges and their founding Quaker meetings; and the challenges to Quaker sensibilities of financially driven, academic prioritization processes.

First, Gary Farlow confronts the persistent trend since the end of World War II of Quaker colleges attracting insufficient numbers of Friends, as students and as faculty, to ensure sustaining a recognizable Quaker ethos. He sees an important role for Friends Association for Higher Education helping its member institutions address this problem by facilitating ongoing discussions regarding the colleges' adherence to values grounded in Friends' testimonies. In particular, Gary prescribes honing in on Friends' commitments to plain speaking, honesty, peace, simplicity, Quaker governance, and equality. By doing so, he believes that the Quaker ethos can be preserved in a manner that makes Friends proud.

Next, Paul Lacey, reprising a remarkably current 1977 talk given to incoming Earlham students, examines the college's response to

145

Howard Brinton's challenging question: "Can a Quaker educational community be conducted on the principles of the Quaker meeting for worship or for business with the consequent embodiment of the social doctrines of community, pacifism, equality and simplicity?" Paul, while humbly laying bare ways in which Earlham often falls short, provides keen insight into how to best proceed and the benefits of doing so. He concludes, "When we are at our best, things are not decided by appeal to authority or challenges to legitimacy, they are decided by meeting–overcoming divisions without eliminating differences, knowing oneself and others in a common search for the truth, going outside one's personal prejudices and wishes to ask what is best for the whole community.

Doug Bennett, Earlham College's former president, builds on Paul Lacey's contribution by raising important questions regarding the vexing impact of variables such as institutional size and complexity and individual expertise and responsibility. Doug points out that, "At Earlham, the Faculty as a whole makes decisions by Quaker business practice, as do its committees, most student organizations and other groups." He notes that "...'Robert's Rules of Order' or other voting processes can become an exercise of power politics (majority wins! others lose!)..." while "...consensus process encourages us to find solutions that win assent and legitimacy from everyone." He goes on to explore the difficulties raised by the institution's response to two questions: " (1) Who is included in the group that reaches consensus, and how do we justify this pattern of inclusion and exclusion? And (2) should we ever allow an individual to make an important decision, and if so, how do we justify that?" Doug examines the complexities introduced by these issues, clearly illustrating the challenges involved, while making a compelling case for Quaker organizations to seek consensus guided by "...transparency, careful listening and constructive speaking..." in order to foster "...broad participation, ...active consultation, and ...care... that every voice is heard."

Governance of Quaker Colleges is complicated by the colleges' affiliations with their "founding" monthly and yearly meetings. The fourth entry in this chapter, again by Doug Bennett, explores the tensions often existing among these Friends organizations, pointing out that Meetings often expect the affiliated educational institutions (whether Quaker schools or colleges) to respond more to their members' needs, while the schools or colleges invariably expect more financial support from the Meetings; misunderstandings exacerbated by the lack of formal, written agreements specifying what their relationships should entail. Doug argues that critical to resolving tensions is realizing that Quaker meetings and Quaker colleges "...stand in some relationship of mutual obligation, but not a relationship where one has primacy or dominance." Indeed, he claims Quaker colleges are far too large and complex to possibly be subservient to their relatively simply organized, affiliated meetings. The 2010 Covenant struck between Earlham College and Indiana Yearly Meeting is offered as a model for addressing the issues raised throughout the article.

The final essay, addressing the current spate of academic prioritization initiatives at financially strapped colleges and universities, focuses on Donn Weinholtz' experiences as director of a doctoral program targeted for divestment in the University of Hartford's institution-wide prioritization effort. In addition to summarizing and illustrating the steps recommended by academic prioritization's most prominent proponent, Robert Dickeson, Donn offers insights into the quandaries encountered by a Friend caught in a particularly non-Quaker-like process. He also questions some of Dickeson's primary suppositions, in particular that there are substantial pools of money hiding in academic programs and ripe for reallocation.

A Quaker-Valued Education: The significance of Quaker Identified Colleges and the role of FAHE in that identification from a 30-year, personal perspective

by Gary Farlow, Wright State University

Historical Context

In 1981, I was asked to sit on a panel exploring the unique qualities of a Quaker college. This panel and its topic presumed that the justification for a Quaker college was that a Quaker college is somehow unique, that it is somehow irreplaceable. I was a green, graduate student worried more about defects in Silver Bromide than defects in Quaker Colleges, and the one from which I had just been graduated (Guilford) seemed perfectly okay to me. I was set up among such thoughtful Quaker worthies as Earl Redding, Linda Eliason, and Ward Harrington. It turned out I had the unenviable task of telling the nescient FAHE–which at that time included educators, administrators, trustees and students concerned by their alma maters drifting from Quaker allegiance–that there was nothing they could do that could not be done by someone else. The text can be found in the proceedings of FAHE–1981.

Consider now the context of 1981. Most Quaker, and other religiously affiliated schools, had alienated their putative sponsors, e.g. yearly meetings, through the liberality of thought that had become the norm on college campuses. My God, whatever became of a "guarded education"? Well, Quaker families after World War II were less tied to their Quaker institutions having become more 'of this world' than merely 'in it'; and these good Quaker families quite frankly preferred the testimony of frugality to the one of Quaker peculiarity. As a result, fewer Quaker students were showing up at Quaker Schools at the same time the Quaker schools had grown to the point where there was no possibility of populating these schools with Quakers–even if you included the attendees who decided to become Quaker based on their experience at that Quaker school. As the number of Quakers declined relative to the population, and as many of us academics found more lucrative positions or more challenging research careers in state or other non-sectarian institutions, there was also no way to populate the faculty at a Quaker School with a 10% leavening, much less a majority, of Quakers. It looked to the old timers of 1981 like the next event in the sequence was taps for the Quaker college as a Quaker College. Does this resonate with the present?

However, thanks to Canby Jones (Wilmington College) and Charles Browning (Whittier College), the trumpet was sounded and the dead-in-despair were raised with an enthusiasm for rescuing the Quaker College from the amorphous identity of 'a liberal arts college'. A number of colleges re-embraced their Quaker roots with considerable purpose. Great interest arose in the social testimonies of Friends on the campuses of Quaker Colleges–so long as it was not the testimony on temperance. Quaker governance practice, with its protection of minority view, became a cause celeb among faculty in particular. At least four Quaker schools instituted Quaker Scholars programs, and others strengthened their library holdings. A few even attempted to make peace with their Yearly Meetings. This looks good.

But, there is no new thing under the Sun, and as of Fall 2011, no Quaker college will have a Quaker president. Only five of the eleven will have a majority of the board of trustees who are Quaker. (May I say, one can be very creative in identifying Quakers when looking for trustees.) Only three Quaker colleges have trustees who are appointed by a Yearly Meeting. Three have dissolved all ties with any organ of the Religious Society of Friends (not counting FAHE). The sad reality is that there are still not enough Quaker students, educators, or influential citizens to maintain either institutional or cultural control of one Quaker college, much less eleven. Periodic tiffs aside, there really is no interest among Quaker judicatories (the official National Council of Churches designation of a denominational organization) in trying to assert institutional or cultural control over any one of the Quaker colleges, much less all of them. We find however, increasingly prestigious Quaker library holdings at Quaker schools and increasingly prestigious Quaker Studies programs. We find an institution as prestigious as Haverford College asking itself, "What is our Quaker identity?" Does this sound like something we have heard before?

Where Do We Go From Here?

So, what will it mean to be a Quaker college in the 21st century? Or, as most of our institutions so coyly put it: "Colleges founded by the Society of Friends".

Some semantics: if the designation 'founded by Friends' were adequate; we could include Johns Hopkins, Cornell and Brown Universities since a majority of the original endowment of these schools was provided by wealthy Friends. Presumably there was even some Quaker influence in their early days. In the present day "Quaker-affiliated" would stretch our testimony on honesty, if not break it.

I prefer to use the term "Quaker-identified colleges" as being those colleges who were indeed founded by Friends and who choose to continue to hold some identification with the Society of Friends, its practices, and its values. All the institutional members of FAHE fall into this category. In the remainder of these remarks I will propose what I believe is a proper and fruitful identification with the Society of Friends for our time, as well as the role of FAHE in promoting, informing and eldering such an identification.

Parameters

First, it is impossible to make the Quaker identified colleges be naturally Quaker. We have established that there are not enough Quaker students, nor faculty to establish constitutional operation nor cultural domination of a Quaker identified college. The demography of the populations does not allow enough role models for this to be practical and to survive economically, nor to allow the kind of academic freedom to which academia has become accustomed. Despite the number of books written on the subject, being Quaker is not something that can be learned from a book or rule ledger. This identity is learned by living in a practicing faith community and cannot be prescribed. You must talk the talk, walk the walk, and meet God in the private places of your heart and mind. Modern colleges are not intrinsically faith communities, so they will not naturally be Quaker.

Second, Quakers are not going to 'own' the Quaker identified colleges. As more and more of the alumni of Quaker-identified institutions are non-Quaker and live in a secular, professional world, their vested interest in the institution is its professional, academic, and athletic reputation. A religious or spiritual culture is not high on the list of vested interests for such institutional stake-holders. Donors are needed to keep these institutions economically alive, and the vast majority of donors are not Quaker. Donors are also significant stakeholders in the reputation of the Quaker College and their interest need not be intrinsically Quaker. Alumni and donors eventually drive much of College function and identity. This must be acknowledged.

Nevertheless, a college's culture is appreciated as a distinguishing mark and is part of its reputation. I believe for Quaker-identified colleges one of the principal, if not the principal, distinguishing mark is a Quaker ethos; that it is in the interest of a Quaker identified college to maintain this ethos as a distinguishing mark; and that this ethos will form the basis for a Quaker identified college continuing to have an interest in identification with the Society of

Friends. A Quaker ethos forms an added value to the degree and can form a non-sectarian community spirit for alumni even though it has sectarian roots. It can be a tool for institutional promotion, or should I say branding, in a time when competition for students demands any effective tool for recruiting that is available. It is a recognizable Quaker ethos that will make the larger Quaker community proud of the Quaker identified colleges and want to claim them.

This, however, poses a problem. Without an adequate practicing core, how does a Quaker identified college sustain a distinguishing character that can honestly be recognized as a Quaker ethos? I believe that this ethos will be driven explicitly by the values that Quakers hold and for which we are known through our testimonies. It will be expressed by practices for which we have also become known. It should additionally be informed by the spiritual foundations from which these values are derived. It can be effectively promoted and made genuine by the involvement of FAHE because 1) as Quakers we understand the foundations of Quaker values and practices and 2) as academics we understand the academy.

The Prescription

I will now review some of these testimonies and practices that ought to be part of a Quaker ethos, and will address the ways that I believe Quaker values can be articulated and made comprehensible to an academic environment.

I will start with Plain Speaking, because it is integral to the academic enterprise, as well as public Quaker spirituality. More importantly, unless we exercise this testimony ourselves what comes after will not connect with our putative audience, the academy, and therefore will be fruitless. 'Saying what you mean, and meaning what you say' is a basic part of what scholars do in trying to explain an insight that is the result of deep thought, research, or experience. It should be a natural connection between non-Quaker academics and Quaker culture. However, "plain speech" and "Quakerisms" are mostly 19th century relics. As such, they are not at all plain in the sense of universal comprehensibility–which was the original testimony. Acknowledgement of this linguistic evolution will mean that we must give up some of our favorite slogans. Consider "as way opens." To render this saying into modern usage for non-Quakers one must say something to the effect of : "as opportunity or circumstance is provided by divine agency." This version doesn't ring true, but it is plain, and it is not particularly subject to awkward misinterpretation. By the same token, we must call our academic brethren to account when they obscure their exposition in pursuit of eloquence, equivocate in the name of precision, or claim "I can't possibly explain this to you because you don't have my experience." We also should not forget that the testimony of plain-speaking derives from Jesus's admonition (in paraphrase): "let your yes be yes and your no be no, for equivocation has its roots in evil."

Academic honesty has been too much in the news of late: fabrication of data in the laboratory, failure (intentional or not) to recognize others' work, and massive cheating on entrance and course exams in prominent institutions. The academic community responds to these failings with outrage: Honesty is the foundation of its credibility. The Quaker testimony on honesty should thus be immediately recognizable by our non-Quaker brethren. One of my fondest memories of Guilford was when a professor passed out an exam and then walked out of the room. Contrast this with the honor code, "I have neither given nor received help on this exam," as a statement that one would be required to sign. The former is a clear testament to the expectation of honest work from knowledge honestly gained. The latter is a demand for a declaration that "while I could have been bad, I wasn't." The Quaker take on honesty is that we expect it. The basis for this view is the Quaker assumption that the soul of man yearns for nobility. It need not be second-guessed. When someone fails to be honest we are not so much outraged as wounded. Indeed John Donne's admonition, "Ask not for whom the Bell tolls, it tolls for thee" expresses the Quaker view of how dishonesty affects the academy and life in general.

Peace is the hallmark Quaker testimony in the public mind, and deservedly so. Quakers and Quaker Schools were in the forefront of establishing the legitimacy of conscientious objection to war. One of the ways that Quaker schools can and do promote peace as part of their Quaker ethos is to tell the stories from WWI and WWII about how they provided outlets for alternative service when it was a new idea. There are also stories of how students from Quaker Schools went to Europe to help bind up the wounds of war. These can be compared to the efforts of students on campus to do the same today by publicly objecting to warfare and studies showing how military expenditures are inflationary. There are also the evidences of student mediation in crisis and in community building in the environs of the college. Who will collect and tell these current stories? What are the fora in which they can be told? I believe it is a proper function of FAHE to collect these stories and help organize events on campuses where they can be told.

To those of us who are Quaker, however, just telling stories seems pale because for us the peace testimony grows out of a deep appreciation for the holiness of the other person. Stated this way, the peace testimony seems rather hopelessly old fashioned; yet if not communicated to students and institutions, the Quaker ethos of peace becomes just more do-gooder-ism. One of the functions of FAHE should be to find ways to say that the other is holy, in a manner that can be, and will be, heard by modern students and modern academic institutions.

I am told by my colleagues on Quaker campuses that simplicity is the hardest of our testimonies to convey. Outwardly, it looks 'simple' enough–doing without. This is not naturally a high value at highly valued institutions. Frugality gives us the reputation of tight wads. Plain dress makes us look Amish. Yet the bedrock of the practices arising from the simplicity testimony is in choosing clothing, food, and amusements that are of good quality and long service. Why? Because items so chosen add measurably to an ennobled life, and sometimes to a spiritual life. Simplicity includes temperance as well, in the context of an ennobled life. Not only do we wish to avoid spending our treasure on wastrel goods, we want to avoid spending our lives on wastrel activities. Of course it does not hurt that this quality-based simple living is good, long-term economics. Our function as FAHE is to explain, in plain language, the importance of unadorned quality and unadorned living to those who educate at Quaker institutions and to their students. Most importantly, FAHE should help our Quaker schools understand that by living well within our means (there is a pun here–living well, within our means), we have the ability to charitably serve others as God would have us.

Faculty tend to like Quaker Governance. Reverence for the minority voice allows us to 'put our foot in it' when we don't like something. Younger faculty like that everybody has their own say independent of rank. It seems the ultimate in democratic, reason-driven governance. It has been described as an anti-political, consensus-based governance by a Jesuit priest. Quaker governance, however, has never been democratic in its traditional form. There have always been "Weighty Friends." The clerk has enormous power to guide and direct the conversation. The process is not really consensual.

Modern gurus of Quaker governance have delighted in promoting the practical benefits of having the whole body in one accord, of synergistic ideas and of having the lone voice in the wilderness pulling the group back from a precipitous or thoughtless decision. But, they frequently forget to point out that Quaker governance is a pursuit of a higher understanding of truth and proper action–not the lowest common denominator of our individual wills, nor a bland synthesis of proffered ideas. Now how do we explain to a group of academics, whose DNA is dispute, that they are gathered as a faculty to seek an almost metaphysical higher understanding and a more excellent course of action? I am told that the faculty at Whittier gave up this model, finding it just too bizarre.

It is too much to hope that a group of non-Quaker academics will admit that they are actively seeking to implement the insight of a higher being. It should however be possible to convince our colleagues that faculty governance is ultimately driven by the considered and humble pursuit of a goal higher than ourselves or our disciplines. I would suggest that goal should be what will best ennoble and best empower the student. But whatever the goal, the role of FAHE should be the explainer, the exemplar, and perhaps even the advocate of governance based on that in the academic environment which can truly be said to be higher than ourselves. There are many more Quaker testimonies and practices to examine, but I want to address only one, equality. I think this testimony is the most problematic for the academy, which is constitutionally a meritocracy. The academy celebrates rank and prestige, which are acquired only by their pursuit. The term 'equality' also is problematic in the modern context. In the modern world it carries significant connotations from the civil rights movements of the last half-century which semantically include "equality of opportunity" and "equality of value." Both of these goals get muddied in application by how they are measured. I will not address that question because neither value is directly related to the Quaker testimony.

Historically, the testimony of equality had its origins in the rejection of "hat honor" to one's social betters, in the rejection of "pronoun honor" to one's superiors of class, and in the recognition that women and the untrained could speak on behalf of the Almighty. In each case these were manifestations of equality in how people are treated. The historic Quaker testimony on equality therefore has to do with way we treat people, not the standing we accord them, nor the recognition we give them. If FAHE is to properly represent the testimony of equality to our colleagues at Quaker schools, I propose the following test. Consider the student who is in your office yelling at you for keeping him out of Medical school because you did not assign one problem on one homework set its full credit. We must be able to convey to our colleagues that this student is wonderful in God's sight, if not in ours, and deserves to be treated so. Treatment may seem like a lower standard, but if it is based on the holiness of the other, then standing and recognition will be afterthoughts.

154

Is this effort worthwhile?

If FAHE can convey the foundations of Quaker testimony and practice, which is the same as conveying the depth of the tradition on which these schools were founded, then I believe FAHE will have justified its worth and its existence to its member institutions. If our Quaker colleges can infuse through practice these insights into the human condition and human relationships, I believe they will be a light unto all the academic world, they will be true to their foundations (even without any Quakers present), and we Quakers can be proud to claim them. I believe this is a worthwhile effort and a tribute to FAHE's founders.

Decision-Making in a Quaker Context

by Paul A. Lacey

I am going to begin what I have to say by quoting the Jewish philosopher Martin Buber, who said that "all real living is meeting." That may be a grim idea for some of you. You are sitting in a meeting, and I am addressing a meeting. Perhaps some of you are dreading a meeting with some distant relative whom you have an obligation to visit. Hall meetings, class meetings, business meetings, meetings for worship–if that is the sum total of all real living, things are worse than we thought.

Of course that isn't exactly what Buber meant, but it has a connection. Think of what it means to meet another person. What we are aware of first is difference between us, separation. I am *here* and you are *over there*. But when something good and meaningful happens between us, we come together; we find similarity, mutuality, perhaps a high degree of identity in common. I am here and you are there, but we are also someplace together, in a center which we share. Certainly a number of you have already met people you can call friends and some others who give promise of being friends if you meet often enough. That is the sense in which I want to talk about the phrase "all real living is meeting:" the great possibilities for knowing meaning in our lives come through encounters with other people, strange situations, new demands, in which we experience difference which leads to identity, conflict which leads to reconciliation. We have a meeting of the minds, we say, or we really met someone where he really lives.

Now, I describe the experience this way to emphasize that meetings are not guaranteed successes, and that they can be hard unsatisfying work. If you meet your mother's second cousin Arthur, you could be discovering a wonderful life-long friend, but you could also be meeting a complete dud. The same, of course, is true for him.

You have heard a certain amount about Quaker methods of governance and decision-making, and if you know nothing else you know that we do things in the pattern of the Quaker business meeting–that word again. I want to tell you something more about our methods of arriving at decisions, but I want you to have in mind both the risk-taking and the frustration and the satisfaction implied in the word "meeting," as I have been using it.

To begin with, Quaker business procedure grew up in the early days of the Religious Society of Friends as a way of resolving the most practical matters in a religious context. That is, the group which met to consider committee reports, the treasurer's report, and the like, sat in a meeting for worship in which business was held up to the Light for guidance. Every meeting was held in the expectation of Pentecost. Friends spoke literally of being led to action, of feeling the way open. They met each other in that which is eternal; they also met God.

The business procedures presupposed a highly homogeneous group, for whom both the vocabulary of action and experience were held in common. Edward Burrough, an early Quaker leader, wrote a letter of advice on business meeting which is cited in Arnold Lloyd's *Quaker Social History.* First of all, these were meetings "for the management of truth's affairs." As Lloyd describes it, "All members who were sound of principle and judgment were to feel free to attend. They were particularly urged not to spend time in needless, unnecessary and fruitless discourses,' but equally were not to reach quick decisions by vote. They must determine, not in the way of the World by hot contests, by seeking to outspeak or overreach one another in discourse..... but in love, gentleness and dear unity."

Now this is a tall order. Friends were to wait and try to open themselves to God's leading, because they knew the wisdom and power of God directly. If they earnestly sought to be led, treating each other in love, gentleness and dear unity, the truth would be revealed to them all. They would express the sense of the meeting as a single unified perception of what they should do. That is a statement of the ideal, but of course the fellowship of the saints rarely approached the ideal.

Howard Brinton, writing on Quaker education, distinguishes what he calls three classes of doctrines which are characteristic of Friends. The first is the doctrine of the Inward Light which can lead every human being who will be open to leading; the second concerns the meetings for worship and business, social institutions created so that the group can search for a corporate understanding of the leading of the Light; the third doctrines concern the social testimonies of community, pacifism or peacemaking, equality and simplicity. Brinton says Quakerism is unique only in the second class of doctrines, those having to do with meetings for worship and business which are laboratories in which we can test the leading of the Light of Christ and express them in the social testimonies. Those meetings also shape the small community of believers who exemplify in their life together what the larger community can be like.

Howard Brinton emphasized that these doctrines are closely interrelated and animated Quaker schools and colleges when those

157

were homogeneous communities. He goes on to note that Quaker schools and colleges face a dilemma whether to allow themselves to develop "solely as institutions of excellent standing, meeting the needs of families who can afford the luxury of private schools, or shall they appeal to a more limited constituency by discovering and applying the distinguishing characteristics which a Quaker school ought to embody today?"

As long as I have been at Earlham, we have been on the horns of that dilemma, and I assume we will remain in that awkward position for as long as any of you are here. That is to say, we cannot resolve the question in an either-or fashion. We wish to discover and apply the distinguishing characteristics appropriate for a Quaker college today, but for a heterogeneous student body like yourselves, many things early Friends took for granted are in serious doubt. For that matter, you know that the Society of Friends is highly heterogeneous.

We have stayed on the horns of this dilemma because no other position was more tenable–if the mental image that conjures up isn't too awkward to contemplate. Howard Brinton asked "Can a Quaker educational community be conducted on the principles of the Quaker meeting for worship or for business with the consequent embodiment of the social doctrines of community, pacifism, equality and simplicity?"

In a fumbling, tenuous, imperfect fashion, we have tried to answer that question in the affirmative, particularly by the way we govern ourselves. I want to emphasize this point: we often do the job badly, we are often inconsistent and mistaken, sometimes unfaithful to the principle we enunciate, but as an institution we try to be a Quaker educational community, we try to conduct our affairs on the principles of the Quaker meeting for business, and we hope to see the social testimonies embodied in our life together. It is easy to dismiss our failings as hypocrisy–a word which springs much too readily to the lips of people at Earlham–but I want to emphasize that even when we fail there are a substantial number of people trying to understand how to be faithful to Quaker business procedures.

Now, what is the business meeting like? I have already described it as a meeting for worship in which practical matters are held up to the light. Let me describe it in a bit more detail. A clerk presides over the meeting whose job is both to introduce the business and to gather the sense of the meeting about what should be done on each subject. The clerk calls on people who wish to speak and from time to time he or she may try to express what is being said and the direction the meeting is going in its quest for agreement.

That is, the clerk will try to phrase in words acceptable to the group whatever measure of agreement there is. If that is well done, the group can recognize what is still to be considered, what it has unity on, and what is still a matter of doubt, disagreement, or lacks clarity.

Notice I spoke of the clerk expressing the *sense* of the meeting. We speak often of consensus, or the substantial agreement of the whole group, but it is also important to think of what is meant by the "sense of the meeting." The clerk does not count votes, but it is his or her duty to weigh what is said, to take into account the weight of experience and wisdom behind each contribution in the discussion. This is very hard to do well, and it can be very frustrating to everyone. At times it seems clear that a great deal of wisdom and judgment are on one side of a question and that there is less on the other. The meeting may be moving toward a very definite sense of what should be done, even though several people are opposed or unconvinced. When that happens, the meeting as a whole may want to postpone action until those who are unconvinced have more time to consider their position, or until they can convince the others that the sense of the meeting is mistaken, but that is not an absolute requirement. I make this point with some vigor because a number of people get the idea that they can always have a personal, private veto over what everyone else wants to do. That is not the case. The sense of the meeting does not have to be unanimously agreed on.

If there is still division, the meeting has to consider whether it should proceed when there is not complete unity, and those who disagree on the action being considered must ask whether they shouldn't unite with the meeting, agreeing that the sense of the meeting is to go ahead.

In practice, meetings can be so concerned with achieving unanimity or overwhelming consensus that they search for compromises to make everyone feel better, or they put decisions so vaguely that the decision commits no one to anything significant. Some times meetings get so vague and indirect that no one says anything significant. Sometimes meetings get so vague and indirect that no one knows what is really being said. You may have heard of the Friend who, when he heard a name of which he disapproved suggested for a committee, said, "That is not a name which would have occurred to me." Now that is a strong expression of disapproval in some circles, but no one could be blamed for thinking it isn't so direct as it might be. I noticed another way Quakers have of arriving at consensus through compromise when I attended a meeting of Meeting for Sufferings in London Yearly Meeting last spring. A statement

159

was brought forward which had substantial support, but also some strong disagreement from a few weighty Friends. Of course, whenever we talk about the text of a statement, there are suggestions for additions, corrections and other improvements. At the end of the discussion, the meeting did something as typical as it is frustrating. It enlarged the drafting committee to include some of those who were opponents, so that the statement which came forward next time would be more evenly-balanced. The meeting also asked that the statement be shorter. Think about the action: the meeting enlarged the committee and therefore the scope of the statement *and* asked that the statement be shorter. The effect will be to make the statement more general, but it will also require the opponents to take their share of responsibility for the statement.

I have been describing meetings of Quaker groups, but of course when we talk about decision-making at Earlham we are talking about a method, which is not understood only, or even primarily, as a religious activity. Not everyone who goes to community council meetings, (where student-elected representatives and a small number of appointed faculty and staff members meet regularly to deal with issues of general community concern) or who attends a dormitory hall meeting, does so expecting to be led by God to make the decisions before the meeting. There is, in fact, a very great danger to our life together if we try to make every issue a supreme moral or ethical test of ourselves and of the business method. A friend of mine who has lived a number of years in experimental religious communities once said to me that he was never able to see that there was a way of determining what color the Holy Spirit wanted the community to paint the dining room walls. If asking for divine guidance on a matter essentially neutral in its meaning or–at the worst–if you happened to have people with strong opposing views, you painted the walls half one color, half the other. Now if there is anything worse to imagine than the discussion of the moral implications of paint colors, it is the effect on people who have to dress up their personal preferences for blue, white or green in high-flown moral language. Yet I can assure you that over-using the method of arriving at decisions lets us in for that kind of excess. Parliamentary business methods encourage long-windedness, pretentiousness, trickiness perhaps, but Quaker business procedures can encourage all of that *and* self-righteousness as well. In the recent past we have seen people argue not just against the *wisdom* of a decision taken perhaps years before they thought of coming here as student or faculty member, but against its very *legitimacy*–as though the Quaker procedure required not only an absolute democracy, but also behaving as though this is the first day of creation.

Let me emphasize these points. Quaker business procedure, even when it is following the principle of one-person-one-vote, is more and less than that. Greater wisdom and greater experience receive greater weight in a decision, but wisdom and experience are not merely assumed to belong to the older people here. I remember a faculty member from another college telling me about a proposal in their faculty meeting that failed because it was proposed by an assistant professor. All the assistant professors were for it, but all the associate and full professors were opposed. Even now, when it is harder to get tenure and younger faculty are more conscious of their exposed situation, you could not determine weight by rank in the Earlham faculty, and certainly there is no sense that the person speaking to business is an assistant, associate or full professor. Neither does the procedure require that every decision be reopened just because someone new has arrived. You join an on-going institution whose direction and shape you may have some opportunity to influence, but the obligation is greater on the newcomer to know and understand what has happened, to cover more of the distance in reaching a meeting with others.

Let me illustrate my point with an example. Several years ago, when I was an administrator, we were trying to decide between two candidates for a position on the faculty. The department was divided between a majority and minority view, based largely on two different conceptions of what the department program should be. That is, the majority were saying, "We need someone who can teach Shakespeare." And the minority was saying, "No, never mind Shakespeare, we need someone to teach creative writing, someone who is a writer." I use this example as an illustration–the department was *not* English. Both Faculty Affairs Committees, the committee elected by faculty members and the Student Faculty Affairs Committee, were in favor of the majority's candidate, primarily because that candidate seemed a stronger teacher. Students in the department, however, agreed with the minority and demanded their preferred candidate. We had, therefore, what I came to call a monster meeting, where everyone with an interest had a chance to present his or her point of view to everyone else. After two hours, it was evident that there was no possibility in the short run of reaching agreement and that Academic Dean Joe Elmore and I were going to have to take the advice of all these other participants, weigh the arguments, including our own, and make a decision, or the department would begin the next year one person short. As I was leaving the meeting, I asked one highly vocal student whether she thought she has been heard. She answered, "that will depend on what you decide." My reply was, "No, that wasn't what I asked. I asked whether you were heard, not whether you convinced me. If I *heard* you I should be able to restate your argument and conclusion well enough that you recognize it as your own. That is a preliminary requirement to trying to *weigh* it against other points of view in order to determine what seems best given *all* these arguments for doing two mutually exclusive things."

I tell this story because it illustrates how easily we can do violence to the whole system of consultation, advising and recommending on which our decision-making rests. That student was so sure she was right that she was already preparing to accuse me of not listening, of pretending to consult, if I didn't come to the conclusion she had arrived at. Perhaps she would have called me a hypocrite if I didn't agree, or she might have argued that my decision lacked legitimacy if I came out with a conclusion she didn't like.

I am not trying to blame one student for a reply to a question. I am showing how easy it is to refuse to meet another person. I could cite examples of administrators or faculty members being just as arrogant, doing just as much damage to the process of reaching decisions. It is very tempting to believe that anyone who can't be convinced by my passionately argued beliefs is not acting in good faith. It is also tempting to block action until everyone comes to my point of view, or to railroad through a decision against my opponents because they are not acting in good faith.

Now, it is reasonable to ask why we go about decision-making this way, if it has so many headaches. There are several reasons which are persuasive to me. The first is that it is an expression of my religious faith–my faith that when people are open to being led to do the best or the right thing, they will be led. But beyond that, I believe our way of consulting and arriving at decisions is both politically and educationally valuable. I believe the statements in Earlham's compendium of rules and practices for community life, The Little Read Book, fail to do justice to the political aspects of our method. "Political" is too often contrasted with "religious" as though one was always a synonym for dirty and the other a synonym for clean. Quaker principles have always held that political process can also be an expression of God's will, and I believe that about the political system which is imbedded in our methods. I am not one of those who thinks that voting is a dirty activity. It is another way of getting at decisions, and it is worth noting that the same religious ferment which led to the Quaker business meeting also led to other forms of religious democracy, including that of the Congregationalists and other groups who place great emphasis on the equal participation of each communicant in the business affairs of the church. "Vox populi, vox Dei"–the voice of the people is the voice of God. The Book of Acts tells us the first Christians cast lots to determine who would take Judas's place as an apostle. They believed that God would use the laws of chance to make God's will known. There are a number of ways with a better or worse chance of showing us God's will–including voting or seeking the sense of the meeting. And every method of consulting on decisions is also political in the sense that many different groups' interests have to be taken into account in order to arrive at actions that gain the assent of those affected by them. When we say "let's enlarge the committee to include critics" that is a political act–not necessarily to co-opt people or neutralize them but to make the possibility of effective consensus greater. I believe the Quaker business procedure has much to offer as a purely political system: it makes people realize that a majority is a frail thing, so it is better to aim for the widest possible acceptance of actions than to force them through just because 51% of the voters want them; it puts a high premium on considering one's opponents as people also trying to achieve the common good, so it also emphasizes arriving at decisions by appealing to what is noblest in people, not just to the narrowest self-interest. It also puts emphasis on careful reflection, reasoned argument–not hasty emotional decisions. It can enhance the possibilities of a good life in community rather than exacerbating disagreements.

The method is also educational, in the way that meeting is educational–meeting other people, meeting new ideas, even meeting oneself by thinking through what one really believes or wants. We can learn from what others believe and want. Perhaps their vision of the way we should live together is so admirable that we become convinced. Perhaps our practical solution to a problem is so persuasive that we can serve ourselves and everyone else by presenting it for consideration. Perhaps asking for the widest expression of opinion will reveal terrible weakness in a plan which made good sense to the few who were least affected by it. And, as important as anything, we may learn how to behave respectfully, democratically, wisely in a lot of other areas of our lives as a result of working together to decide about life together at Earlham.

There are dangers in building up our method too much. When you consider that perhaps 90% of every year's budget has been committed by previous decisions, for example, it may be frustrating to think of such an elaborate system being used for making decisions about the remaining 10%.

I want to acknowledge such difficulties, but I also want to emphasize that any opportunity we have for making decisions about making our life together more meaningful is an opportunity worth taking. You will spend a great deal of time in your dormitory hall, so it matters that you learn how to confront and resolve issues *there*, whatever else is happening around you. Learning to live together with mutual respect, learning how to confront the thoughtless or selfish roommate, learning how to shape your living situation to be supportive of your personal and educational needs–these are very important goals. Don't disparage them because someone tells you that all the power is in the faculty or administrative council. You may notice that this is the first time I have spoken of power. It is not a word which sufficiently speaks to our situation. In a sense, no one here, from the president to the newest student has a lot of power to make the institution do anything. We all can have a certain amount of power to prevent things from happening. We can get around rules, or make such a fuss that people abandon their wishes. We may have a lot of power to neutralize one another, but that is ultimately the most frustrating kind. The faculty has the power to compel all of you into humanities classes; those who are compelled into my class have the power to frustrate the goals of the course by refusing to do the work, refusing to take part in discussions or write the papers; I have the power to fail you if you don't do the work. But what will have been gained if we operate only according to our power? Nothing, unless you think of anger and frustration as a gain.

Of far greater positive impact, I believe, is the influence we have with one another. Teaching rests on persuading and influencing people, rather than on compelling them alone. And we are influenced by persuasive arguments, by good examples, by our respect and affection for the people who are making their case to us. And I am influenced primarily by people who seem to me to care about me, my opinion, what I value in life. Why should I change my mind to agree with someone who gives no evidence of trying to understand why I hold the views I do? If he can show he has heard through my views and tried to accept them, I will be much more willing to do the same for his views. And perhaps the result of such an encounter is that we are both persuaded to a position neither of us saw before.

In such a sense it is possible to say you can all be involved in decisions-making at Earlham. You can have influence as you show that you have more than narrow self-centered desires shaping what you recommend, as you listen to others and try to practice respecting them, respecting your own integrity, searching for what is best for everyone. And of course what I am saying about you I would say of every faculty member and administrator, from the newest to the president, the faculty as a whole and the community council. When we are at our best, things are not decided by appeal to authority or challenges to legitimacy, they are decided by meeting–overcoming divisions without eliminating differences, knowing oneself and others in a common search for the truth, going outside one's personal prejudices and wishes to ask what is best for the whole community. We invite you to join us in this process, because we believe it will help both you and the rest of us.

Quaker Governance of Quaker Colleges

by Douglas C. Bennett, President Emeritus, Earlham College

Since I arrived in 1997, there have been perhaps six occasions when the Earlham Board of Trustees had significant difficulty coming to unity.

On each occasion, the matter at hand was important and the Board had been prepared for the agenda item in advance. On each occasion, the Board deliberated with care, each person speaking constructively, no one dominating, and all listening attentively to one another. On each occasion, the clerk proposed a minute after about two hours that, at first, seemed to draw approval from those gathered. On each occasion, one member and then another asked to be recorded as standing aside, noting that the rest of the group seemed in substantial unity. But on each occasion, when a third or a fourth also asked to be recorded as standing aside (we are a Board of 24, with several honorary life trustees also participating at most meetings), the clerk withdrew the proposed minute. Generally he asked the group to return to the matter the next day, and after further deliberation, the Board did come to unity, always a different decision than the proposed minute of the day before, and a decision that everyone present agreed was superior.

This is Quaker governance at its very best: not only better decisions, but also deepening trust and respect for one another. On another college board, the decision of the day before would have been approved by an overwhelming vote, perhaps leaving some with misgivings. At Earlham, the Faculty as a whole makes decisions by Quaker business practice, as do its committees, most student organizations and other groups.[1] Consensus governance may well be the most unusual aspect of Earlham, and the one that seems, to many, most closely connected to our being a Quaker College. (Many Friends prefer to speak of unity rather than consensus, but in my experience, most Quaker organizations tend to talk of consensus governance.) I mostly want to celebrate our consensus governance, but also to note some confusions in the practice that arise among Quaker organizations like schools, retirement homes, social service agencies, and the like.

---

[1]You can see our Governance Manual at `http://www.earlham.edu/policies/governance/`. In addition to key governance documents, the manual also includes a series of short essays on Quaker governance, most of them written by members of the Earlham community for various purposes over the past several decades.

For Friends, Quaker business practice involves listening for the leadings of the Holy Spirit. Even at Earlham, we can hardly understand it this way, since many members of our community are not themselves Quakers and may not even believe in God. Nevertheless, we believe the process "can be effective in any group whose members share hopes and beliefs about their ability to engage in collective action for the common good." [2]

Consensus decision making is much more than finding ourselves all inclined to vote the same way; it is a set of commitments to work together to construct shared understanding and agreement. These four bracing commitments are especially important.

1. Transparency. We need to take care that all relevant information is made available to all who will participate in decision-making. This requires active habits of regular disclosure and information sharing.

2. Listening carefully. We need to listen unusually carefully to one another. We gather in silence (or stillness) to prepare ourselves to listen carefully and to empty out distractions that may linger in our minds. And we leave moments of silence between spoken messages to allow each contribution to be fully comprehended.

3. Speaking constructively. We need to speak constructively, not in opposition to one another, but constantly seeking to find and widen a firm ground of shared agreement. (This can be especially difficult in academic settings because of ingrained professional habits of criticism.)

4. Good clerking. We need to put ourselves in the hands of a clerk who will help us find the best we collectively have to offer. Clerking is a mutual relationship: the clerk should trust that each participant will speak only when s/he can move the discussion forward, and the participants should trust the clerk's judgment in acknowledging speakers and in formulating and reformulating where we are in the deliberation.

At its best, consensus process can be seen as a collective exercise of reason: many minds working together to think through a complex or vexing problem. Perhaps this is why it can work so

[2]That quotation is from Monteze Snyder et al., *Building Consensus: Conflict and Unity*, Earlham Press, 2001; a valuable handbook "for using consensus processes in workplaces, community organizations, schools, families and other social settings."

well at an academic institution. Where Robert's Rules of Order or other voting processes can become an exercise of power politics (majority wins! others lose!), consensus process encourages us to find solutions that win assent and legitimacy from everyone.

So what mars this celebration of Quaker decision-making?

In practice we recognize some potential drawbacks. It can be very slow in reaching a conclusion. It can be sabotaged by bad faith (which could undermine each of the commitments noted above) though we rarely experience this. It can work poorly where self-interest is engaged among some participants. It probably asks too much of human frailty to ask or expect some individuals to put aside their own self-interest in this process; better that such individuals recuse themselves. We recognize these practical difficulties, and yet we are still deeply attached to the idea of consensus decision-making. But none of these are the main difficulty, which is more conceptual than practical.

Grasping the conceptual difficulty requires focusing on these two questions: (1) Who is included in the group that reaches consensus, and how do we best justify this pattern of inclusion and exclusion? And (2) should we ever allow an individual to make an important decision, and if so, how do we justify that?

Our ways of thinking about Quaker decision-making processes arise from the monthly meeting for business. In this setting, we have clear answers to these two questions. Who is included in the group that reaches consensus? All members. Should we ever allow an individual to make an important decision? No. But are these the right answers in Quaker organizations?

It is one of the glories of Quakerism that we have created so many vital, effective, purposeful organizations: schools, colleges, retirement homes, hospitals and hospice services, and social service and advocacy organizations. We want these Quaker organizations to follow Quaker business practices. But if our standard model for such decision making arises from the monthly meeting for business, we risk (and I believe we regularly experience) recurring issues around the legitimacy of authority in Quaker organizations. I believe we have some conceptual work that needs to be done so that Quaker business practices can be adapted to the different circumstances of a Quaker organization.

Monthly meetings for business generally involve a few dozen people, and rarely more than 100. Many Quaker organizations (even if small) can be a good deal larger in terms of total people involved. Their functioning requires specialized roles (teachers and students, professionals or managers and support staff, boards of directors and paid staff, etc.). Those specialized roles sometimes involve valued expertise. And Quaker organizations often have specific missions that put them in regular engagement with those who are not members of the organization. There may be legal requirements that prescribe how the organization does its work. Put another way, the different circumstances of a Quaker organization (as against a Quaker meeting) involve size, complexity, expertise and responsibility. These differences make it difficult to adapt the standard model of Quaker decision-making to Quaker organizations.

Consider again the two questions. I'll use Earlham as a running example. (1) Who is included in the group that reaches consensus, and how do we justify this pattern of inclusion and exclusion?

Although we often provide an opportunity for anyone in the community to voice his/her opinion to whoever is making a decision, no decisions at Earlham involve every member of the community: all 1500 persons, including faculty, students and staff. No one seriously argues we should make decisions in this way, though it is not uncommon to hear that someone doubts the legitimacy of a decision because "s/he was not involved."

Many of the decisions we make involve careful thinking (not just tallying of preferences) so it makes sense to focus the decision-making in a relatively small group of people to whom we entrust the responsibility to listen carefully and weigh thoughtfully.

At Earlham, our Governance Manual has a good deal of black letter text that specifies who makes which decisions. The pattern turns out to be quite complex. Most of the time there isn't much controversy about who's included and who's not. The Faculty make decisions about the curriculum, for example; the Board of Trustees gives final approval to the budget. These delineations of "whose decision is it to make? following what process?" generally arise from sensible thinking given the location of relevant expertise (e.g. The Faculty with regard to the curriculum) or bearing of responsibility (e.g. The Board with regard to the budget, in light of its ultimate fiduciary responsibilities).

Some controversies about inclusion and exclusion arise because someone may object that they should participate in making a decision because "it will affect them." Note that this argument that anyone potentially affected by a decision should be involved in making the decision could be used to justify the involvement of a great many people (if not everyone) in the making of every decision. And it flies in the face of the admonition that Quaker process may not work well where self-interest is involved. The controversy arises because the standard account of Quaker decision making process has virtually nothing to say about who should be involved in making a decision, and certainly says nothing that helps draw the lines of inclusion and exclusion. The default understanding is that "everyone" should be involved.

(2) Should we ever allow an individual to make an important decision, and if so, how do we justify that?

Many decisions at Earlham follow a compound process: a committee that includes faculty and students makes a recommendation to the President or to another officer of the college. In these situations, the ultimate decision will be made by the administrative officer based on considerations of expertise or responsibility, but the officer is charged to "consult broadly" before making the decision. The committee is the group charged with the consultative responsibility and will normally make its recommendation by consensus. Nevertheless, should the officer make a different decision after receiving the recommendation, we often hear that "the President has overturned a consensus decision." The problem, again, is a not a lack of clarity in our governance documents. Rather, it is a lack in our standard understanding of Quaker decision-making that could ever justify any single individual making a decision or that could justify any further step ever following a consensus process.

In an important 1969 joint statement by the Faculty and the Board of Trustees there appear these two sentences: "Earlham is an open community within the context of a Quaker pattern of search for consensus. We realistically recognize the necessity for division of labor and for weighted allocations of responsibility." I quote these because the second sentence is remarkably wise, in my experience, among Quaker writings about decision making. And yet the document provides no elaboration. It provides no justification for the "realistic recognition" of either a "division of labor" or for "weighted allocations of responsibility" in making decisions. These are precisely what we need.

Every Quaker organization I know (schools, colleges, retirement homes, social service and advocacy organizations) frequently finds itself in governance wrangles. Just as the good exercise of Quaker business process (like the instances of the Earlham Board working to find unity with which I began) can strengthen bonds of trust and group cohesion, these wrangles about the legitimacy of decision-making can weaken trust and tear apart cohesion.

These wrangles arise, I believe, not because Quaker organizations do not seek to follow the broad understanding of consensus-seeking decision-making. They arise, rather, because the way Quakers articulate decision processes makes no provision for size, complexity, expertise or responsibility–all features of any serious organization. When a decision-making process is sensibly shaped around these, it is vulnerable to being attacked as illegitimate–to being attacked as unQuakerly.

Within Quaker organizations, consensus should be the process we use within groups when they are charged to participate in the decision making process, but the decision-making process is certain to be more complex than one in which every individual gathers together in a single group to make all decisions. Within Quaker organizations, the guiding principles for consensus decision-making should light our way: transparency, careful listening, constructive speaking. We should seek broad participation, engage in active consultation, and encourage care to be taken that every voice is heard.

Quaker Meetings and Quaker Colleges: What Should They Do for One Another?

by Douglas C. Bennett, President Emeritus, Earlham College

When I first became a member of the Religious Society of Friends at Germantown Meeting in Philadelphia in the mid-1980s, I was surprised to discover that there were recurrent tensions between the meeting (which I had grown to love) and Germantown Friends School, the splendid k-12 day school it sponsored. Sponsored? Even finding the right word is a little tricky. Certainly the meeting appointed members of the School Committee (GFS's Board), and the school used property belonging to the meeting. Many members of the meeting worked at the school or were alumni or had sent their children to GFS, but that simultaneously soothed and aggravated the difficulties.

I soon grew familiar with the tensions. I encountered them again at Wilmington Meeting and Wilmington Friends School when I moved there; came to be more aware of the tensions between Haverford College (where I am an alumnus) and Philadelphia area Friends; encountered them again at 15th Street Meeting and Friends Seminary when I moved to New York City; and lived very much in the middle of the strained relationship between Earlham College and the two FUM Yearly Meetings (Indiana and Western) when I was President of Earlham.

The common threads in these various situations are mismatched mutual expectations. The Meetings expect the educational institutions under their care (again the language is tricky) to be more responsive to their concerns, and to do more for their members. The educational institutions, on the other hand, expect more support, especially more financial support, from the Meetings that sponsors (?!) them.

Another commonality is the lack of any statement of the appropriate expectations on either side of the relationship. Each assumes it knows what it has a right to expect of the other, and feels disappointed when this isn't forthcoming. The disappointments (and simmering anger) can endure for decades.

While the issues are similar for Quaker k-12 schools as for Quaker colleges, I want to focus here on the mutual obligations of Quaker meetings and Quaker colleges. Should Quaker meetings and their members feel an obligation to support Quaker colleges? And if so, what forms should that support take? And on the other hand, should Quaker colleges feel an obligation to support Quaker meetings (monthly and yearly) and their members? And if so, what forms should that support take?

I'll mostly try to excavate the tensions, but at the end I'll describe an effort between Earlham and Indiana Yearly Meeting to achieve some shared clarity through a Covenant.

What do I mean by a Quaker college? Eight U.S. Colleges officially acknowledge a religious affiliation with Friends: Barclay (KS), Earlham (IN), Friends (KS), George Fox (OR), Guilford (NC), Malone (OH), William Penn (IA), and Wilmington (OH). Each grew out of a relationship with a Yearly Meeting, and most of these still have Board members appointed by the Yearly Meeting(s). Four other U.S. Colleges were founded by Friends and still (to some degree) think of themselves as Quaker colleges but have no formal religious affiliation and no connection to a Yearly Meeting: Bryn Mawr (PA), Haverford (PA), Swarthmore (PA) and Whittier (CA). All of these institutions are members of the Friends Association of Higher Education (FAHE).

The default (perhaps unthinking) perspective of Quaker meetings toward Quaker colleges is to think of the meetings as primary, and the colleges as subservient. "We created them; they should do what we ask them to do," or something along those lines. The meetings expect the colleges to be straightforward outreach efforts of the meetings.

The obverse default perspective of Quaker colleges toward Quaker meetings (also perhaps unthinking) is to consider themselves as independent organizations, in no way subservient, capable of steering themselves without interference, but at the same time expecting a greater level of material support than they receive. From this perspective, their founding by Quakers is a sufficient warrant to call themselves 'Quaker;' they need no help to think through what this entails.

It is easy to understand why Quaker meetings might easily fall into thinking of themselves as having primacy in the relationship. After all, the Religious Society of Friends is a gathering of religious communities; the meetings, monthly and yearly, are how we organize ourselves to worship together.

It is easy to slide into thinking of Quakerism as a tree where the yearly meetings are the trunks, the monthly meetings the branches, and the array of schools, colleges, service organizations and retirement communities as fruits that hang from these branches. How can we not consider the meetings as primary? And what can Quaker colleges mean by calling themselves Quaker if they insist on complete independence, acknowledging no relationship to the worshipping communities of Quakers?

On the other hand, the Quaker schools, colleges, service organizations and retirement communities are much too large and too heavy to hang from the branches of a Quaker tree so conceived. As organizations, most monthly meetings have a staff of a few, and a budget under $100,000; most yearly meetings are only a bit larger as organizations. A Quaker college, on the other hand, will have hundreds of employees and a budget in the tens of millions of dollars. How can we look at them as delicate emanations budding from the worship life of Quaker meetings?

Each Quaker college (or other organization) may have started as a project of some monthly or yearly meeting, but the successful ones grew well beyond that beginning to have their own primary substance and identity. And let us note that many newcomers find their way to Quakerism by first encountering it via a school or college or service project.

So let us start with a fresh conception. Let us look at Quaker meetings and Quaker colleges as two kinds of Quaker organizations that stand in some relationship of mutual obligation, but not a relationship where one has primacy or dominance. What might be the substance of these mutual obligations? Let us consider the possible mutual obligations under three headings: governance, mission, and support.

Governance

In most relationships between Quaker meetings and Quaker colleges, it is governance that is most often the focus of attention. The substance of being a Quaker college becomes primarily a matter of a yearly meeting appointing a certain percentage of members of the college's board of trustees. At its best, such a governance relationship can knit together a college and a yearly meeting. Over time, however, the college can come to feel that it cannot build the board of trustees it needs because the yearly meeting lacks sufficient talent or well-resourced individuals, or seeks to impose its own directions on the college.

Mission

A Quaker meeting provides a community for worship together; a Quaker college provides an education that has some grounding in the faith and practice of Friends. These are not identical missions. But what does "some grounding in the faith and practice of Friends" mean? Every Quaker college has found itself in some turmoil over this question; Quaker meetings can become overbearing participants in that discussion seeing the college as having a responsibility to enact its Quakerness in a manner expected by the meeting.[1]

Does this grounding mean explicitly teaching and expecting all students to learn Quaker beliefs? Does it mean that the college expects all students to attend Quaker worship services, or simply that it provides an opportunity for students to do so? Does it mean that the college employs some practices common among Friends, for example consensus governance, no use of titles, or regular employ of moments of silence? Or does it simply mean that the college pays deference to its founding by Friends? There is quite a wide spectrum of possibilities here, and the twelve Quaker colleges that have membership in FAHE show considerable variety in where they fall along that spectrum.

With respect to mission, the question of mutual obligation can especially arise over the use of the term "Quaker:" Quaker meetings may object to a college describing itself as Quaker when the college allows expression or activity that meeting members consider un-Quakerly. (Of course the embarrassment can run the other way.)

A different kind of mission issue arises over the question of whether a Quaker college should feel an obligation to provide privileged access (preferential admission? extra financial aid?) for Quaker students. How about Quaker faculty? In either case, how should such privileged access be granted? As an affirmative action category? Or as a component of excellence in making judgments about best candidates?

The obligations that Quaker colleges owe to Quaker meetings are generally mission issues. Quaker meetings expect Quaker colleges to be exemplars of Quaker beliefs or to be instruments of outreach. On the other hand, the obligations that Quaker meetings owe to Quaker colleges are generally support issues.

Support

Quaker colleges hope that yearly and monthly meetings will provide them with financial support, but the colleges have long since abandoned any expectation that such support will be at all significant. (From time to time I would be dismayed to hear an Earlham student surmise that the reason the college didn't take some hoped-for action was because the college worried we would lose financial

---

[1]I have considered at greater length what it means today for a college to be Quaker in "The Idea of a Quaker College," a Convocation address I gave at Earlham in August 2000. http://dougbennettblog.files.wordpress.com/2011/09/idea-of-a-quaker-college1.pdf.

support from Indiana or Western Yearly Meeting.) In the absence of financial support, Quaker colleges hope and expect that yearly and monthly meetings will urge their young members to apply and enroll at the college.

Earlham's New Covenant with Indiana Yearly Meeting

After more than a century of friction between Earlham College and Indiana Yearly Meeting, the two made a dramatic change in the character of their relationship in the summer of 2010. The two came to a mutual agreement that Indiana Yearly Meeting would no longer appoint members of the Earlham Board of Trustees. In revising the college's Articles of Incorporation to make this change, Earlham obligated itself to continue to have a board of trustees more than half of whose members are Quaker.

Indiana Yearly Meeting arrived at this decision because many of its members had come to feel ill at ease about any governance relationship, and largely for mission-related reasons. Appointing trustees made them feel 'responsible' for the college, but the college had a conception of its mission with which they disagreed. Simply stated, the college was committed to allowing its students a high degree of autonomy in seeking the truth and a high degree of responsibility for their own conduct. Yearly meeting members wanted a more didactic and directive approach to education, one in which the college would tell students what to think and how to behave. Earlham came to this decision wanting to be able to draw Quaker trustees from across the geographical and theological spectrum of Friends.

The change in governance was accompanied by the signing of a Covenant in which each side made promises about what it would do for and on behalf of the other.[2] With governance no longer an aspect of the relationship, the Covenant addresses both mission and support issues. Earlham promises, for example, to actively seek Quaker students and faculty, to support research by and about Quakers and to maintain a Quaker archives, to continue preparing pastors for Quaker churches, and to be an exemplar in its organizational behavior of Friends testimonies. The promises from Indiana Yearly Meeting are more modest, but they include a commitment to provide tangible support for a Christian ministry presence at the college.

What is most noteworthy about the Covenant is that it gives both Earlham and Indiana Yearly Meeting an explicit statement

---

[2]You can see a copy of the Covenant at http://dougbennettblog.files.wordpress.com/2011/10/earlham-covenant-with-iym1.pdf

of mutual obligations. In so doing, it also provides Earlham with a statement (something, surprisingly, it has never had before) of what it means for Earlham to be a Quaker college.

The Earlham-IYM Covenant took two years to write and approve, but these were two constructive years. It may be useful for each Quaker college to develop a similar statement of mutual obligations with whatever Quaker meeting(s) it is situated in a relationship of mutual accountability. Both Quaker meetings and Quaker colleges would be the better for it.

Academic Prioritization as a Response to College and University Financial Challenges

by Donn Weinholtz, University of Hartford

Tuition-driven colleges and universities throughout the United States continue to experience substantial financial distress due to their high costs, the lingering effects of the Great Recession and competition from online programs. In *The Innovative University*, Christensen and Eyring (2011) conclude that most colleges and universities can no longer afford to maintain their organizational, curricular, extra-curricular and residence models. In particular, they challenge the viability of common approaches to: 1) face-to-face instruction; 2) rational/secular orientation; 3) comprehensive specialization, departmentalization and faculty self-governance; 4) long summer recess; 5) graduate schools atop colleges; 6) private fundraising; 7) competitive athletics; 8) general education and majors; 9) academic honors; 10) externally funded research; 11) up-or-out tenure, with faculty rank and salary distinctions; and 12) admissions selectivity. They point out that most of these expensive features originated at Harvard and were subsequently copied by colleges and universities around the nation. Currently, they argue, even extraordinarily endowed elite institutions are having difficulty maintaining the complete model; and that financially less robust institutions are going to have to change dramatically in order to survive.

Although Christensen and Eyring claim that program pruning will not be an adequate long-term survival strategy, prioritizing programs and reallocating funds are logical first steps for most colleges and universities moving forward in uncertain times. In *Prioritizing Academic Programs and Services: Reallocating Resources to Achieve Strategic Balance*, Robert Dickeson (2010) offers a detailed program review and reinvestment strategy. Here, I briefly summarize both *The Innovative University* and *Prioritizing Academic Programs and Services*, offering a few criticisms of each. I then describe my own university's experience with Dickeson's prioritizing model, concluding with my reactions–as a Quaker–to the model.

The Innovative University

Christensen and Eyring explore conditions affecting much of modern higher education–excluding community colleges–guided by the theory of disruptive innovation, the perspective Christensen previously applied to examining how fledgling competitors in the steel and auto industries overtook the giants in their fields. Until the advent of online learning, they argue, residential, 4-year colleges and universities did not have the competition necessary to force them into convulsive change. They then explain how industries causing disruptive innovation initially deliver inferior products, cost-efficiently; thereby obtaining a market foothold, subsequently refining their products, and eventually putting the more expensive, dominant suppliers on the defensive. Think of Toyota and Honda versus General Motors. Then consider the University of Phoenix and other online purveyors versus traditional colleges and universities.

While laying bare the existential threat posed by online education, Christensen and Eyring also argue that there are many aspects of the traditional college experience that remain far superior to online options. They claim that the great challenge facing the traditional institutions will be to maintain what they do best, while harnessing online technology for their students', and their own, best interests.

Briefly, Christensen and Eyring recommend altering traditional colleges and universities in the following manner: 1) transitioning from face-to-face instruction to a mix of face-to-face and online instruction; 2) replacing the dominant rational / secular orientation, with increased attention to values; 3) moving from comprehensive faculty specialization to an increased focus on interdepartmental cooperation; 4) initiating change via goal-specific innovation teams, rather than depending on departmentalization and traditional faculty governance; 5) eliminating the long summer recess in favor of year-round learning focused on specific learning outcomes; 6) replacing comprehensive graduate schools atop colleges and universities with smaller, streamlined schools made up only of strong programs; 7) refocusing private fundraising efforts to emphasize fundraising for mentoring students, especially undergraduates and those requiring needs-based aid; 8) de-emphasizing competitive athletics, while greatly expanding other student activities; 9) replacing general education distribution requirements and concentrated majors with cross-disciplinary, integrated general education, and customizable majors with certificates and associate's degrees nested within bachelor's degrees; 10) increasing emphasis on student competence with regards to learning outcomes as opposed to traditional, GPA-based, academic honors; 11) scaling up undergraduate involvement in research; 12) eliminating up-or-out tenure, substituting customized scholarship and employment contracts, while minimizing faculty rank and salary distinctions; 13) moving away from admissions selectivity towards expansion of capacity, especially through online learning.

This is an extraordinarily heavy dose of change, rightfully daunting to most college and university faculty and administrators. Yet, Christensen and Eyring argue that leaders refusing to confront the current existential challenges expose their schools to great peril.

Even though *The Innovative University* is an engaging read full of provocative insights and recommendations, the authors' primary case study for large-scale change (the transformation of Ricks College into Brigham Young University-Idaho) is a flawed example. Christensen and Eyring salt their book with many brief snapshots of single-shot changes at colleges around the country, but they only dive deeply into the Ricks/BYU metamorphosis. The case is intriguing, but its generalizability is hopelessly limited. The change was launched via a sudden, top-down directive from Gordon B. Hinckley, at the time the powerful President of The Church of Jesus Christ of Latter-day Saints (Mormons.) Hinckley's command was implemented with the authority and resources of the Mormon Church behind it. Few schools, if any, are capable of undergoing change on this scale, without encountering crippling blowback from students, faculty, administrators and alumni. The vast majority of college and university administrators could never attempt so much change, so fast.

If you are trying to decide whether or not to delve into *The Innovative University*, a brief video of Christensen and Eyring explaining why they wrote the book is available online.[1] Alternative, compelling explanations of the problems confronting modern colleges and universities are available in Jeffrey Selingo (2013) *College (Un)bound : The Future of Higher Education and What it Means for Students* and in William G. Bowen (2013) *Higher Education in the Digital Age*.

Prioritizing Academic Programs and Services

> Many institutions have been operating in a financially unsustainable way for many years. Now that economic conditions are forcing institutions to reduce or restructure their program offerings, critical questions and challenges face campus leaders. Which programs are most important to the institution's mission, overall financial health, and competitiveness? How do I ensure the institution is stronger as a result? Join Bob Dickeson and Larry Goldstein for an in-depth examination of a

---

[1]http://www.amazon.com/Innovative-University-Changing-Education-Jossey-Bass/dp/1118063481/ref=sr_1_1?s=books&ie=UTF8&qid

proven method for prioritizing academic and administrative programs.[2]

So reads the online promotion inviting college administrators to
a workshop spelling out the key steps of Robert Dickeson's prioritizing model. Briefly, there are nine stages to this approach: 1) recognizing the need for reform; 2) identifying responsible leadership;
3) reaffirming institutional mission; 4) defining what constitutes a
program; 5) selecting appropriate criteria; 6) measuring, analyzing, prioritizing; 7) anticipating process issues; 8) implementing
program decisions; and 9) achieving strategic balance. An important aspect of the model involves recruiting trusted faculty to do
much of the initial prioritizing work, although some administrators, preferring a more top-down approach, may choose to have the
administration take on the bulk of the work.

Dickeson came early to the academic prioritizing, consulting
marketplace with a clear, implementable package of recommendations (a previous edition of his book appeared in 1999). In the more
recent version he touts a "proven" method and provides brief case
studies from a range of colleges and universities to illustrate how
prioritization can be accomplished. However, to me, the cases seem
too carefully selected to support his arguments. Without the benefit of longitudinal evaluation studies documenting the strengths and
shortcomings of Dickeson's approach, it seems too early to judge its
overall merit. Nevertheless, Dickeson has captured a wide audience
of administrators anxious for solutions to the vexing problems confronting them. Indeed, he has attracted many hundreds of college
and university officials to the workshops at which he markets his
model.[3]

As I previously mentioned, longer-term evaluation studies of the
Dickeson model's effectiveness are unavailable; however, a small
body of anecdotal information is emerging. The most celebrated
case has been at Columbia College of Chicago, where staunch faculty and student opposition resulted from a top-down version of the
prioritization process.[4]

---

[2]From: http://www.academicimpressions.com/conference/
prioritizing-academic-and-administrative-programs-october-2012?
qq=7459v274891yT

[3]You can read more about the sorts of issues and recommendations
Dickeson addresses at: http://www.academicimpressions.com/news/
report-what-higher-ed-leaders-are-saying-about-program-prioritization

[4]You can review some materials critical of Columbia
College's prioritization process at the following web-
sites: http://www.insidehighered.com/news/2012/03/06/
restructuring-proposal-columbia-chicago-prompts-criticism and

Academic Prioritization at the University of Hartford

I have been employed at the University of Hartford–a non-sectarian, co-educational institution of approximately 7,000 undergraduate and graduate students–for 23 years; first as a college dean, then as a full professor, department chair, and program director. I have also served as secretary, vice-chair and chair of the Faculty Senate, and as a member of the university's Board of Regents. During the last three years, the university has faithfully proceeded through Dickeson's prioritization process. This has involved reviewing every academic and administrative program in the entire university. Below, I explain this process in some detail in order to illustrate how complicated and difficult it can become.

Initially, two large committees, one focusing on *academic programs* the other addressing *administrative programs*, carefully progressed through the steps presented in *Prioritizing Academic Programs and Services*. Sworn to secrecy regarding their deliberations, the committees worked throughout the 2012 spring semester, including a lengthy set of June meetings–several hours a day, four days a week–culminating in two, early-summer reports which the University's central administration kept under wraps until the end of September 2012. For every program in the University, recommendations were offered for investing, maintaining, restructuring or divesting (eliminating.)[5]

Upon completion of the committees' work, a goal of $3,108,000 was established for savings and reallocation on the administrative side, while $3,780,000 was targeted for the academic side. These figures were substantially lower than what the university administration had initially hoped could be reached; but after arduous deliberations, neither committee could find further savings. As administrative programs are not revenue generating and because there is no mechanism at the University of Hartford for a shared governance review of administrative cuts, streamlining and reallocation procedures were quickly implemented based on the Administrative Task Force's recommendation. Following some minor adjustments by University vice-presidents, plans were approved by the president to invest in 7 programs, maintain 52 programs, restructure 34 programs and divest 7 programs; all resulting in a reallocation pool of approximately $2, 500, 000. By January 2014, this amount increased to approximately $3,000,000 . It provided the University

---

https://www.youtube.com/watch?v=SRIBbb-cXMO

[5]A description of the initial phases of the entire University of Hartford process, including an extensive President's message, is available at: http://www.hartford.edu/aboutuofh/office_pres/committees/foundation_future/

with funds that could be rapidly applied to pressing needs, such as deferred salary increases. However, this was accomplished at a substantial cost in staff morale. The elimination of various staff positions, along with the restructuring of others from twelve to ten months of employment, caused administrative staff to correctly perceive that they were experiencing the brunt of the cuts, while faculty were generally being spared.

While the administrative reallocation process was breathlessly efficient, a very different picture emerged on the academic side. To meet their $3,780,000 goal, the Academic Task Force recommended that 10 programs be targeted for investment, 78 be maintained, 29 restructured and 41 divested. In spite of the secrecy requirement placed on the committee, word leaked out that the decision-making process was tortuous for those involved.

After reviewing the committee's report, the university provost issued a revised set of recommendations primarily concurring with the committee on the investing, maintaining and restructuring targets, but departing substantially from the committee on divesting 41 programs. The provost recommended divesting 25 programs, deferring divestment decisions on 13 programs, and merging 2 programs. While at first glance this appeared to involve shutting down a substantial number of programs, thereby freeing up a sizable pool of funds for reallocation, 16 of the programs that the provost advocated closing were essentially programs on paper only, generally not offered and costing little. As required by the university's *Manual of Academic Policies and Procedures*, and given the president's long-time commitment to shared governance, the Faculty Senate reviewed the closure recommendations. Over the course of the spring 2013 semester, the Senate reached strong agreement with the provost on closing 16 programs. Regarding the remaining closures, however, the Senate engaged in a very thorough, time-consuming review and recommended maintaining 7 of the programs, all of which cost little and generated moderate revenue. Meanwhile, the "deferred" divestment programs were not reviewed as the provost granted them anywhere from 6 to 18 months of self-study and planning time. The "restructured" programs were ignored by the Senate, as the "closings" issue dominated the spring agenda. Finally, from a faculty perspective, many central administration and collegiate deans' plans for using reallocated funds appeared to be ad hoc or confused, as the university had not yet begun a scheduled strategic planning effort.

When the fall 2013 semester began, the senate and the provost awaited the president's final decision regarding the programs recommended for closure by the provost but retention by the senate. He eventually agreed with the provost on the majority of the programs, but aligned with the senate on two programs remaining open. Meanwhile, the provost and the senate could not reach agreement regarding when "restructured" programs had to come to the senate for approval, and various programs (deferred by the provost) remained under self-study with the charge of proposing financially viable, innovative plans for the future. Significantly, after two full years of implementation and a remarkable amount of energy expended, very little money had been targeted for reallocation due to program changes on the university's academic side. At the completion of this essay, no clear dollar figures had been released, but savings from academic reallocation were expected to be very modest.

My own program, the Doctoral Program in Educational Leadership, was included on the Academic Task Forces divestment list. For multiple reasons, this recommendation was problematic to the university. In particular, the program annually graduates the largest number of university students completing a State of Connecticut approved *research* dissertation, thereby making the program central to the university's efforts to obtain and maintain a Carnegie classification as a research institution. Furthermore, the program has very strong alumni support. Also, following one very lean admissions year, occurring during the three-year window when the Academic Prioritization Committee examined costs and revenues, admissions have been robust for three years in a row. In fact, enrollments have been strong for 21 out of the program's 22 years. Finally, the program recently concluded a smooth transition from focusing on both K-12 education leadership and higher education leadership to focusing on higher education alone; thereby, making it the only such program in the state.

For all of these reasons, the provost granted the program an additional 18 months for self-study and planning regarding future directions, while granting permission to continue admitting students. Collaborating with my three faculty colleagues, I wrote a report, requested by the provost, which we submitted to our college's dean and subsequently the provost, nearly seven months ahead of its June 2014 due date. At the completion of this essay, the provost had not reached a decision about her recommendations for the program's future. If closure is recommended, which I believe to be highly unlikely, the program will have to be reviewed by the Faculty Senate, prior to any action taking place. Closure might eventually free up approximately $600,000 in expenses for reallocation to other academic units, but there is no guarantee that such reinvestment will yield more than the $150,000 of revenue per year (after expenses) that we project for the Educational Leadership program. Also, it will take seven years to grandfather out the recently admitted doctoral students, thereby long delaying the availability of reallocation funds.

While many consequences of academic prioritization at the University of Hartford have yet to play out, I have discerned a number of lessons that are perhaps generalizable to other schools attempting a "textbook" adoption of the Dickeson model. Briefly, they are:

- Administrative / staff restructuring can be accomplished in corporate-like fashion, but at a substantial cost in staff morale.

- Prioritization of academic programs is effective for eliminating low-cost and no-cost programs; but few academic programs are likely to provide ample pools of money that can be reallocated for more profitable spending. Furthermore, preliminary financial targets will be difficult, perhaps impossible, to meet.

- Commitment to shared governance substantially slows the academic review process, while ignoring it causes great hostility. Also, substantial differences of opinion are likely to exist between faculty and administrators about what program changes require faculty review.

- Much long-term and hard-earned trust in the administration is likely to quickly dissolve during the prioritization process.

- Arguments for effective reallocation are unconvincing in the absence of clear, recent strategic planning.

Personal Reflection

When colleges and universities engage in academic prioritization and financial reallocation, there are substantial human costs. For example, at the University of Hartford some administrative staff who had been at the university for as long as seventeen years lost their jobs. Also, while faculty were informed that tenure would not be broken, such assurances provided little comfort to untenured faculty who feared their programs might be eliminated. Furthermore, although the university guaranteed that it would fulfill its obligations to students by *teaching-out* all divested program, some students feared that faculty in these programs would flee the university and seriously questioned the quality of the instruction that they would receive. Finally, students and alumni of endangered programs expressed substantial concern that value of their degrees

185

would be diminished appreciably by the elimination of their programs.

In response to such concerns, as director of the Educational Leadership program, I sent a letter to the program's faculty, staff, students and alumni. Below is an excerpt.

> I would like to stress that our program remains strong. We have outstanding students and graduates who provide important leadership throughout Connecticut and beyond. The research conducted within the program has resulted in many important contributions to the literature and to our various communities. Our faculty is bright, committed, and caring. We continue to attract ever-increasing numbers of diverse and talented students from around the region, the nation and the world.

> Please be assured that, should the ongoing review process have any negative impact on the Educational Leadership program, the university is committed to providing ample time and instructional support, including dissertation advisement, for all current students to complete their degrees. Also, it is important for you to understand that the released report contains recommendations, not final decisions, and the process is still unfolding.

It was very difficult for me to write this letter. At the time, many of my students and colleagues thanked me for my day-to-day efforts at remaining optimistic in the face of very disturbing events; but they often shook their heads, indicating that they fully expected the worst. I inferred that they saw my actions as naïve; but I continued forward, not knowing if I was correct or not about the prospects for our program's future. I also, as a member of the Faculty Senate Executive Committee, tried my best to provide support to my colleagues elsewhere in the university whose own programs were threatened.

Recently, I read David Ross and Ed Dreby's essay, *Microeconomics: Markets and Choices*. They wrote:

> Change can hurt: Innovation, ingenuity, and the human capacity to learn are constantly expanding our understanding of what is possible. New enterprises are created while others shut down in a process Joseph Schumpeter named, "creative destruction. ....many are hurt by innovations and the social change that results. Not

186

only can change destroy communities and jobs, it can destroy the ecosystem. The balance between innovation and stability is hard to find (Ross and Dreby, 2012, p. 34).

As their reference to the ecosystem shows, these Friends were addressing changes well beyond those we are encountering at our colleges and universities. Nevertheless, much of their message applies well to what many of us are experiencing on our campuses. Those of us who are Quakers must discern how we are called to act when confronted with the circumstances that lead to calls for prioritization and reallocation. We must search deeply for ways that can we remain true to our testimonies under these conditions; seeking ways to sustain community, maintain integrity, foster equality and adhere to simplicity. While situations will vary substantially from campus to campus and from program to program, our spiritual commitments must guide our individual and corporate actions.

Bowen, W. G. (2013). *Higher Education in the Digital Age*. Princeton University Press, Princeton, NJ.

Christensen, C. and Eyring, H. (2011). *The Innovative University*. Jossey Bass, San Francisco.

Dickeson, D. (2010). *Prioritizing Academic Programs and Services: Reallocating Resources to Achieve Strategic Balance*. Jossey Bass, San Francisco.

Ross, D. and Dreby, E. (2012). Microeconomics: Markets and choices. In Dreby, E. and Lumb, J., editors, *It's the Economy, Friends: Understanding the Growth Dilemma*. Quaker Institute for the Future, Caye Caulker, Belize.

Selingo, J. (2013). *College (Un)bound : The Future of Higher Education and What it Means for Students*. New Harvest, New York.

Chapter 6

Liberal Arts Education

Quaker colleges and universities are, at their core, liberal arts institutions. They may house some professional programs in education, business or health professions; but they are first and foremost dedicated to the traditional liberal arts. However, in an era of rising costs and diminishing resources, how must liberal arts colleges adjust to survive? And what concerns must Friends' schools attend to if they are to remain Quakerly? The four articles in this chapter examine aspects of these issues.

Julie Meadows opens the chapter reflecting on her experiences while teaching philosophy at Presbyterian College. She notes regretfully "...the rhetoric of academic sacrifice for the economic competitiveness..." that pervades the country, along with the simultaneous "...creeping dehumanization of work." What good, then, is a liberal arts education? After wrestling with this question, Julie decided that her teaching should focus on values rather than just skills, concluding that she should teach the values she loves–such as humility, ethical responsibility and courage–those that make life worth living, even if they do put you at odds with the prevailing ethic of our market driven system. In doing so, she found common ground with Friends' articulation of the spiritual life–one that we are called to "... pursue as passionately and tantalizingly and seductively as we possibly can."

Patricia Berg, from Walsh University, follows, exploring in detail what can be done to engage business students in an education truly reflective of the liberal arts. Patricia asserts that "... there is a way to connect the dots so that a liberal arts education in business not only educates students with the how-to technical aspect of business, but adds real world skills and adaptability..." She believes that a well-designed business education can spark a deep thirst for learning in a diverse array of areas. Drawing on two methods for integrating business skills into the classroom, Findlay University's Partnership Model and The Corporate Classroom, she examines how business curricula in liberal arts institutions can deliver both breadth and depth of learning. She also examines the educational responsibilities of colleges/universities and business communities, emphasizing the need for ongoing collaboration in the design of high quality programs.

University of Hartford Architecture professor, Theodore Sawruk, describes the traditional liberal arts model, examines the increasing infusion of professional programs into liberal arts curricula, and offers a staunch defense of the liberal arts, advising that liberal arts colleges "... should not be quick to abandon centuries old, tried and true methods of education, as the return on their students' investments..." continue to increase well after graduation. Among the colleges integrating occupational skills into the liberal arts, Ted lauds the ability-based model adopted at Alverno College, which has led to in-depth teaching and evaluation approaches. He also cites studies conducted by the Annapolis Group and by the Office of Institutional Research at Dickinson College indicating that liberal arts education yields long-term personal and professional benefits.

In the chapter's final essay, Lonnie Valentine, from Earlham School of Religion, looks piercingly at the responsibility of religiously-grounded schools, including Quaker liberal arts college, to address the needs of the worlds poor and oppressed. Lonnie argues that, "Though religious institutions often begin at the margins of society and offer alternatives to that society, most of us now work in settings that are established within the larger social and economic order." Drawing on Latin America liberation theology, he asks readers to consider that, by not being marginalized, "...even persecuted by society, we are doing education for the oppressive status quo instead of for liberation." He then offers strategies for breaking down class barriers between those in our colleges and the poor, asking self-critical questions, and finding meaningful ways of adopting a preferential option for the poor.

Seduction and the Liberal Arts

by Julie Meadows, Presbyterian College

The starting place for this paper is deep concern about the terms in which education is being described in this country. Young people are told that they should get at least an associate's degree in order to improve the economic competitiveness of their country.[1] That education might matter for other reasons is largely absent from the national conversation on these issues. This is troubling, but more troubling still is the message it sends to our students about who they are and what role they have in the world. The rhetoric of academic sacrifice for the economic competitiveness of one's country is only a stone's throw away from the rhetoric of personal sacrifice for the military success of that same country. In either case, young people are called upon to sacrifice their own well-being for a "higher good" whose claim on their lives is never justified.[2] In the absence of any alternative rhetoric, they may not even think to question these claims.

The same rhetoric is being used to dismantle a century of work toward humane working conditions. Where jobs are so scarce, employees should be grateful for whatever they can find. Arguments about jobs numbers drown out any examination of job quality. The professions are by no means immune to this creeping dehumanization of work. Doctors are assigned targets for how many patients to see and how little time to spend with each one; more and more professors are adjuncts who teach for a pittance and have no job security.

In its turn, higher education in the U.S. is under attack by the advocates of "accountability"–that is, countability. Colleges and universities are pressured to conform as much as possible to a business model under which the "outputs" are satisfactory employees.[3] From this increasingly powerful perspective, only measurable things are valued; only quantifiable things are real.

Faced with this context, liberal arts education needs eloquent champions indeed. But defenses of the liberal arts run aground in several places. Problems arise whether we argue for its practicality, defend its importance to Democratic society, or appeal to the model of "whole person" education. I will explain why I think each is

---

[1]See, for example, Wood (2012).

[2]Paul Krugman (1996) made the point long ago that a country is not a company. Countries do not compete against each other economically: individuals and companies do.

[3]See, for example, Dickeson (2010).

problematic, then explore a way forward that begins with careful scrutiny of the term "liberal." My experiences in the classroom have forced me to choose between competing definitions of "liberal" education, and this has changed my understanding of my own role, and of the larger role of the liberal arts.

To adequately defend the liberal arts, we have to be able to address the charges of snobbery and exclusivism–charges that a liberal arts education is all very well for affluent young men and women whose future is already safely assured, but that no such luxury is practical for others. The current economic realities bring into question whether such an education is valuable even for the elite.

We have to admit, first, that these charges are partly fair–higher education is exclusive; it is, in our society, increasingly a luxury item. It's also fair to ask questions of value, and of quality, when it comes to education. What are students learning? Are they learning enough? What's not fair is dictating ahead of time a very narrow range of possible answers, or even a single possible answer: success in consumer capitalist terms.

If we capitulate to the demand for "practicality" by citing job placement statistics and lifetime earnings figures, we present liberal arts colleges as a gateway to social status and economic well-being, a somewhat shaky claim and one that offers no hint of why such a system should be preserved.[4]

In our justification of the liberal arts, would it be better to see our students as future citizens, hopefully a broader view than seeing them only as potential employees? Certainly there is abundant evidence that the weakness of American public education is problematic for our attempts to maintain a working democracy. In this case, everyone should receive something like a liberal arts education, in or maybe just after high school. This is not at all a bad idea (and not at all a new one, either), but it still leaves open the question of the purpose and value of selective liberal arts colleges.[5]

Perhaps we resist both categorizations, and say that we aim to

---

[4]There is a debate now about whether it will still hold in the future, but the old advice is that college graduates earn more than non-college graduates, so it's in students' economic interest to get a college degree, even if they need to take out a loan. What may be good advice for individuals, though, won't work for the whole country: if everyone has a college degree, it doesn't give anyone a competitive advantage. John Marsh (2011) makes this case–he is explicit that the rhetoric about improving schools is a way of avoiding more direct talk about class: it's a false hope to think that we will eliminate inequality through better schools. Furthermore, we open ourselves up to being evaluated on the same grounds. See Barret (2012).

[5]Some recent examples: Nussbuam (1997, 2010); Gutman (1987).

address our students not just as prospective employees or future citizens, but also as "whole people." We point to the life-changing, liberating nature of a liberal arts education. We may believe strongly in this; it may have been true for us. Certainly it was true for me. But this way of talking about what we do is still problematic. It suggests that the lives of those who have been educated at liberal arts colleges are more worthwhile than the lives of those who have not. Do we believe this to be so? Are the lives of those who have been educated at liberal arts colleges more worthwhile than the lives of those who have not?

Without ever clearly articulating what exactly the value of a liberal arts education is, and without meaning for it to happen, we have landed ourselves back in the snobby and exclusivist camp. You'd understand if you had one, we sometimes seem to be saying. Ouch. We have to do better.

Fortunately students press us to explain the value of everything we do, over and over again. When I began teaching, I would describe the liberal arts in more or less classical terms: a liberal arts education trained one to read carefully, write clearly, and care about the exploration of questions of meaning and value, an exploration that was best pursued in community. This ran me into a problem, however. Unlike the community where I was deeply and persuasively indoctrinated into the deep mysteries and rituals of the liberal arts–I mean, "went to college"–the one where I found myself teaching lacked the communal ethos that had supported these enterprises.[6] In their absence, it became obvious how extensively values and community undergirded the teaching and learning of the skills I was calling "the liberal arts."

I increasingly came to see my teaching in terms of a set of values, not just a set of skills, and I began to articulate these values to my students. To read a text well, we have to be willing to listen carefully before imposing our own ideas or making our own judgments–that is, we need humility. To write clearly, we have to think in terms of the ethical responsibilities we bear to those who will read our words–that is, we need to practice a kind of hospitality. To explore ideas in community, we need to be willing to change our minds–but also willing to stand by our convictions. In either case, we will need courage.

The confusion of values and aims in my new academic setting opened up a space for me to clarify my own goals. How should

---

[6]My undergraduate degree is from St. John's College, in Annapolis, MD. To be fair to my current employer, I should note that few institutions have the clarity of purpose of that one.

justice, my central concern as teacher and scholar, be incorporated into my teaching? To answer that question, I had to work through some confusion about the multiple meanings of the term "liberal."

In one sense, the "liberal" in liberal arts carries the sense of liberation, of freedom from prejudices and the ability to see the world as it really is, avoiding the many forces (advertisers, politicians) that would deceive and mislead us. I believe that a liberal arts education at its best can and does do this; this is what my own liberal arts education wrought. I was eager for my students to experience this kind of liberation, but hesitant to press any specific point of view upon them. Even as I explored the potential of contemplative pedagogies, I worried about the extent to which, merely by assigning personal reflection as a task, I was already imposing values on my students, whose freedom from such impositions was somehow sacred to my role as educator.[7] This hesitation stems from the other meaning of "liberal": implying a kind of forward-thinking political stance that does its best to remain neutral as regards to questions of value. While reasoned argument is respectable, passionate defenses are suspect, as somehow impinging on a person's freedom of choice. To lure, entice, or even seduce someone is intellectually and morally suspect.

The world does not allow us to remain neutral for long. A conference on Environmental Ethics exposed me to the fear and grief that anyone paying attention to the state of the natural world discovers.[8] I noticed that the business professors who took BB&T Foundation funding for a course on the Moral Foundations of Capitalism that included reading *Atlas Shrugged*, in full, were not similarly concerned about preserving the freedom of their students to think for themselves.[9] Rather than advocating passionately for justice, I had

---

[7]This question arose during a discussion in the new Contemplative Studies Group at the 2012 Annual Meeting of the American Academy of Religion. One scholar raised the concern that such assignments were "invasive," and went beyond the appropriate bounds of the academic enterprise. While I do incorporate contemplative exercises into my teaching, I do so with serious reflection on this question, and serious respect for the power of these exercises, in mind. Information about the Group, and about Contemplative Studies as an emerging interdisciplinary field, is available at http://www.sandiego.edu/cas/contemplativestudies/aar.php.

[8]"Human Flourishing and Restoration in the Age of Global Warming" at Clemson University in September of 2008, http://people.oregonstate.edu/~thompsoa/web/confrn.html. It was here that the grim outlook of our natural world hit home, and here that I was introduced to thoughtful philosophical responses. I met Roger Gottlieb, whose teaching and writing have been an inspiration.

[9]If, as Wayne Booth (1989) so beautifully argues, the books we read affect us not just after we read them, but while we read them, *Atlas Shrugged* can

stayed on ground that now seemed to me disappointingly neutral.[10] Lastly, the language of business started to assume a dominant role at my college. It was presented as some kind of exciting new magical key, a tool that could solve our problems without requiring that we mire ourselves in thorny discussions of value. This was not in itself surprising. What was surprising was how few people questioned the values implicit in these "measurements," measurements that, to me, seemed directly opposed to everything that we claimed to stand for.[11]

I'd like to say that my teaching became dangerously radical. That's not the case. But it *did* become increasingly *erotic*. If you've been persuaded by the division of kinds of love into eros, philia, and agape, I'll have to ask you to suspend that set of categories for just a few minutes. By the erotics of teaching I mean the energy of human beings who are physically present to one another, and whose work is to share with one another things that they love–to lure, entice, and maybe even sometimes seduce.[12]

I found that this new way of approaching my job involved two things. The first, as happens in Plato's *Republic*, that most liberal and illiberal of texts, was an awful lot of promise-making. That is, teaching the liberal arts requires some way to persuade students that there are some worthwhile things, maybe even the *most* worthwhile things, that must be actively pursued *before* one can experience them. This is directly at odds with the consumer model of the self, in which we face an array of options among which we "freely" choose. The general education program at my college works something like this–its purpose being to expose students to a range of academic disciplines so that they can then choose the one they like best (or find easiest, or get the best grades in) as they major. How, in such a situation, do we tell our students that the hardest classes, or the ones they have the least facility for, might prove the most

---

only be seen, using Booth's metaphor of books as friends, as a very bad friend: the kind that intends us harm.

[10]For the point of view I disagree with here, see Fish (2008).

[11]For example, the measurements we used pitted academic departments against one another, by counting numbers of majors as a measurement of "success." But the liberal arts aim to soften, not solidify, the distinctions between disciplines. See Robert C. Dickeson (2010). My purpose here is not to blame my colleagues, but to describe a problem that I believe to be widespread.

[12]This view of eros relies heavily on the work of Cynthia Willett (2001). I am grateful to my friend Duane Davis, Professor of Philosophy at UNC Asheville, for pointing out that Platos *Symposium* offers a commentary on the erotics of teaching. I reject the emphasis on *agape* as somehow distinct from and better than other forms of love. The Incarnation seems to me profoundly *erotic*, and to ascribe to it some form of love that has been 'purified' of bodily desire is to deny its very essence.

rewarding?

I found myself becoming very explicit: we will practice conversation about important human questions in this course, because conversation about important human questions is one of the great pleasures of being human. I believe in this and I want you to get a taste of it, before the semester is over. While that taste often comes in week thirteen, it's something to hear my students say, ah, if only we could start over, now that we know how to talk to each other. Too many people *with* liberal arts educations have never had this experience. How will we recognize the loss of experiences we have never had?

The second was a constant search for beautiful models of writers who paid attention, who showed us how to pay attention, and who showed us that paying attention reveals things as yet unseen and maybe even unsuspected. I started to pepper my students with invitations to fall in love, and in doing so recognize their own erotic nature. But this bears striking resonances to the work of contemplatives from Ancient Greece onward; this is spiritual work. I had to admit that my aim was not just to develop my students into good thinkers or communicators or even into people freed from prejudice. My aims as an educator had far more content than that.

My hope was to help them develop into persons who would be attentive to each other and the world around them, and whose attentiveness might lead them to try to be just. This was not simply treating them as "whole people," it was treating them as people who were, *most* importantly, people with souls. It was to take a clear stand *for* some ways of life, and a clear stand against others. In simplest terms, we might say, with Kant, that we ought never to treat people as things, as turning students into prospective employees ("outputs") is wont to do. In fact, we may become very bad at "outputting" prospective employees. Liberal arts education, at its best, will tend to mis-fit students for easy integration into our current economic system. They will want to live human lives, not sub-human ones.[13]

---

[13]Martin Luther King, Jr. called for us to be "maladjusted." "But there are some things within our social order to which I am proud to be maladjusted and to which I call upon you to be maladjusted...God grant that we will be so maladjusted that we will be able to go out and change our world and our civilization. And then we will be able to move from the bleak and desolate midnight of man's inhumanity to man to the bright and glittering daylight of freedom and justice" (Martin Luther King, 1986, p. 12-15). A speech by Dr. Martin Luther King, Jr. at the YMCA and YWCA at the University at Berkeley on June 4, 1957. In the same speech, King identifies *agape* love as the heart of nonviolent resistance, distinguishing it from *eros* and *philia*. While I disagree with this sharp distinction, I see King as a model of passionate public

If we claim, perhaps courageously or outrageously, that our work is always, whatever else it is, spiritual work, work of love, work imbued with values, and that our students, whoever else they are, are always human beings with spirits that respond to careful attention and nurture, this changes the nature of the game when it comes to defending the liberal arts. Being clear about what we do opens up the problem, and brings with it a challenge. It places liberal arts education in a larger category, that of the education of the spirit–*a category to which it has no exclusive or even primary claim*. If the hope is that human beings become persons who are attentive to each other and to the world around them, there are other ways to reach that goal. Disciplined attention and care can be developed in a number of ways, and academics might find that they share a sense of purpose with a much broader range of people than we could have guessed.

Furthermore, academia may not even be the most effective of these communities in terms of providing alternatives to the dominant narratives that would reduce our students to their measurable outputs, de-valuing their bodies, their relationships, their communities, the natural world that sustains them, and their souls. Poet and farmer Wendell Berry writes movingly–and justly–about academia's contributions to the destruction of our land and our communities (Berry, 2010). So, such a stated goal opens up liberal arts education to a degree of scrutiny. How well are we meeting that goal? And, how does our pursuit of that goal differ from others'? The absence of a lively and serious debate about the nature of our aims is one mark of our failure to pursue them adequately.

I can think of at least three risks of this approach. First, there is the fear of being accused of doing "woo-woo." A recent editorial in the New York Times proposed that Philosophy "get over" its claim to be about "love of wisdom," since such fuzzy and pseudo-spiritual claims detract from the authority of a discipline that's really about the *science* of being. "Ontics" as a title would make philosophy's purpose and value clear, and crucially, respectable.[14] My response to this problem is simply to say that we need to get over this particular fear. What we do *is* "woo-woo," and, furthermore, we claim that "woo-woo" is vitally important to the future of humankind and the planet.

Second, there is the claim that academics should not engage

---

argument, and wish we read more of his work today.

[14]Colin McGinn, "Philosophy by Another Name," The Stone (blog), New York Times, March 4, 2012. His response to responses in Colin McGinn, "Name Calling: Philosophy as Ontical Science," The Stone (blog), New York Times, March 9, 2012.

politics. My response here is that if we're so obviously turning all of our students into political liberals, where have they all gone? The continual accusation of "political bias" in academia forces too many of us to quell our own political impulses, leaving our students with no sense of themselves as political beings. Humane education is not clearly Democratic or Republican. It values tradition and community, even as it values the common good, and the rights of minority groups. It helps us see what's not being said at all, even as we weigh the truth or falsehood of what is. The most crucial topics for national debate are left unclaimed by either party.[15]

Third, it raises the question of our own status, as practitioners and exemplars. We need to explain more clearly the nature of our work and the resources it requires. But we run the risk of facing squarely the real limitations of our jobs. Contemplative pedagogy demands contemplative practice, but who can be contemplative with a 4/4 load and research requirements? What community supports us? How are our own erotic needs–for community, for friendship, for renewal–being met? A recent article in the *Chronicle of Higher Education* asks, "Why are Associate Professors So Unhappy?" In interviews, mid-career academics describe themselves as isolated, overworked, and underappreciated. They have too little time for scholarship, and the scholarship they do isn't as important as they thought it would be (Wilson, 2012). Academic life is not sustainable for us, as academics. If we were clear about what we are trying to do, what would we need to change to make that possible?

If you've been listening for resonances here between the classroom and Quaker practice, you will have heard a few. I assumed that, after setting up the problem, I would be writing a paper about the resources Friends have to address that problem. But as I wrote this essay, I noticed that the same problems threaten Quakers as threaten the liberal arts. We, too, suffer from confusion about the meanings of the word "liberal," so much so that it's seen as inappropriately interfering with the freedom of others to suggest that they show up on time for Meeting.[16] This gets in the way, not just of our corporate worship, but of our corporate witness.

On the other hand, Quakers *do* have something vital to offer when it comes to describing the value of the spiritual life, and the value of the liberal arts, and the value of the human person, in terms that neither offend Christians nor enrage atheists. And this is what we must do, over and over and over again, as passionately and tantalizingly and seductively as we possibly can.

---

[15]For example, the many issues linked to poverty. See John Marsh (2011).

[16]I speak, of course, from experience.

For his ongoing support of my passion for education, as well as his generosity in hunting down references for this article, I am grateful to my husband, Jim Thompson.

Barret, D. (2012). All about the money: What if lawmakers and students used starting salaries to evaluate colleges and their programs? *The Chronicle of Higher Education.* September 18.

Berry, W. (2010). An argument for diversity. In *What are People For?* Counterpoint, Berkeley, CA.

Booth, W. (1989). *The Company We Keep: An Ethics of Fiction.* University of California Press, Berkeley, CA.

Dickeson, D. (2010). *Prioritizing Academic Programs and Services: Reallocating Resources to Achieve Strategic Balance.* Jossey Bass, San Francisco.

Fish, S. (2008). *Save the World on Your Own Time.* Oxford University Press, New York, NY.

Gutman, A. (1987). *Democratic Education.* Princeton University Press, Princeton, NJ.

Krugman, P. (1996). A country is not a company. *Harvard Business Review*, pages 40–51. January/February.

Marsh, J. (2011). *Class Dismissed: Why We Cannot Teach or Learn Our Way Out of Inequality.* Monthly Review Press, New York.

Martin Luther King, J. (1986). The power of nonviolence. In Washington, J. M., editor, *A Testament of Hope: The Essential Writings and Speeches of Martin Luther King, Jr.*, pages 12–15. Harper San Francisco, San Francisco, CA.

Nussbuam, M. C. (1997). *Cultivating Humanity: A Classical Defense of Reform in Liberal Education.* Harvard University Press, Cambridge, MA.

Nussbuam, M. C. (2010). *Not For Profit: Why Democracy Needs the Humanities.* Princeton University Press, Princeton, NJ.

Willett, C. (2001). *The Soul of Justice: Social Bonds and Racial Hubris.* Cornell University Press, Ithaca, NY.

Wilson, R. (2012). Why are associate professors so unhappy? *The Chronicle of Higher Education.* June 3.

Wood, P. (2012). Supersizing: Obama's higher education agenda, part 1 of 8. *The Chronicle of Higher Education.* February 15.

Connecting the Dots: The Long Term Impact of a Liberal Arts Education in Business

by Patricia E. Berg, Malone University

"In a teacher's consciousness the child has been sent to his telescope to look at the stars, in the child's consciousness he has been given free access to the glory of the heavens" (Whitehead, 1929, p. 33). A technical education in business contradicts what a liberal arts education in business should be. But there is a way to connect the dots so that a liberal arts education in business not only educates students with the how-to technical aspect of business, but adds real world skills and adaptability that opens access to the "glory of the heavens."

A liberal arts education in business is a form of delayed gratification, which seems to have gone out of style in today's fast-food-get-it-now, online and degree completion culture. This poses a challenge for liberal arts universities who are striving to compete for market demand without sacrificing the value of the liberal arts educational journey.

The Purpose of a Business Education

The purpose of a business education at the undergraduate level goes beyond merely training in a skill for immediate application in the corporate world. The impact may not be realized until long after graduation has occurred. This is where a liberal arts education stands apart from technical training. A liberal arts education creates a spark for learning and a well-rounded knowledge base in diverse topics, avoiding the focused memorization approach to knowledge that Whitehead (1929) described as "packing articles in a trunk" (p. 33).

If universities only train in technical business skills, a student may be able to create a balance sheet, financial report or marketing plan, but he would be ill-prepared to face the daily challenges of managing staff, setting and reaching goals, critically thinking or developing contingency plans for when things inevitably go wrong. Life is messy. Business is messy. Careers are messy. If higher education becomes a neatly wrapped package of memorized technical skills, students are not prepared for the messiness of the corporate world.

So what should a liberal arts education in business include? Takei (2011) studied best practices within the liberal arts education at Central Washington University and concluded that there were two educational components crucial to the overall success of a liberal arts education: teaching (class-wide technical skills) and mentoring (one-on-one managerial skills). The class wide teaching is what we are most comfortable with. However, the individual mentoring is just as important, and involves working with students outside of the classroom on projects, presentations, securing internships and connecting them with business leaders in the community.

This approach merges together two diverse and distinctive venues of higher learning only available in the liberal arts education in business and the strength of this educational journey lies in that diversity. Together, they create a well-rounded student who becomes trained in his field of interest as he journeys into becoming a lifelong learner.

Corporate Influence

From the very beginning, universities have been influenced by corporate America. The University of Chicago was funded by corporate investors (mainly John D. Rockefeller), and so began the concern about the corporate influence on higher education. The question then becomes whether the purpose of education is about pleasing corporate America by teaching specific, technical skill sets and preparing the graduate for the here and now or educating students in the broad sense to become lifelong learners, preparing them to be the leaders of tomorrow. One is a quick fix and the latter reflects long term gratification.

The reality is that the corporate world has a great deal of impact on what we teach our business students. They hire them. They train them. They promote them. They fire them. They could, in essence, be considered the ultimate university customer. Students go from a desk in our classroom to a desk in their offices, and if they are ill-prepared for what the corporate world offers, no one wins, and our enrollment may suffer as well.

Connecting the dots between these two diverse worlds involves a two-step approach: both Co-Ed–Coordinating with and educating business as to the value of a liberal arts education in business and Co-Op–Cooperating with and integrating business skills in the classroom.

Co-Ed–Coordinating and Educating Business

The corporate world does impact the classroom world, and it should. However, it is the university's responsibility to educate the corporate world about the value of a liberal arts education in business.

This involves building relationships with corporate leaders, asking them to sit on university committees, guest lecture in business courses, and help to develop curriculum that reflects their needs. But it also involves educating business leaders about the advantages of having a well-rounded, liberally educated student to work for their company. The corporate world must realize the value of the depth and breadth of knowledge needed to grow successful business leaders who will shape the face of tomorrow's corporation.

Depth – Depth of knowledge must include technical skills. However, technical knowledge (such as planning, leading, organizing and controlling) changes over time and technical skills quickly become outdated. It is the ability of graduates to be lifelong learners which allows them to contribute and to grow our corporations. This is where knowledge breadth comes in.

Breadth – Technical knowledge is merely the baseline from which students begin their educational journey, but it is adaptability (the ability to adapt to change) and coachability (the ability to be lifelong learners) which helps them succeed in the dynamic and chaotic business world.

Business students must be educated in both technical skills (depth) which gives them a firm foundation and a liberal arts education (breadth) which gives them the ability to adapt and thrive in today's corporate world. The key is not to produce amateurs, but to graduate experts who are leaders, not merely managers. As Whitehead (1929) stated, "During the school period (K-12), the student has been mentally bending over their desk. At the university they should stand up and look around." It is the liberal arts education in business which asks students to stand up and look around and hold together what Palmer (2007) referred to as diverse paradoxes, like breathing in and out. What universities are struggling to accomplish is difficult, but necessary if the liberal arts education is to survive this fast-paced, fast-food, degree completion and online era. Universities must join together what has been historically separated:

We separate head from heart. Result: minds that do now know how to feel and hearts that do not know how to think.

We separate facts from feelings. Results: Bloodless facts that make the world distant and remote and ignorant emotions that reduce truth to how one feels today.

We separate theory from practice. Results: Theories that have little to do with life, and practices that are uninformed by understanding.

We separate teaching from learning. Results: Teachers who talk but do not listen and students who listen but do not talk (Palmer,

2007, p. 68).

As educators, when we merge these paradoxes, we add to the breadth and depth of the educational journey. Then, as we work with business leaders (through building relationships and integrating them into our classrooms) we work to develop curriculum that reflects their needs. In the end, we help shape the face of tomorrow's corporation.

Co-Op–Cooperate with and Integrate Business Skills in the Classroom

There are various methods of integrating business skills in the classroom. The two that will be presented here are Findlay University's Partnership Model and The Corporate Classroom.

Findlay's partnership model. This partnership model pairs small business owners with student teams who make three presentations throughout one semester. This works well for an upper level business course, integrated business course or free enterprise course. The three presentations are (1) a SWOT analysis of the small business, (2) a marketing and financial analysis of the small business and (3) a complete business action plan with recommendations. According to Yates and Ward (2009), this model engages students with business owners/leaders in active learning by doing which is a great way to integrate real world business skills in the classroom.

The Findlay partnership model provides several benefits to students. As students engage with business owners/leaders, they are better able to see how their academic skills can be implemented to improve real world business achievement. Students are also able to work in a professional setting, build their resume attributes and begin to network within industry. The model also provides benefits to business owners/leaders who gain a free business consultation, adding an outside perspective and analysis of their current business strategy and market position. Business owners/leaders also have the opportunity to improve the liberal arts education process, benefiting all with stronger business leaders for tomorrow.

The corporate classroom. This teaching model involves establishing corporate hierarchies in the classroom as students complete a team project. Professors establish their class as a corporation with the professor serving as the CEO. Students are invited to apply to be Group Managers (GM), giving some leadership experience and others teamwork experience. GMs then interview and hire group members, using managerial skills such as decision making, organizing, empowering and delegating. Groups choose and complete their project as GMs serve as hierarchical managers, scheduling all group meetings, organizing the project, delegating tasks and reporting regularly back to the CEO (professor).

GMs are expected to handle all group conflict as it arises, only involving the CEO if needed, and are responsible for group progress just as a manager would be in industry. At the end of the semester, the CEO (professor) evaluates the GMs, and the GMs evaluate group members, and all evaluations are factored into the final project score along with the project completion and success.[1]

Conclusion

The conflict between the corporate world and the liberal arts classroom lies somewhere between cooperation and consternation. It is the liberal arts university's obligation, the professor's calling, to connect the dots between the two diverse worlds through a two-pronged approach: Co-Ed (Coordinating with and educating business as to the value of a liberal arts education in business) and Co-Op (Cooperating with and integrating business skills in the classroom). By merging these paradoxes, both depth of technical knowledge and breadth of adaptability are integrated into the educational journey.

The challenge for today's liberal arts university is to continue to value the long term impact of a liberal arts education in business, while also competing in today's fast-food-get-it-now, online and degree completion culture. Educators must stand firm to value long term educational gratification to give students "free access to the glory of the heavens" (Whitehead, 1929, p. 33). The question then becomes whether or not today's liberal arts universities are bold enough to hold out the telescope.

---

[1]For additional information, see Berg (2003)

Berg, P. (2003). Group leadership project teaches corporate skills. *The Teaching Professor*, 17(6):8.

Palmer, P. J. (2007). *The Courage to Teach: Exploring the Inner Landscape of a Teacher's Life*. Jossey-Bass, San Francisco, CA.

Takei, H. (2011). Teaching effectiveness and educational components in business education for liberal arts students. *International Journal of Education*, 3(1 E8):1–11.

Whitehead, A. N. (1929). *The Aims of Education and Other Essays*. The Macmillan Company, New York, NY.

Yates, D. and Ward, C. (2009). Staying on the cutting edge of student active learning through real world engagement. *American Journal of Business Education*, 2(1):101–114.

The Morphing of America's Liberal Arts Colleges

by Theodore Sawruk, University of Hartford

Higher education has recently come under significant attack from various external and internal aggressors. Academics and administrators are being forced to reassess the value, construct and cost of education. Colleges and curriculums are asked to be more accountable, more affordable and more germane. A number of articles in educational journals and *Inside Higher Education* have addressed a growing crisis targeting liberal arts education, and the shrinking number of colleges and universities that offer the traditional liberal-arts model. In May 2010, *Education Digest* printed a condensed version of *The Morphing of America's Liberal Arts Colleges* by Frank DiMaria[1]. This review article sought to more fully understand the nature of liberal arts education and to respond to aspects of the current commentary.

Although established in Europe, the ideal of a humanist curriculum grounded in classical languages, literature and critical thinking found its home in small colleges throughout the United States. Some noted prominent examples include the Little Three: Colby, Bates and Bowdoin; the Little Ivy Colleges: Williams, Wesleyan and Amherst; and the predominantly female Seven Sisters. These institutions promote an educational experience characterized by three primary aspects: a) a smaller scale with individual attention provided to each student, b) a residential experience that supports a variety of cultural, political and intellectual events, and c) a two-year general education foundation before declaring a major. Important to this discussion, the term "liberal arts" generally refers to the humanities or an education not relating to a professional, vocational or technical curricula.

In 1990, David W. Breneman published a controversial study, *Are We Losing our Liberal Arts Colleges?* (Breneman, 1990) He found only 212 liberal arts colleges in the United Sates. He cited a growing trend, where many of the historic liberal arts colleges were evolving into "career-oriented professional colleges" (DiMaria, 2009). Baker et al. (2012) re-examined the state of America's liberal arts colleges in a study, *Where Are They Now? Revisiting Breneman's Study of the Liberal Arts Colleges.* Using the same criteria as the 1990 study, Baker et al. (2012) found that of the 212 previous schools, only 130 could now be classified as liberal-arts colleges. They went on to explain that many of the schools had

---

[1]For original article, see DiMaria (2009)

not closed, but had instead transitioned into new versions of themselves. "In order to survive, all organizations must adapt. The question becomes: how... in this environment to remain viable and attractive...?" (p. 13) Many colleges added professional or graduate programs, others simply merged with larger institutions. Thirty-six had experienced "mission creep," an education term used to describe a dramatic change in an institutional mission, usually a shift towards a research focus. Baker et al. (2012) considered these transformations more of a necessary evolution than a grave loss.

Baker et al. (2012) understood that, though it may drastically reduce educational options, some small schools are naturally morphing in response to the current financial crisis, peer pressure and market influences. (In August 2012, the Kiplinger Report listed the Liberal Arts as one of the worst college majors for your career, based on low salaries and high unemployment.[2]) They implied that some liberal arts colleges have survived intact due to strong reputations and large endowments. In turn, many enrollment-driven or tuition-dependent schools have found it fortuitous to weave a traditional liberal arts core with more vocational preparation. They state that vocationally oriented students are more concerned with financial rewards than with "common liberal arts goals, such as developing a meaningful philosophy of life or promoting tolerance and understanding among diverse groups" (p. 12).

Yet, these remain important goals. The definition of a liberal arts model is not just determined by class size and residential life. If that was the case, all small colleges could provide professional and technical education, within a personal and communal environment. There is more to a true liberal arts education than just student-teacher ratios and physical environment.

Founded in the fifth century BC, the classical liberal arts have provided transformational education for over 2500 years. The original goal was to create "two handed worriers," men and women committed to both the life of the mind and the life of the spirit. In his 2011 article, *The Greco-Roman Liberal Arts: When Students were More Than Just Numbers*, Gary David Stratton[3] wrote, "the liberal arts tradition grew out of the Greco-Roman ideal of developing a life of the mind in a soul nurturing relational environment." Aristotle, building on his experiences with Socrates and Plato, asserted that virtue and friendship were the inseparable foundations

---

[2]http://www.kiplinger.com/slideshow/college/
T012-S001-worst-college-majors-for-your-career/

[3] *Two-Handed Warriors*, July 13, 2011, http://garydavidstratton.com/
2011/07/13/origins-of-higher-education-1-the-greco-roman-liberal-
arts-or-why-students-shouldnt-feel-like-numbers/

of education and that the teacher-friend relationship involved a commitment that affected the student's entire life (Wilkins, 1992). There was once a shared vision of an advanced culture teeming with virtuous truth-seeking leaders (Reuben, 1996), but that vibrant dream appears to have faded. Socrates, Plato and Aristotle would be shocked to find the pragmatic, depersonalized and mercenary approach to education currently dominating many colleges and universities. One can only imagine what they would say about the tragic decline of relationally-based, moral education.

Bruce A. Kimball (1986) when writing on *Orators and Philosophers: A History of the Idea of Liberal Education*, identified two discernible streams in the liberal arts traditions, the philosophical and the oratorical. Initiated by Socrates and refined by Aristotle, the Greek philosophical tradition conceived of the liberal arts as "liberating arts," in that they freed the mind of traditional beliefs accepted uncritically, allowing for the further evaluation of values as true or good. In turn, the Roman oratorical tradition, founded by Cicero, focused on developing citizens as enlightened leaders, and liberating them from the pragmatic concerns of learning a trade. "They were learning to think so that they could lead their culture toward the good, the beautiful and the true" (Kimball, 1986).

Baker et al. (2012) remind us that historically these educational values have produced some of the country's top scientists, world leaders and business leaders. While relatively diverse and even competitive at times, both the philosophical and oratorical educational traditions fostered highly collegial, "spiritual" and communal learning environments.

These two educational streams eventually morphed in the Middle Ages, emerging as the seven liberal arts, a curriculum based on the Trivium–grammar, rhetoric, and logic, and the Quadrivium–arithmetic, music, geometry and astronomy. The aim of these studies was not just to educate, but to produce a virtuous, knowledgeable and articulate "citizen," someone who could actively participate in civic life and public debate. During the Renaissance, Italian humanists restructured and expanded the Trivium, creating the Studia humanitatis. Ethics replaced logic, poetry replaced grammar and rhetoric evolved into history. By the sixteenth century, the educational curriculum of humanism spread throughout Europe and became the educational foundation for society's elite: aristocrats, politicians, clergy and the learned professions of architecture, law and medicine.

However, a sincere understanding of the value of a liberal arts education cannot be reduced to a mere examination of course content, for it is the combination of an educational philosophy with a vital teaching methodology, all set within a nurturing community environment that distinguishes the liberal arts model.

The "morphing" occurring today within liberal arts colleges is therefore not merely a shift in curriculum, but mirrors a greater loss of heritage and the slow decline of long established civic values in American society. In the contemporary quest for job security and higher salaries, can we afford to ignore critical thinking, academic enquiry and ethical debate? In an article posted on *Inside Higher Ed*, "Study Finds that Liberal Arts Colleges are Disappearing," Scott Jaschik (2012) commented on Baker and Baldwin's 2009 article. Victor E. Ferrall Jr., president emeritus of Beloit College, was quoted by Jaschik (2012):

> The problem is not that some places (that still) call themselves 'liberal-arts colleges' really aren't any more, but rather that the number of Americans who see the great value a liberal arts education provides is dwindling.

The crisis is that "fewer and fewer (Americans) value the liberal arts education the colleges provide." If liberal arts colleges are going to survive they need to do a better job articulating and justifying the value of the education they offer. "Parents and children want to know that the education and professional outcomes are there and worth the high price tag associated with a liberal arts education" (DiMaria, 2009, p. 15).

Many critics have heralded the achievements of Alverno College, where a distinctive ability-based curriculum advances the merit and relevance of a liberal arts education. But what sets this liberal-arts college apart from the others? The foundation of the Alverno experience is made-up of eight building blocks: Communication, Analysis, Problem Solving, Valuing, Social Interactions, Developing a Global Perspective, Effective Citizenship and Aesthetic Engagement. The college argues that this core of abilities are needed "to create an effective and relevant learning experience," and "it is what sets us and you apart from the crowd."[4] Each student is expected to master each of the eight abilities. The "mastery" requirement goes beyond the more usual academic experience of "exposure" or "understanding" and demands a more rigorous curriculum, one that leads to a more dramatic impact on a student's education.

Alverno believes that its ability-based education is a model for the real world, and it provides a learning experience that is more

---

[4]http://www.alverno.edu/academics/ourability-basedcurriculum/

valued by graduate schools and the professional world. It is this valued-added, enhanced content/experience that gives their curriculum significance in a contemporary market. If a student considering Alverno understands that her liberal-arts degree will be seen as superior by graduate programs nationally, then the Alverno degree has a career value above and beyond that of a more focused curriculum from a less expensive college or university.

Additionally, Alverno College has opted to initiate its own internal assessment and evidence-based learning methodology, which is expected of both teachers and students alike. Assessments are entrenched in the school's pedagogy; thereby imposing self-evaluation and documented achievement on the curriculum, course delivery and performance outcomes. These actions, aggressively advertised to the public, preempt any requirement of a curriculum accreditation. Alverno has wisely taken the steps to salvage its reputation and advance the merit of a liberal arts education. It is setting a new standard and providing a prime model for other liberal arts colleges to follow.

A positive, recent report related to the liberal arts was an article by Michelle Simmons (2012), in which she championed the continued value and impact of the liberal arts college experience.[5] Based on a study by The Annapolis Group (a consortium of 130 liberal-arts colleges and universities), 2,700 alumni of top-tier private and public schools were interviewed in 2002 and 2011. Three critical questions were asked related to: value for cost, method of content delivery and value of product. The findings gave vital ammunition to those defending traditional liberal-arts colleges. Almost eighty percent of those polled rated their undergraduate experience as excellent and reported benefiting from the high-quality, teaching-oriented model. Factoring highly in the report were small class sizes, personalized attention, undergraduate-teacher research opportunities and service-learning activities. Overwhelming evidence showed that the alumni of private liberal arts colleges, where residential life was a part of the core experience, say "they benefited dramatically personally, professsionally, academically and socially from their college experience" (Simmons, 2012).

In a separate study conducted by the Office of Institutional Research at Dickinson College, a recent survey of the 2006 graduating class showed that 94% of alumni were either working full-time or enrolled in a graduate program. Eighty-two percent of those working full-time reported they were more than satisfied with their current job. Jason Gong, now working for American Express, credited his

---

[5]http://www.dickinson.edu/news/article/432/liberal_direction

Dickinson experience for his professional success, "I developed the confidence to take risks and learned to trust my instinct–these are lessons that have yielded tremendous rewards in my professional and personal life" (Simmons, 2012).

In conclusion, it appears as though liberal arts schools should not be quick to abandon centuries old, tried and true methods of education, as the return on their students' investments "continues to grow long after graduation" (Simmons, 2012). Such schools may, instead, need to become more competitive, actively securing and validating their curricula and more rigorously promoting the advantages intrinsic in their transformational approach to education. In an age where students are expected to change their career five times in one lifetime, a solid, broad-based and humanist education may just be what is needed to survive professionally and prosper financially.

Baker, V. L., Baldwin, R. G., and Makker, S. (2012). Where are they now? revisiting breneman's study of liberal arts colleges. *AAHE Bulletin*, 98(3).

Breneman, D. W. (1990). Are we losing our liberal arts colleges? *AAHE Bulletin*, 43(2):3–6.

DiMaria, F. (2009). The morphing of americas liberal arts colleges. *The Hispanic Outlook in Higher Education*, 19:24–25.

Jaschik, S. (2012). Study finds that liberal arts colleges are disappearing. *Inside Higher Education*. October 11.

Kimball, B. A. (1986). *Orators and philosophers: a history of the idea of liberal education*. Teachers College, New York, NY.

Reuben, J. (1996). *The making of the modern university: intellectual transformation and the marginalization of morality*. The University of Chicago Press, Chicago, IL.

Wilkins, M. J. (1992). *Following the master: a biblical theology of discipleship*. Zondervan, Grand Rapids, MI.

The Challenge of Liberation Pedagogy

by Lonnie Valentine, Earlham School of Religion

At the University of Central America in San Salvador a rose garden flourishes in memory of eight Catholic educators massacred by the Salvadoran military with US government support. The six Jesuits along with their housekeeper and her daughter died just because they were educators who challenged the systematic oppression occurring in their country and throughout Latin America.[1] For the students from the Earlham School of Religion, a Quaker seminary, who visited El Salvador, the memory of this rose garden has pain, power and beauty. Part of the struggle for students–and me as a teacher–is being confronted with this scene where martyrdom came because of the way these Jesuit educators practiced education. These suffering servants were engaged in teaching and learning based upon a pedagogical method developed in Latin America that they understood to be foundational in educating for liberation.

Though religious institutions often begin at the margins of society and offer alternatives to that society, most of us now work in settings that are established within the larger social and economic order. The challenge from Latin America liberation theology is this: How can we do education that takes account of the oppression around the world, including in our own country? For, to put it bluntly, if we are not marginalized, even persecuted by society, we are doing education for the oppressive status quo instead of for liberation. This is the challenge that Latin American and other forms of liberation theology make to educational practices in Catholic and other religiously grounded educational institutions.

Here is a summary of the constructive recommendations I see from liberation pedagogy for those of us in the United States who are concerned with liberation issues:

First, we need to break down the "class" space between students, their teachers and those in our society who are poor and oppressed.

Second, from such de-centering experiences with oppression, students, teachers and perhaps the institution itself will raise the self-critical questions about the realities we have seen in contrast to the educational reality we are in.

Third, and most problematically, we need to embrace what is called in Latin American liberation theology, "the preferential option for the poor."

---

[1] For a detailed account of the murders, see Jon Sobrino (1990), Introduction and Part I.

This essay first situates the liberation challenge to our teaching and learning in relation to the U. S. Catholic Bishops 1986 statement on "Economic Justice for All." Then each of the above three recommendations are explored.

U.S. Higher Education and the "Economic Justice For All"

In their 1986 statement on economic justice, the U. S. Catholic Bishops went a long way towards embracing the challenge of Latin American liberation pedagogy, but did not fully explicate what their statement might mean for post-secondary educational institutions, especially religious based institutions. Further, it was not their task to say what implications there are from their statement to specifics of pedagogy. Rather, their challenge was to stimulate all institutions to think about economic issues as they engage in their stated missions. So, this essay seeks to draw out some of those implications for pedagogy and this section seeks to highlight the connections between the U.S. Bishops' concerns and education in religiously based institutions, generally.

The bishops state that the reason they wrote the pastoral letter on the economy is because of the challenge that the economic system of the U. S. raises about how we are "to live our faith in the world." Their fundamental premise is: "The life and words of Jesus and the teaching of his Church calls us to serve those in need and to work actively for social and economic justice" (Bishops, 1992, pp. 572-573). Such a foundational principle can of course be found in other denominations. From this starting point, the bishops present the six basic moral principles that they elaborate. These, also, are not only relevant to Catholic institutions. With each, we can begin to infer what they might mean for educational institutions.

The first basic moral principle is: "Every economic decision and institution must be judged in light of whether it protects or undermines the dignity of the human person" (Bishops, 1992, p. 574). For the bishops, it is the fundamental dignity of all persons that ought to guide economic decisions. Such dignity comes from God and so any economic system is to be judged by what it does to that dignity. This means that educational institutions must be aware of how they are situated in the economic system and what their role as an economic actor means for the dignity of all persons. Attending to such questions in relation to the various activities of an educational institution is quite revealing. Starting with a school's Mission Statement, what is stated or implied about how the institution sees itself as an economic agent in the larger society? What is its stated goal for educating the students that attend and how does that purpose relate to the larger economic system in which the school finds itself? So, for example, this question ought to be asked as the school engages in recruiting and admitting students and the criteria for the scholarships it offers. Specifically, what is the institution doing to reach out to those who are the economically marginalized regardless of race and ethnic divisions? Then, what is the institution doing to be aware of its economic and social location in relation to those who have been thus marginalized? Of course, many other questions might arise, but the point is that the bishops' stated principle can help us think about such questions in relation to our institutions.

The second basic moral principle is: "Human dignity can be realized and protected only in community" (Bishops, 1992, p. 574). This raises the question of how we view our mission in terms of educational practices. If we see it as educating individuals as solitary agents in their life, we might miss the bishops' challenge to us and not even realize it, since much of our economic system can be said to presuppose individual economic actors. This may be as clear as explicit statements of purpose that say the school wants their graduates to be successful competitors in the economic system, or in more subtle ways indicating that students and graduates are seen in isolation from one another. For example, this might lead us to raise questions about the reduction of "liberal arts" education, residential educational institutions, and the increase in online education insofar as these developments reduce the sense of community and social responsibility.

The third principle is: "All people have a right to participate in the economic life of society" (Bishops, 1992, p. 574). Here the foregoing emphasis upon the fundamental commitment to human dignity is connected explicitly to economics. That is, for the bishops, the economic situation of people is directly related to the realization of human dignity. Though certainly they do not equate more wealth with more dignity, they do state that people must "be assured a minimum level of participation in the economy." Of course, educational institutions can help individuals prepare to participate in the economy, however, this principle ought to lead institutions to self- critically reflect on their status in the economy and how they are working to change the larger system insofar as it is unjust and denies individuals and groups their right participation in the economy of the society. This begins to move towards the challenge of liberation pedagogy to be explored later, and the bishops' next principle faces that challenge directly.

This next principle is the key to opening up the challenge of Latin American liberation pedagogy for us: "All members of soci-

215

ety have a special obligation to the poor and vulnerable" (Bishops, 1992, p. 574). They state that "the justice of a society is tested by the treatment of the poor" and they make reference to biblical texts for their warrant, citing, for example, Luke 4:18 where Jesus is presented as reading from the scroll of Isaiah which says: "The Spirit of the Lord is upon me, therefore he has anointed me. He has sent me to bring glad tidings to the poor." Upon this basis, the bishops, using a phrase from Latin American liberation theology, state that institutions as well as individuals "are challenged to make a fundamental 'option for the poor."' This means we need to assess our institutions as well as our own life styles in terms of their impact upon the poor. For the bishops, "this option for the poor' does not mean pitting one group against another, but rather, strengthening the whole community by assisting those who are most vulnerable." Though those "with the greatest needs require the greatest response," the needs of all are to be addressed (O'Brien 574). Implicit in this statement is a tension between meeting the needs of everyone and the preference for addressing those with the greatest needs. This tension is explored in terms of pedagogical issues later in this essay.

The next basic moral principle that the bishops lift up is that "human rights are the minimum conditions for life in community." They go beyond listing only civil and political rights, citing Pope John XXIII: "all people have a right to life, food, clothing, shelter, rest, medical care, education, and employment" (Bishops, 1992, p. 575). This highlights the tension between meeting everyone's needs, while at the same time giving preference to those most in need. What do we do when some claim that their needs preclude meeting the fundamental economic needs of others? How do we consider the range of needs claimed by all segments of society if we perceive that some are meeting what they claim as needs upon the backs of the marginalized? More pointedly, what is the role of educational institutions in exploring this question and how are such institutions to give preference to those most in need? Whatever the answer that institutions work out for themselves, the final basic moral principle of the bishops clearly states that this is the task of all social institutions.

The U.S. Bishops' final statement places the responsibility of searching out the aspects of the question of the preferential option and also acting upon the answers to that question: "Society as a whole, acting through public and private institutions, has the moral responsibility to enhance human dignity and protect human rights" (Bishops, 1992, p. 575). That is, what educational institutions do is more than a matter of raising the questions. Rather, as an economic actors in a larger society, how they conducts themselves on such questions is to be a matter of moral concern. There can no longer be a claim that educational institutions are neutral about such questions, exactly because they are institutions involved in the economic order of the society. Therefore, not only must they ask what it means for their students to "enhance human dignity and protect human rights," the institution is to ask this question of itself and act upon the answer to this question.

The U. S. Bishops' statement on "Economic Justice for All" is in itself a challenging document for individuals and institutions that are doing education. It is clear that aspects of Latin American liberation theology have entered already into the thinking of U. S. Bishops, specifically the difficult charge that individuals and institutions ought to act with a preferential option for the poor. This is not only vital for academic discussion in our educational institutions. The bishops' statement also means that educational institutions decide how they will be actors, based upon the answers they give to what it means to embrace the "option for the poor."

The next three sections of this essay explore the implications of the bishops' statement for specifics of pedagogical practices that emerge from Latin American liberation theology.

Breaking Down the "Class" Space

Most of the education we do is located in a classroom space within an institutional space set apart from the surrounding society. The first challenge of liberation theology to this way of teaching and learning is to, at least, regularly move beyond this space that insulates us from the issues of the larger society. Further, since most of our institutions have "made it" in this society, we can be blind to the context in which we are doing education. The claim of liberation theology is that educational institutions, like all other social structures, tend to become captive to the prevailing cultural powers. Even as we might critique them, we are in a situation that gives little or no direct challenge to those structures. For many in oppressive situations, when you are attacked, then you know you are onto something important! Certainly, the danger to the students and teachers at the University of Central America was clear and the military government's way of responding was extreme. However, our society and government have more subtle ways of keeping institutions in line, though we are now experiencing a bit more attention regarding, say, international students, than we have had before. For example, institutions of higher education were pressured after September 11, 2001 to turn over lists of international students to the government.[2]

Therefore, this first task is to put students, teachers and the institution itself into direct contact with the social problems of our society and the world. Though we could talk about these realities and read books about them within the walls of our institutions, the challenge from the liberation educators is that our common context will tend to leave such realities at the classroom door. Such problems might be interesting to read about, but we need not get our hands too dirty by being immersed in such situations. I imagine that in many of our institutions, many students participate in volunteer work with local social service agencies and many have the opportunity to study in other countries. Such experiences provide a great basis upon which to build, but are not sufficient themselves. For example, often the volunteer work is done from the perspective of "helping the poor." Helping them to do what? Helping them survive in an unjust situation? Helping us feel good about ourselves so we can maintain our station in life? Helping take the pressure off of government agencies that should be using taxes from the wealthy to change social structures? These questions are not rhetorical: they need to be asked.[3]

A missing link with the use of volunteer programs and international programs is that the student then returns to the dominant structure of the institution. Hence, it is easy to leave behind, to put in a scrapbook, the experiences they had off campus. I see two things that can help in connecting these experiences with what then goes on in the institution. First, ask the students, including teachers who participate, what troubles them in the settings where they have been. How do such experiences challenge how they see themselves in the larger social context? How do they view their place in society, given the contact with neighborhoods or countries that are different and less privileged? What research questions could they pursue to clarify their experience? That is, do not let the experience get cut off from the return to campus. Second, to help make sure this separation of experience from self-critical reflection does not happen, bring some of those with whom students have been in contact onto the campus and into the classrooms. Not just as guest lecturers or convocation speakers, but as participants in the classroom dialogue. Further, try to make these visits happen over an extended time, so that they become part of the class and not just an occasional event.

---

[2] I am proud to say that my institution, Earlham, did not turn over the list of international students, and we have had a number of students from Palestine.

[3] See Master's thesis by Elisabeth Beasley (2007), that raises such questions in the context of Study Abroad programs in Africa.

The issue that has been argued about for a long time now, and raised again by the recent Supreme Court decision about the University of Michigan, is how we are to handle making our campuses more diverse in terms of race, ethnicity and class. Of course, most of the discussion has been around African Americans, but it applies to other groups as well. Further, recent discussion has turned more to the issue of class. Many are raising concern that our institutions are class bound, even if we are able to get under-represented minorities to our campuses without running afoul of the Supreme Court (Sachs, 2007, B9-10). The desire for such diversity may be argued for in terms of letting those at the margins into the status quo economic order. However, in terms of liberation theology, the question about the justice of that economic order must be raised. If we get a representational number of minorities into the middle and upper economic classes, is that justice? That is, the unexamined assumption is that the intent is to allow the racially and ethnically diverse students and faculty who enter such institutions to full participation in the status quo that has been determined by the larger white, male economic order. Here's a reflection by bell hooks on how this works, even with good intentions for diversity:

> The banking system of education (based upon the assumption that memorizing information and regurgitating it represented gaining knowledge that could be deposited, stored and used at a later date) did not interest me. I wanted to become a critical thinker. Yet that longing was often seen as a threat to authority. Individual white male students who were seen as "exceptional," were often allowed to chart their intellectual journeys, but the rest of us (and particularly those from marginal groups) were always expected to conform. Nonconformity on our part was viewed with suspicion, as empty gestures of defiance aimed at masking inferiority or substandard work. In those days, those of us from marginal groups who were allowed to enter prestigious, predominately white colleges were made to feel that we were there not to learn but to prove that we were the equal of whites. We were there to prove this by showing how well we could become clones of our peers. As we constantly confronted biases, an undercurrent of stress diminished our learning experience (hooks, 1994, p. 5).

Therefore, from the perspective liberation educators, even our efforts racial and ethnic diversity can mask the assumption that the

status quo is to remain in place. Even if there were equal distribution of racial and ethnic groups in the economic class structure,
this would not mean that the structure is just. The questions about
this structure are hard to ask, since many of us in such institutions
benefit from such a structure. In Freire's classic work on such problems, *Pedagogy of the Oppressed,* he describes the tendency of such
successful educational institutions to treat the oppressed as those
marginalized from the norm of the good society. Therefore, "the
oppressed are regarded as the pathology of the healthy society" in
the sense that such people must change their mentality to conform
to the society so that they will be successful, too. The problem
of course is that the society itself, not those who are oppressed by
its structures is unhealthy: "The solution is not to integrate' (the
oppressed) into the structure of oppression, but to transform that
structure so that they can become 'beings for themselves'" (Freire,
1990, pp. 60-61).

From De-centering to Self-Critical Reflection

Once the experiences from beyond the walls of the classroom are
brought back into the class and institutional space, there remains
the problem that the setting of the institution as part of the dominant social order will restrict or eliminate the tough questions that
have arisen. As bell hooks notes, even those within such institutions who are not part of the dominant social order have a hard
time being recognized as other than those who ought to aspire to
"the equal of whites." If it is this difficult for most in such institutions to even see those among them who are different, then it is far
more difficult for texts that do their best to reveal these realities to
be comprehended by most students and their teachers. As Paulo
Freire indicates, there is a separation between reading the school
words of the "closed world" of the academy and reading the reality
of the larger facts that shape the lives of most of the population:

> The other world, the world of facts, the world of life, the
> world in which events are very alive, the world of strug-
> gles, the world of discrimination and economic crisis...do
> not make contact with students in school through the
> words the school asks students to read. (Shor and Freire,
> 1987, p. 135)

So, even after students have gone into this larger world for their
experiential education, as discussed in the prior section of this paper, that is not enough for those concerned with liberation pedagogy. They may have found themselves challenged–if they have not

bracketed the experience as something completely separate from their lives–but then return to the relative safety of the school world where the realities that they briefly experienced are not there or at least are not so visible and can be ignored. What now?

First, courses can attempt to build upon the experience of the de-centering world that has been introduced by applying academic skills for reflection and research. Journaling and research on social problems experienced outside the walls of the classroom can help maintain the connection between the larger world and the college world. Those who are attempting to do liberation pedagogy do not dismiss the world of the academy, though it is immersed in a dominant and often unjust social world. Rather, the abilities unique to the university, the resources of knowledge, critical thinking, analysis of causes, and so on can be applied directly to the questions that emerge from the experience of those who have gone outside the classroom. What can we now learn from the de-centering experience of having been in another world?

Second, encouraging student activism on these issues, both directed towards that larger world, but also towards the university itself can help students practice seeing the larger social system. Of course, there are many student groups on campuses addressing issues of social justice, but often these are rather separate from what goes on in the classroom or in discussions among faculty, administrators and trustees. It is often seen as an extracurricular activity, disconnected from the core mission of the school. Liberation pedagogy would argue that such motivation being expressed by students needs more institutional support. Compare the amount of institutional money put into such student activism compared to, say, the athletic budget.

The institutional problem with student activism is that it often turns its attention to the institution itself. Even at my small institution, there have been a number of issues over the past few years that have made us who work in the place uncomfortable, as we should be. Here are some examples of issues raised at Earlham that reveal the connection of the institution to the larger world: living wage for hourly staff, food service ties to for-profit prisons, endowment investments, sweatshop labor making college apparel, and vendor connections to unjust labor practices or environmental issues. Imagine what these efforts could do in terms of education about the world if they were supported as much as some of the other extracurricular activities. For such efforts to develop as part of the educational mission, they need support so there can be continuity. At least at my institution, the students involved in such issues often become exhausted by the amount of work they attempt with little support, and subsequently get discouraged and quiet. Further, because of this dynamic, the concerns also do not get passed along to new students. Would we run the theater program, the orchestra or sports teams in this fashion?

Now, this recommendation does not mean that what any of the student group says must be agreed with or that only those of certain views are to be allowed to participate. Rather, by involving institutional resources, including faculty support, these groups can begin to explore the questions they raise in a deeper way, as expected in a university. Instead of leaving the students at their initial level of thinking, such institutional support might lead them further into the questions, to see aspects they did not initially recognize. That is, such support would help students connect their concerns to the intellectual resources of our institutions.

As part of this deeper engagement with student activism, encouraging interactions between student groups that might not share views would be important. In whatever ethos students find themselves, they might feel silenced or fearful of raising their questions. This can be true both of "liberal" students in what they perceive as more conservative institutions, as well as "conservative" students in what they perceive to be more liberal institutions. If an institution is not careful, then student voices that are different can be unintentionally suppressed making for a less rich intellectual environment. Creating opportunities for those of differing perspectives to discuss their views and the reasons for them can inspire students to do their homework. As a part of stimulating such dialogue, trying to make sure that speakers brought to the institution have a range of perspectives on issues will help foster such exchanges, even though some constituencies might be upset.

In addition to making sure all the various voices on campus have a place to be heard, and are supported in the deepening of their self-reflection, the school needs to encourage more continuous contact between the school and the larger world that is suffering from unjust social and economic structures. After all, though we can say that many of the more "conservative" voices are representing that system, even the "liberal" voices are in large part also part of that system. This means that those who are outside the educational system, living and working in the real world, need to be continually present in the campus atmosphere. This would mean not only increasing guest presenters who bring their life and world into the class, but having such people be a regular part of class discussions. That is, if a class is discussing relations with Islam or immigration from Mexico, then having representatives from those groups present in the class would help keep it pertinent. This is not to say that whatever such a person says is automatically correct just because he or she is from that group, but it does mean that voices not usually heard will be present. For example, if the many service learning programs developed a speakers bureau of those who are clients as well as workers for the various social service and advocacy groups, then it would be easier for teachers and students to make connections with those on the outside of the "ivory tower."

Preferential Option for the Poor

This final step in the model of liberation pedagogy explored here closes the circle of praxis. However, it is the most controversial of these recommendations, since it appears to contradict the task of the university to stay open to critical reflection and not take sides in debates. That is, are we not to be neutral or objective and not begin with a bias such as a "preferential option for the poor"? Indeed, the prior stage of this model says that even the voices of those who we might say are in the class of the oppressors need to be heard. However, for a university to take the "preferential option for the poor" simply recognizes that the school stands in a social location always and is never free from its social location. Thus, for such an institution to articulate its stance only makes clear where it stands. This does not mean that all dialogue is closed for those who do not share its stance, but that this is part of the mission of the institution where students are choosing to come. Such a preference for the poor appears difficult because it is often understood as prejudging the situation and not promoting free academic inquiry. To have already decided to prefer the poor seems to lack objectivity and so bring in prejudgment to any critical reflection on the situation.

However, for the form of liberation pedagogy argued for here, there is an error in both the assumption of objective inquiry and the inference that critical voices must be cut off. First, as often noted these days, the place of objectivity is denied given the social location and social construction of all knowledge. However, this does not mean that we either resort to an unreflective advocacy for the poor or that we retreat to a purported benign relativism. Rather, by subjecting the positions and claims emerging from such a commitment to the poor to critical appraisal, reality is made more understandable and relevant to students. It is as mistaken to allow students who have what we might see as correct positions to go unquestioned as it is for students who have what we might see as incorrect positions to go unquestioned. The task of the university in this respect is not altered by embracing a commitment to the poor. Indeed, by being clear as to the institution's social location and commitments, the better we can reflect critically about this stance. If it is assumed that any educational institution can be unaffected by its social location, then these self-critical questions can remain unasked.

Of course, we might say that we can do this by introducing readings and course assignments that will raise such self-critical questions. This is vital, but from the perspective of liberation theologians, insufficient. Why? Because our social location as an institution and individuals who compose the institution are often hidden, we need to make it more clear to ourselves and our students. The prior recommendations here about going beyond the "class"room space and de-centering ourselves gets at this. In this final recommendation, however, the next step is to commit ourselves to standing in the social location of the poor until we can see things from their perspective. That is, it is to be more than a merely challenging reading assignment or an immersion experience, but the development of enough empathy to see what we look like to these others who are at the margins. Just as we desire students to be able to clearly understand what an author is saying before reflecting upon a text, so too do we want students and teachers to understand things from the margins. So, there are many practices now in place and many colleges and universities that can be the vehicle for this. However, it is not enough to have direct experience of the marginal world or to read about it or to work with advocacy groups. We need to come to the place of seeing our teaching and learning done with the poor and not just for the poor. It is not a matter of charity, but of transformation. In this sense, the preferential option *for* the poor means we stand *with* the poor, realizing our human dignity together.

This is the place where the educational method of liberation theology may appear to contradict the academic pursuit of truth we cherish. Further, this approach seems to leave unsettled the tension imbedded in the U. S. Catholic Bishops statement between the commitment to the well being of all and the commitment to the poor. Critical analysis would seem to require not accepting an option for the poor, since we appear to begin with a pre-commitment that would determine conclusions already assumed. However, if we believe we can remain neutral in our inquiry, we will fail to really grasp the reality of the poor and merely reinforce the status quo of an unjust economic order. However, the theological basis for taking the option for the poor in education and action in the context of education does not mean we uncritically accept the views of the poor as automatically true. Yes, it does mean we must enter deeply into their situation with a willingness to see things as they do, but this does not mean we must end up agreeing with how others see things. Ignacio Ellacuria, one of the Jesuits murdered at the University of San Salvador, argued that the task of a Christian university ought to be about changing the unjust world in which it exists in the way appropriate to such social institutions:

> The university must carry out this general commitment with the means uniquely at its disposal: we as an intellectual community must analyze causes; use imagination and creativity together to discover remedies; communicate to our constituencies a consciousness that inspires freedom of self-determination; educate professionals with a conscience, who will be immediate instruments of such a transformation; and continually hone an educational institution that is academically excellent and ethically oriented (Ellacuria, 1990, p. 149).

This pedagogical approach assumes that we cannot be objective knowers, free from our social location and unchanged by how and what we know. However, it does assume we can still engage and must engage in critical reflection on our empathetic engagement with the poor.

Recently, advocacy for certain positions critical of the status quo by educational institutions has led to calls for educational reform. Education ought to be balanced and fair, objective, and by no means take sides according to these critics. The response from liberation pedagogy is that education is never interest free, never balanced and fair, objective and neutral. Thus, it is exactly the vociferousness of these critics that begins to reveal the hidden assumptions that have been guiding most educational institutions as embedded within the larger economic order. If nothing would happen but that assumptions about truth, objectivity and neutrality were examined, this would go far in meeting the concerns of liberation pedagogy. As one of the murdered teachers form the University of Central America had said, the university's task as a place for critical reflection is not set aside, more is demanded of such reflection. It is not required that the views of the poor or any marginalized group be accepted as true, but it is demanded that such views be heard. The educational method of liberation theology presents us with a hypothesis to be tested: *If we attempt to live and learn in the world as the poor do, what do we see about their world–and ours?*

In conclusion, the three components that compose the challenge of liberation pedagogy to our religiously based educational institutions form a hermeneutical circle that comes to break open ques-

225

tions about not only the larger economic system, but the place of our institutions and us as individuals within that system. This goes beyond experience and reflection, but poses questions of personal and institutional transformation. Some our institutions have gone some ways along this path, raising critical issues about the system, providing experiential education and service learning opportunities. However, without the final step, the embracing of the preferential option for the poor, these other efforts can become lost in the larger institutional stance in the social order. In raising such questions of ourselves and our institutions, the method of education offered by liberation theology does not determine what the answers will be for all students. Therefore, the university itself must answer and act on them, since the institution is already occupying some stance. Finally, it is a question of empathy for the dignity of others. Jon Sobrino, one of the targets for death at the University of Central America who escaped, put it this way:

> It would ask all universities, and especially those of the First World, to be universal, to see the whole world and not merely their own world, to look at the world from the perspective of the Third World majorities, and not only from the exceptional islands of the First World. And I ask that, in looking at this, their hearts be moved to compassion (Sobrino, 1990, p. 172).

For such education, compassion does not mean letting your heart rule your mind, but asking that our minds not forget our hearts.

Beasley, E. (2007). The "I" of the institution: An american learns americanism abroad. Master's thesis, Earlham School of Religion, Richmond, IN.

Bishops, U. C. (1992). Economic justice for all (1986). In O'Brien, D. J. and Shannon, T. A., editors, *Catholic Social Thought: The Documentary Heritage*. Orbis Press, Maryknoll, NY.

Ellacuria, Ignacio, S. J. (1990). The task of a christian university. In Sobrino, J., editor, *Companions of Jesus: The Jesuit Martyrs of El Salvador*. Orbis Press, Maryknoll, NY. presentation at commencement at University of Santa Clara.

Freire, P. (1990). *Pedagogy of the Oppressed*. Continuum, New York, NY.

hooks, b. (1994). *Teaching to Transgress: Education as the Practice of Freedom*. Routledge, New York, NY.

Sachs, P. (2007). How colleges perpetuate inequality. *The Chronicle of Higher Education*, LII(19).

Shor, I. and Freire, P. (1987). *A Pedagogy for Liberation: Dialogues on Transforming Education*. Bergin & Garvey, Westport, CT.

Sobrino, J. (1990). The university's christian inspiration. In Sobrino, J., editor, *Companions of Jesus: The Jesuit Martyrs of El Salvador*. Orbis Press, Maryknoll, NY. presentation at the University of Deusto, Bilbao.

Chapter 7

Instructional Methods

Colleges and professors, everywhere, are confronted with ongoing challenges regarding how best to teach. In a world of ever-changing technology and widely varying levels of student preparation, selecting optimal instructional methods involves a greater array of demands and options than any previous era. The articles appearing in this chapter do not provide a comprehensive set of strategies for making instructional decisions, a task well beyond the scope of this book. Rather, they attend to a few specific problems professors in Quaker colleges, and elsewhere, are likely to encounter. The first two articles offer concrete suggestions suitable for use in many college classrooms. The final three articles pay particular attention to providing what is often referred to as "developmental education" for underprepared students.

First, Don Smith describes a technique, "Just In Time Teaching," that he has applied in his physics courses and his interdisciplinary classes at Guilford College in Greensboro, N.C. "Just In Time Teaching" confronts the vexing problem of students not doing their reading prior to class. The method, which involves having students complete advanced quizzes on the web, has yielded promising results: dramatically increasing completion of reading assignments; allowing for the redesign of classroom presentations based on students' performance on the quizzes; and promoting students' critical thinking and problem-solving. Don analyzes these benefits in light of Quaker values.

Peter Oliver teaches educational psychology at the University of Hartford (Connecticut.) He explores applying "Mindfulness" techniques with students. Citing the theorists Piaget and Vygotsky, Peter explains that disequilibrium, accompanied by ambiguity and frustration, is an important antecedent condition to valuable learning. Recognizing that a predictable reaction to disequilibrium is to turn away from learning situations, he identifies a four-step process for developing students' and teachers' capacities for recognizing disequilibrium, accepting it and skillfully adjusting to it in ways that yield personal growth.

Susan McNaught, from Kentucky State University, turns the focus to working with underprepared students in developmental education programs. Susan emphasizes the need for Quakers to live up to their testimonies in this work: in particular practicing integrity; being sensitive to community needs; engaging in plain speech; and minding "the Light" in all students. While fleshing out how Quakers might do so, she reveals many of challenges facing underprepared students, as well as the organizational complexities encountered in delivering developmental education.

Douglas Burks, from Wilmington College, and Mike Moyer, from William Penn University, further explore issues involved in teaching underprepared students. They offer the results of a national survey of Quaker colleges and FAHE members regarding percentages of underprepared students at their institutions, as well as the areas of greatest academic need. Arguing that providing high quality education for underprepared students is a social justice issue, they go on to describe the best practices at their own colleges at both the college and individual classroom levels. They close by referencing the cutting edge work at Cabrillo College (in Santa Cruz, California) by Diego Navarro, the author of the final contribution in this chapter.

Diego James Navarro founded Cabrillo College's "Academy of College Excellence" (a program formerly known as the "Digital Bridge Academy"). It is a carefully researched and meticulously designed program growing out of Diego's own experiences as an "at-risk" youth. He freely acknowledges that his time spent at Young Friends Retreats provided the transformative experiences that served as the inspiration for the Academy. The Academy's mission is to give underprepared community college students the opportunity to improve their lives by helping them develop the academic qualifications, professional skills, and personal attributes necessary to succeed. The students' "bridge" into regular community college courses via a full-time, semester-long transformative learning environment focused on academics and self-efficacy. The Academy aims to increase the number of students who emerge from community college prepared for a professional career with a future. (Editors' note: Diego's article is published with the permission of "Western Friend," where it first appeared in the June 2012 issue.)

A Way to Get them to Do the Reading: Just In Time Teaching

by Donald A. Smith, Guilford College

Just in Time Teaching (JiTT) is a technique developed in the mid-1990s by four Physics professors at widely different institutions as a way to use the then-new technology of the World Wide Web to enhance active learning in the physics classroom. They describe the technique in their book, *Just in Time Teaching*, by Gregor Novak, Evelyn Patterson, Andrew Gavrin, and Wolfgang Christian (Prentice Hall, 1999). I embraced their ideas when I encountered them in 2003, and I have used them in a variety of courses (Physics and otherwise) at Guilford College and at the University of Michigan. In 2009, I organized a workshop around the technique at the June gathering of the Friends Association of Higher Education (FAHE). The FAHE workshop led to this article to share the ideas of JiTT to a wider audience than just Physics educators, in the hopes that you will find them useful. I cannot take credit for the invention of the technique, but I have expanded the application into the interdisciplinary courses I teach, where I have found it to work just as well.

The core idea of JiTT is to use the world-wide web to pose reading quizzes that are to be answered by the day before the class sessions that are scheduled to deal with the corresponding material. The professor can then read the answers the morning of the class. Evelyn Patterson, of the US Air Force Academy, calls them "pre-flights", by analogy with the checking you need to do before a plane can leave the ground. This choice of terminology alone will convey the importance of the exercise: you don't want the plane to crash! Even if there were no other benefits, this would free up class time that would otherwise be used in administering quizzes. However, this extra time is the least of what you gain.

First of all, with the carrot of credit and the stick of assessment, students are much more likely to actually do the reading ahead of time. I imagine (although I have been assured otherwise) that humanities professors have an easier time getting them to read ahead of time than we physical science types. After all, if your class is discussing *Beowulf*, it might make sense to have read the book before class (you humanities types are probably laughing at my naiveté). In Physics, there is a pernicious perception that you should encounter the ideas for the first time in the classroom, and then go to the book later to try to make sense of them. Offering credit for answering the questions provides a much clearer incentive for them

231

to do the reading first. 10% seems about right. Much less, and it won't seem worth their while to participate. It is important that the credit be based purely on participation: the pressure of needing to get the right answer (and for many of the most interesting questions, there isn't one single right answer) leads to stress and motivates cheating. I have never (that I know of) had anyone cheat on these pre-flights.

With the pre-flight checks, the students gain exposure to the ideas, so they are more prepared in class to engage where they know they are confused or need attention. In fact, I have found that you need to reassure them repeatedly that you don't expect them to be able to answer all the questions all the time; if they knew all the answers, they wouldn't need to take the class! I find students often apologize for not getting it the first time, or they blame the textbook for their frustration. They need to hear affirmation that this is just the first step, not the last. The pre-flights also provide a space for them to share a connection they've made or an interpretation they've realized. Ideally, it's a tool of affirmation.

For the instructor, there is an even more important benefit: you receive, when you wake up that morning, an assessment of what your students do and don't understand about the material you plan to teach. If you are willing to adjust your lesson plan that morning (hence the name of the technique), you can tailor your attention right to where they most need it. In Physics classes, I have used this to decide to skip certain topics, or make sure to spend more time on a subject I thought I would be able to skip! The first time I tried it, I was teaching a class on cosmology for non-majors. I thought I wouldn't need to waste class time on how exponential numbers worked (10^2 is ten times smaller than 10^3, and so forth), but the pre-flights showed me that they really didn't understand exponents, so I made sure we spent time on that in class. In discussion classes, their answers will not only prime the pump of the students' critical thinking about the issues you want to tackle, you can see what aspects grab their attention, and you can leave room in the pre-flight for them to ask the questions they find most engaging.

To be most effective, the way in which the students' answers to the JiTT quizzes have shaped the class time needs to be transparent. If you use Powerpoint, incorporate their answers into your slides. If you are discussing, turn to someone and say "Patrick, you asked a fascinating question in your preflight answers. Could you explain further how you felt Eddington was begging the question?" When discussion lags, you have concrete contributions from each student that you can use to draw them in and get the conversation moving again. When they see how seriously you take their answers, and that their answers have a direct and important impact on the class time, they become more invested in the quizzes and take more ownership of the class time. This, in turn, makes it more likely they will do the reading.

Based on the recommendations of Novak et al., I use two short-answer and one multiple-choice question for each pre-flight quiz. For physics classes, I make one of the questions conceptual and another based on a simple calculation. The web-based nature of the exercise makes it easy to embed photographs, movies, or even Java applet simulations into the quiz page, so the quiz can be more interactive than just reading comprehension. For discussion-based classes, I try to use a mix of questions that simply assess whether they did the reading (e.g. "Which of these concepts is not one of Aristotle's four causes?"), whether a difficult concept was conveyed clearly (e.g. "What is the anthropic principle?"), or to prompt them to think about the topics I want to discuss (e.g. "Would you characterize Ibn Tufayl's work more as science or more as religion?").

It's also very important to have a fourth question that is simple and open-ended, i.e. "What did you find challenging and/or interesting about this reading?" This is where they ask me questions, and this is usually the most productive place to find ideas that affect my lesson plans. This is where they express the ideas that are important to them, and if I can incorporate these ideas into the class time, I know they will be invested in the topic. Sometimes they simply state their reactions to the text (e.g. "Galileo was tough to read."), but often they will go on at some length about an idea they encountered that sparked their thinking. One student wrote, "the reading of McGrath made me want to delve further into the writings of Thomas Aquinas." Another student reacted to Ian Barbour with passion: "Barbour talks about the idea of design leading to a sense of gratitude for the gift of life and the idea of chance leading to a feeling of futility and alienation. I feel EXTREMELY grateful about the idea of chance though. The idea that SO MANY THINGS had to fall perfectly into place for ME to experience existing and that this was never a given blows my MIND! I don't know what the guy who says otherwise is even talking about!" These questions are a wonderful way to gain insight into our students' mindsets and backgrounds.

I find JiTT particularly intriguing from a Quaker perspective, because it has two priorities that I find align beautifully with Quaker ideals. First of all, it's not hidebound. You have to be willing to go out on a limb to a certain degree and improvise. You might be completely smitten with a particular topic, or plan, but if the students' answers show they're not ready for it, or aren't connected to it, you have to be willing to adjust your plans. This reminds me quite a bit of how we, as Quakers, have to be willing to let go of our own agendas to hear the sense of the meeting. Secondly, JiTT affirms the value of letting all the voices of the class be heard. Even the shy kid in the back who never says anything has to write something in the pre-flights. Sometimes that kid will amaze you, and sometimes you can figure out which ones are quiet because they're shy, which ones are struggling, and which ones just don't care. This enables me to be a better teacher because I can address the needs of each of those students separately, which makes for a stronger classroom because all voices are heard and valued.

There are a few downsides to JiTT. It's a pedagogical technique, not a piece of software, so implementation may not be easy. I wrote my own CGI/Perl/HTML code to handle the quizzes, tabulate answers into an easy-to-read table, and track participation. Even so, it takes about a day of work at the beginning of each semester to set up the files for new classes, give students login passwords, initialize the databases, and so on. I have to change those files as students add and drop courses. I'm not aware of any easy, plug-and-play software version. Some educational software, such as Moodle or Blackboard, offers similar features, but at least with Moodle, I have found their version insufficient. Moodle only allows me to view one student's answer to one question at a time, and for a large class, that's just not practical. However, it's also quite possible that the fact that I write my own code has kept me from exploring what commercial software might be available for those who can't or don't want to do it themselves.

In conclusion, I have found that if you're willing to rework your lesson plans on the fly in the morning, and if you're willing to manage the software, the benefits are enormous. It doesn't get every single student to read every single page, but in my experience the participation rate has been close to 99%. The increase in students' attention and ownership of class time is palpable. Although the technique was developed by physicists for physics instruction, I have found that the approach works just as well in my discussion based courses such as "Magic, Science, and Religion", or "Science through Science Fiction". If you're interested, I encourage you to visit the JiTT web site www.jitt.org. It does actually get them to do the reading!

Mindfulness in Classroom Learning: Centering Disequilibrium

by Peter V. Oliver, University of Hartford

Learning is an interactive process, whether it is between two (or more) individuals or within individuals themselves. Jean Piaget and Lev Vygotsky, both cognitive developmental theorists, wrote eloquently and extensively about this process.

For his part, Piaget argued that individuals apply "schemas" or categories of perception, strategy, or experience to solve problems. For instance, when faced with a familiar problem such as tying one's shoelaces, individuals apply existing schemas, that is, strategies that have been used previously and successfully. Thus, in theory, you could put on any pair of shoes with laces and, without having to think about it, tie them without a problem. The process of applying existing schemas is referred to as *Assimilation*. When faced with novel situations that are unfamiliar, existing schemas may not be applicable and the original schema (in this case, tying shoelaces) must be re-shaped or abandoned in favor of another strategy. So, imagine if you were to put on a pair of boots that had buckles instead of laces, and you had not seen buckles before. Your ability to tie shoe laces would not be relevant to this new task and you might experience frustration or confusion as you struggle to make sense of your task and, more importantly, solve it. Piaget referred to the cognitive tension or frustration (when existing schemas do not serve a purpose) as *Disequilibrium*. You need to come up with a new strategy to fasten the boots. The process of revising or creating a new schema is called *Accommodation*. Disequilibrium, then, provides the necessary tension to motivate someone to seek out new solutions to solve problems. To Piaget, the learning process is intra-psychic, meaning that individuals must essentially figure things out on their own and construct personal meaning through experience. In the classroom, teachers can offer suggestions, hints, or ask useful questions, but short of taking over and completing the task for you, they can't do it for you.

On the other hand, Vygotsky's approach to problem-solving is less about intra-psychic processes and more about interactive ones. Specifically, Vygotsky argued that learning occurs in the zone between an individual's current level of independent functioning and what he/she can do with guidance or support from more skillful or knowledgeable others. He called this space of learning, the *Zone of Proximal Development*. Therefore, to Vygotsky we learn to tie shoes or buckle boots because we have learned these skills from

235

someone else who knows better or more than we do. Disequilibrium would occur, for example, when someone neither possesses the necessary skills to solve a problem, nor is capable of learning the required skill because it is outside of his/her zone.

In summary, then, Vygotsky sees learning as interactive, and Piaget sees learning as intra-active (or within oneself). Despite their differences, however, one commonality between Vygotsky and Piaget is their insistence that when we confront problems or challenges, our habitual ways of thinking and behaving are applied, and if they are not successful, strategies or solutions must be changed or abandoned.

It is the process of Disequilibrium that I want to focus on now. We began with the premise that Disequilibrium occurs in equal measure on both sides of the desk; most students and teachers experience moments of Disequilibrium in the teaching-learning process. As much as students might experience frustration when not knowing something, I would argue that teachers, too, experience Disequilibrium when lessons do not go as planned and students do not learn something. Such experiences may, at the very least, be frustrating and at the extreme, cause an individual to give up completely.

Therefore, it would seem that, to some extent, Disequilibrium is an inevitable part of the teaching-learning experience for both students and teachers and that it would behoove both parties to learn how to "be" with frustration and disequilibrium in skillful and constructive ways.

How then, should teachers support students who are in the midst of these unpleasant emotional states? Put another way, how should teachers encourage frustrated or confused students to remain attentive and on-task? Moreover, how should teachers address their own experience of Disequilibrium? Answers to these questions depend, in part, on whether Disequilibrium is viewed as an undesirable experience to be avoided or overcome, or if Disequilibrium is perceived as a necessary and potentially valuable experience in the teaching-learning process.

To begin to address these questions, let us consider context. We live in a digital age where, with a single click of a mouse or push of a button, we can experience instant gratification in the form of 'overnight shipping,' an instant download, or a tweet or instant message. We can find out everything we want to know about pretty much anything. Want a book or to hear your favorite song? Download it. Want an answer immediately? Google it. While the immediacy and availability of such technology offer distinct advantages in today's world, I think that there is a severe downside to these resources; as humans we are losing the psychological skill of deferring gratification as well as the ability to sit patiently with the frustration of not knowing something. As such, I would argue that frustration tolerance, or the ability to sit with disequilibrium, is a skill that is losing its power to sustain people's attention and interest, and keep them engaged. This ever-widening gap in the human psyche has significant implications for the teaching-learning process and classroom instruction.

I like what Abraham Shumsky (1968, p. 17) describes as "the fear of confusion" which essentially means that effective teaching is regarded as the absence of confusion and frustration. We create student and teacher awards for success, not for the ability to be with confusion in skillful ways. Our culture does not regard confusion and frustration as ideal or sought-after states of being. No, I would suggest that the opposite is true; we generally do not tolerate frustration and confusion with much equanimity because it forces us to confront our own fallible and insecure natures. Thus, I believe that humans do not naturally possess the ability to 'be' with frustration in a positive way or to even see it as a potentially worthwhile experience. Consequently, I would imagine that in the midst of the unpleasantness of Disequilibrium, most individuals (students and teachers alike) would be more inclined to turn away from the experience of Disequilibrium, rather than tuning into their internal 'unpleasant' process with compassion and grace. Shumsky suggests that developing a tolerance for ambiguity and frustration are important skills to cultivate as long as frustration (and presumably Disequilibrium) is not considered a negative trait or quality and that it does not cause someone to withdraw from the teaching-learning process.

I would argue that far from negative, Disequilibrium is a valuable emotional and cognitive state that can actually be transformative in promoting learning and instilling confidence for both teachers and students, as long as they embrace disequilibrium as an important part of the teaching-learning process. Furthermore, it is critical that students and teachers also realize that they possess not only the means to empower themselves to work with disequilibrium, but are instructed how to do so skillfully. The essential point here is that confusion and frustration are not to be avoided in the teaching and learning process. In fact, they should be encouraged! Since negative emotional and cognitive reactions, such as frustration and confusion, are going to occur during the teaching-learning process, it seems wiser to learn how to work skillfully with these unpleasant states, instead of learning about how best to avoid them altogether.

Nonetheless, although awareness of the potential value of disequilibrium is a positive step, awareness itself is not the solution. To cultivate an individual's capacity to be with Disequilibrium skillfully and with equanimity, considerable changes of attitude and perception are required. Toward that end, I have outlined a four-step process (Oliver, 2013). While there is overlap among the steps, each one has important meaning and purpose in the whole experience. In brief, the steps include the following four elements:

1. Cultivating awareness and appreciation for Disequilibrium's ability to teach people that they have the internal means to 'be' with unpleasant states with a fair measure of compassion and patience. Consistent with a holistic model of health and wellness, one would learn to recognize Disequilibrium on the *physical, intellectual, emotional, and spiritual* levels. Here the essential goal is to familiarize oneself with typical reaction patterns to frustration and confusion. The 'spiritual' dimension is about an individual's ability to find a higher sense of purpose and meaning in his or her experiences. This seems consistent with the Quaker concept of seeking *clearness* in the Divine presence.

2. Normalizing the Disequilibrium experience so that it is not met with resistance and negative judgment but, rather, with compassion and optimism. According to the process, as individuals experience Disequilibrium, it is important for students and teachers to become 'aware' of the experience without judgment or shame. In this step, the goal is for teacher and students to normalize disequilibrium as a natural process that is to be expected as they encounter strange and unfamiliar experiences and information that may be confusing or challenging.

3. Mindfulness Strategies: Mindfulness has been defined in many ways and is essentially an individual's capacity to be aware of what one is experiencing in the present moment, i.e., thoughts, feelings, and/or physical sensations. Traced to Buddhism and other contemplative practices that emphasize the value and simplicity of "awareness" as a crucial skill in an individual's health and well-being, Mindfulness is a potentially powerful ally in working with Disequilibrium. There is a significant difference between feeling confused and frustrated and being "aware" that one is feeling confused and frustrated. What may appear at first blush as just a meaningless play on semantics, awareness may quite actually be the difference between a

response of skillful persistence and a reactionary pattern that causes one to tune out from learning situations.

Without the ability to 'be' with thoughts or aware of thoughts, thinking can run rampant, leaving someone more confused and frustrated. The essential point here is that interestingly, and perhaps even paradoxically, thinking can become a contributor to disequilibrium, especially when thoughts do not arise from clear seeing. Thoughts generated by a frustrated mind tend to spiral to more frustration. Some problems with thinking cannot be solved at the level of thinking. By cultivating a clear mind, clear seeing becomes not only possible, but even more likely.

4. Sustained and Regular Mindfulness Practice: The goal of this step is to learn to recognize habitual reaction patterns so that Disequilibrium becomes recognized more readily. Here is where equanimity becomes vitally important so that individuals learn to appreciate the ebb and flow of negative thoughts and reactions as simply a normal part of the teaching-learning process. With diligent practice comes increased familiarity and awareness of one's experiences, so that one can then learn to apply skillful responses to unpleasant states as they arise rather than be driven by habitual reaction patterns that are not apt to yield creative and insightful solutions.

Oliver, P. V. (2013). *Using Disequilibrium to Cultivate Inner Resources: A potentially Valuable Tool in Classroom Learning.* University of Hartford. Unpublished manuscript.

Shumsky, A. (1968). *In search of teaching style.* Appleton-Century-Crofts, New York, NY.

Living in the Light: Ethical Considerations of Developmental Education

by Susan McNaught

Almost anywhere one turns these days in academia, whether in public or private, two- or four-year colleges, there is the discussion of what to do with the under-prepared students flooding in the doors. About 60 percent of entering students in community colleges need one or more developmental courses and the rate is 30 percent for four-year schools (Levin and Calcagno, 2008). The American Teacher reports that over 1.3 million college students are presently enrolled in developmental courses (Anonymous, 2008a). There is no question that this population is changing the face of post-secondary education. There is another question that we can raise: how do we do developmental education ethically? How do we mind the light in all our students, even the ones who are under-prepared?

Using James Hood's definition, "A matter is considered ethical when it presents us with a genuine dilemma, any outcome of which will produce positives or negatives" (Hood, 2008). Developmental education in higher education is a complex matter and must be approached with the strongest ethical considerations. We need to insure that our institutions are structured in an appropriate manner that has integrity. We want to avoid becoming institutions that are their own worst enemies of their own missions because "they operate on signals from another planet.... It is not enough simply to become a more skilled leader or teacher in an institution that is morally as well as functionally flawed" (Palmer, 2008). We may be dealing with students under-prepared to enter college; our institutions cannot be under-prepared to receive them.

As Friends, we embrace several qualities that can apply to a discussion of developmental education. One of those qualities is that we are called to community. We seek harmony and we seek inclusion–not always easy to combine. In the world of developmental education, this means we recognize that we educators are all in the same boat. We need to get past any finger pointing at secondary schools for not preparing the students. Colleges and universities need to work more closely with middle and secondary schools. High school teachers can help college personnel understand how to work more effectively with young students; college personnel can help high school teachers know what skills are needed for college and together they can work toward a more standard approach. We, as Friends, believe in community–and collaboration between secondary and post-secondary education certainly embraces that understanding. As we work together, we find common ground and support. We are responsible to each other.

Quakers understand that all individuals have "that of God" within them, that each student has the potential for good and is worthy of dignity and respect. This belief leads us to the understanding that developmental education is not a euphemism for remedial education, but a more holistic approach. We embrace a paradigm shift–from remediation with its deficit model to a developmental approach with its emphasis on strengths and potential (Boylan, 1995). From status being a problem to life being a series of choices and processes (Kozeracki, 2002). We are not fixing what is wrong, but taking our students where they are and as they are, and finding ways to help them achieve their goals.

Students struggle in college for many reasons beyond academic issues. Graduation rates have more to do with issues of personal autonomy, self-confidence, study skills, and social competence than with how well a student reads or his high school scores in math. Developmental education is a far more sophisticated concept than remedial education; it involves a combination of theoretical approaches that are drawn from cognitive and developmental psychology (Chickering, 1993; Erickson, 1997; Kohlberg, 1981). When we insist on the term "developmental," we are not just substituting one term for another, but insisting on plain speech, acknowledging the scope and complexity of our educational endeavor.

An important ethical issue is that of admissions. While community colleges have open admission, many four-year schools are seeing an increase in the number of developmental students as well. Most schools need developmental students. If they only took students who were totally college-ready, many colleges would have to close their doors. And we would do well to remember that students need developmental courses for many reasons. Some may need developmental courses because they simply did not apply themselves in high school. Some did not expect to have the opportunity to go to college and so did not take the pre-college courses. Boylan (1999) estimates about 30 percent of developmental students fall into this category. Some may be returning students who, because they have been out of school for a while, need a brush up on skills. Some may have learning disabilities–diagnosed or not. Screening them all out is not necessarily the answer. Being realistic about their needs and the school's ability to meet those needs is the issue. Friends believe in equality and in toleration, but this does not mean there should be no admissions standards. It does mean that we do not promise what we cannot deliver.

If colleges admit students with developmental needs, they need to be prepared to meet those needs. Some colleges advocate a student's right to fail. This is wrong; there should never be a right to fail. It is wrong to take a student's tuition, place him in classes he is not prepared for, and watch as he accumulates debt but no credits. Students also need to know when they are being recruited that they will be taking developmental courses if that is where they place. Students and their families have the right to know and the right to succeed.

Best practices tell us that if students test into developmental courses, they need to be placed in those courses, and that placement needs to be mandatory (Roueche and Roueche, 1999). Students who test into, and complete, developmental courses graduate at rates the same or better than those who enter college-ready (Boylan, 2002). And the same mandatory placement criteria should apply to part-time students as well as full-time students. Some colleges have the policy that students taking only one or two classes each semester are exempt from mandatory placement. Many students avoid developmental courses by limiting the number of courses they take each term. It just takes them longer to accumulate the bad grades and debt.

Proper assessment and proper placement means that we also need to eliminate late registration for students needing developmental education. Students who need developmental education are often not as organized as they need to be. When they show up at the last minute, they still need to be properly placed. If all developmental classes are filled, it is wrong to place them in college-level courses because that is all there is. Again, this reflects plain speech–provide the proper classes and have the courage to insist on proper placement.

Advising developmental students is critical. Often, they are first generation–they have no one in the family who has gone through the process and who can help them understand the system. Hirsch (2008) reports that 52 percent of developmental student come from homes where their parents have not gone to college. Developmental students come to college knowing that more education is the path to success, but they do not know how to navigate that path. A core value for Friends is that of authority and truth within–and these students may not understand how to discern their own authority. Most have had very little practice doing so.

Often advisors do little more than schedule and they do not do that very well. What these students need is a relationship with someone who they can trust–someone who sees beyond the courses needed to the whole person. Advising becomes helping students know what prerequisites are required, what courses are offered or not offered every term, what resources are available, how to schedule around work schedules, where the child care centers are, and who can help with transportation.

They need coaching through set backs and role models to inspire. They need someone who will check on their progress and call them into the office to chat about what is going on when the grade or attendance reports suggest a problem. Advising needs to be intense and intrusive. As part of discovering the authority within, developmental students need to learn how to learn, they need introductions to understanding metacognition and self-advocacy.

Institutions must address structural issues. They must focus on teacher performance as well as student performance. They need to address the possibility that the quality of instruction may be a problem. There may be teaching disabilities as well as learning disabilities. There is no excuse for a teacher failing half the class in the name of maintaining unrealistically high standards, or for passing everyone so course evaluations by students are high. Plain speech for administrators means monitoring performance all around and having the courage to have hard conversations–done with kindness, of course–and to follow through.

Institutions need to provide not only the developmental courses, but academic support services as well. Mandatory labs, supplemental instruction, tutoring centers all contribute to student success (Roueche and Roueche, 1999). Counseling centers provide emotional support. If institutions only focus on what happens inside the classroom, they miss the opportunity to see the students as whole beings.

Another ethical issue is how many levels of developmental education courses are offered. This is related to both admissions and to advising. How much pre-college work is appropriate to require? Time to degree is an increasingly important consideration and if a college requires many levels of developmental work, that time increases dramatically. Clearly, one size does not fit all. Students cannot be lumped into categories. Some colleges have integrated skills courses which is a pedagogically sound approach. However, if a student places into a higher level of reading than writing, does he go into the lower level or the higher one? Which classes will provide the most appropriate education? Those questions must be addressed.

Developmental students need the very best instructors, but increasingly, they are not getting instruction from full-time instructors–but from adjuncts. When teachers are not employed full time, they are less likely to be available for consultation with students, less likely to be involved in campus activities, and less likely to be involved in professional development (Anonymous, 2008b).

And finally, developmental education programs need to be assessed regularly. Decisions need to be data-driven. Levin (2008) calls for more rigorous research in the effectiveness of developmental education, citing methodical flaws in many current evaluations. Far too often, research focuses simply on pass rates and grades. We need to look at programmatic structure, support services, admissions policies, advising practices, and other factors that affect student success. We need to look at institutional effectiveness and resource allocation. Are we structuring our programs in a life-affirming manner? Are our programs non-violent: providing structure, clarity, and classrooms where all feel safe enough to drop defenses?

Doing developmental education as Friends simply means doing developmental education in an ethical manner. We embrace the complexity knowing we, and our institutions, are all works in progress. We insist that our systems and policies support chances for student persistence and success and we work to eliminate those policies that undermine. We exercise inclusion and toleration, embrace community, use plain speech, and mind the light in all our students.

Anonymous (2008a). Colleges cope with rising demand for remedial courses. *American Teacher*, 93(4):7.

Anonymous (2008b). Part-time teaching and lower student success. *Journal of Developmental Education*, 32(2):38.

Boylan, H. (1995). The scope of developmental education. *Research in Developmental Education*, 12(4):1–4.

Boylan, H. (1999). Exploring alternatives to remediation. *Research in Developmental Education*, 22(3):1–11.

Boylan, H. (2002). *What works: research-based practices in developmental education*. The Continuous Quality Improvement Network and the National Center for Developmental Education, Boone, NC.

Chickering, A. (1993). *Education and identity. 2nd ed.* Jossey Bass, San Francisco, CA.

Erickson, E. (1997). *The life cycle completed.* Norton, New York, NY.

Hirsch, D. (2008). Access to college degree or just college debt? *The New England Journal of Higher Education*, 23(2):17–18.

Hood, J. (2008). John keats and ethical practice. *Quaker Higher Education*, 2(2):19–25.

Kohlberg, L. (1981). *The philosophy of moral development.* Harper and Row, San Francisco, CA.

Kozeracki, C. (2002). Eric review: issues in developmental education. *Community College Review*, 29(4):83–101.

Levin, H. and Calcagno, J. C. (2008). Remediation in the community college. *Community College Review*, 35(3):181–205.

Palmer, P. (2008). On the edge. *Journal of staff development*, 29(2):12–16.

Roueche, J. and Roueche, S. (1999). *High stakes, high performance: making remediation work.* Community College Press, Washington, DC.

Reaching Unprepared Students

by Douglas J. Burks, Wilmington College
& Mike Moyer, William Penn University

A College Reality: The Unprepared Student

Higher education in the United States has seen unprecedented increases in participation rates in the last four decades. With this increase in participation the percent of students unprepared to do college work as they enter college has also increased dramatically. Compared to the decades before 1950, more students today see the primary purpose of a bachelor degree as preparation for getting a job and essential for employment. The trend toward an emphasis on job preparation and training over obtaining a liberal education has resulted in greater student diversity at colleges and universities in terms of socioeconomic, educational (greater number of first generation college students), and racial backgrounds with corresponding lower levels of entering students' motivation and commitment to broader learning while in college.

It is estimated that 2/3 of high school graduates enter a community college or four year college upon graduation in the U.S. and 1/3 of those students take at least one remedial education course (mathematics, writing, or reading). Ninety-five percent of students taking remedial courses report that they did all the work that was assigned to them in high school; many of these students have a GPA of 3.0 or higher and report that their high school classes were easy (Greene and Foster, 2003). In 2000, close to 3 billion dollars was spent on remedial courses nationally. In Ohio, public universities spent $23.4 million on remedial courses offering some 260,000 credit hours of remedial courses (Bettinger and Long, 2005). In 2007 the U.S. Department of Education reported that the graduation rate (within eight years) for students who had taken one or two remedial courses was one half that of students who took no remedial courses; the graduation rate for students who had taken four or more remedial courses was one third of those who took no remedial courses. Helping unprepared students succeed is a challenge facing all institutions of higher education, not only community colleges.[1]

Shawn Robinson[2] defines three dimensions that describe unprepared students. He classes students as being unprepared academ-

---

[1] 2008. Diploma to Nowhere. Strong American Schools. Washington, DC. http://hub.mspnet.org/index.cfm/17122

[2] Robinson, S. 1996. Underprepared Students. Eric. http://eric.ed.gov/?id=ED433876

ically, emotionally and/or culturally. In looking at academically unprepared students, two areas can be defined. The first academic area is the lack of academic skills such as reading, writing, and quantitative skill along with general knowledge in subject matters. The second academic area of unpreparedness is in readiness skills such as study skills, time management skills, and problem solving skills.

In terms of students being emotionally unprepared for college, Robinson describes three attributes. These attributes are confidence in skills (low self-esteem), abuse problems, and lack of motivation and commitment to learn. Motivation and low self-esteem are considered the most significant factors leading to a student's failure and withdrawal from college. In many ways it is also the most difficult challenge in helping and reaching unprepared students. Without students taking ownership of their own education, all of our efforts in addressing other areas of unpreparedness are for naught. The third area that Robinson describes is cultural unpreparedness. Culturally unprepared students typically are first generation students who may come from a family where education is not valued. Such students come from a family culture in which books and magazines are not present in the house and so, as children, were not encouraged to read. Often such students are clueless about what they need to do to succeed in college and don't know the language or what is expected of them.

In looking at attitudes of today's students we find that high school grade inflation leads many to believe they are better students than they actually are. More students today expect education to be entertaining, easy, and fun. They expect good grades with little effort and are unwilling to delay gratification of needs. Students see education as a commodity to be received in exchange for tuition fees and do not expect the effort and hard work actually required to gain knowledge. These attitudes lead to poor long term planning skills and to a lack of self direction in learning. They lead to lack of effort resulting in underdevelopment of cognitive skills and knowledge.

Experience of FAHE Members and Quaker Institutions

In a survey of "Quaker" institutions and FAHE members in the United States, it is not surprising that most respondents saw the major challenge at their institutions as the growing number of unprepared students they need to serve. Fifty percent of respondents estimated that thirty-percent or more of their incoming students are not prepared to take some college courses (Table 7.1).

Ninety-five percent of respondents indicated that students were

Table 7.1: Estimates of Unpreparedness		
Student %	Response %	Response Number
0-5	0.0	0
5-10	0.0	0
10-20	22.6	16
20-30	26.8	19
30-40	26.8	19
> 40	23.9	17
	Total Responses	71

Estimate of percent of entering students not prepared for some college coursework at institutions at which FAHE members work (data collected in fall of 2008.)

not prepared to write at a college level. Sixty-four percent of FAHE respondents indicated that students were unprepared to do college level mathematics (Table 7.2). It is clear that serving unprepared students at Quaker institutions is a major and important issue.

Addressing the needs of underprepared students: a Social Justice Issue

We support the broadening of the diversity and number of students entering college today. In a post-industrial economy a college education becomes a necessity for obtaining a job that enables one to earn a living wage. According to data presented by the College Board:

> A person who goes to college usually earns more than a person who doesn't. This information is based on the U.S. Census Bureau's 2007 median earnings for full-time workers at least 25 years old. Annual earnings, based on degree, are: high school diploma, $32,500; associate's degree, $42,000; bachelor's degree, $53,000; master's degree, and professional degrees, $100,000+.[3]

Education correlates with wealth and influence. The children of the educated are more likely to value education and become educated. It is a fact that we might not like, but access to higher education is essential for a real possibility of success in the new post-industrial global economy. If the disadvantaged have limited access

---

[3] 2009. Why Go to College. College Board. http://www.collegeboard.com/student/plan/starting-points/156.html

	Response %	Response #
Do quantitative problems	67.1	47
Do mathematics	64.3	45
Write at a college level	95.7	67
Read texts and materials	82.9	58
Critically analyze	85.7	60
Critically think	82.9	58
	Total Responses	70

Table 7.2: Unprepared for College Tasks

Entering students, in the opinion of FAHE members, that are not adequately prepared to undertake tasks at a basic college level (data collected in fall 2008.)

to higher education, there is a real danger of creating a social divide created and maintained between the educational haves and have-nots. This social divide correlates with race and social economic status. This reality has not changed even with a federal push to improve public education and to "leave no child behind." Lowell P. Weicker Jr. and Richard D. Kahlenberg reflect this view in a Christian Scientist Monitor article when they state:

> This fall, American children have returned to schools that are increasingly segregated by economic status. That central reality–that poor children and middle-class children increasingly attend separate schools–is at the heart of America's education problem. Poverty concentrations have a way of defeating even the best education programs. Neither political party, however, has a strong plan of action to address this educational disaster.[4]

All children do not have equal access to a quality education. Though unprepared students come from all races and socioeconomic backgrounds, it is clear that a larger portion come from disadvantaged groups. This is why it is a social justice issue that must concern Friends involved in higher education.

What We Are Doing at Two Quaker Colleges

At most of our institutions, we have developed remedial courses to help prepare students in the basic academic skills that unprepared

---

[4]Weicker Jr., Lowell P and. Kahlenberg, Richard D. 2002. *The New Educational Divide*. The Christian ScienceMonitor. http://www.csmonitor.com/2002/1009/p09s02-coop.html

Table 7.3: Topics from William Penn U. first year students' course

Responsibility	Who is in charge of creating my life the way I want it to be?
Motivation	What are my goals and dreams? What outcomes and experiences do I want to create? What is my educational goal? What legacy do I want to leave?
Self-Management	How do I manage my actions effectively to achieve the life that I want? What self-management tools will assist me?
Interdependence	
Self-Awareness	What are my habit patterns? What habits support my success? Which habits sabotage my success? How can I change the habits that sabotage me?
Life-Long Learning	
Emotional Intelligence	How do I experience life fully, yet manage my emotions so that I stay on course to my goals and my dreams?
Self-Esteem	Who am I? What do I value? How can I feel even more confident? What reputation do I have with myself?

students need to be successful. We have also developed courses to develop time management and study skills. We have developed learning centers where students can go for individual and group help. What we have not done is to transform our faculty and "regular" courses to help unprepared students. At William Penn University there is the Academic Skills Building Program in which students who are accepted conditionally are assigned an academic coach the first year. Also, all first year students must take College Foundations, a course utilizing Skip Downing's text, *On Course: Strategies for Creating Success in College and in Life* (Downing, 2007), that focuses on the theme that success is a result of one's choices, emphasizes "soft skills" and encourages student ownership for one's performance in college (Table 7.3).

At Wilmington College of Ohio there are several remedial and college preparedness courses including: Writing, Mathematics, College Vocabulary, Effective College Study Strategies, and Reading for students identified as needing academic skills enrichment. In addition, for students identified as unprepared, there is a course called Academic Resources which gives freshmen a firsthand introduction to every aspect of the college. In this course, basic academic skills of writing, reading, library use, critical thinking, and basic research are emphasized. Career exploration and participation in campus activities are encouraged. Wilmington College also has a program to identify students who are having academic difficulties early in every semester. Faculty members are asked to send notices to the academic dean's office after every course evaluation (such as a test or a paper) is completed listing students who are failing or are having difficulties. The student's advisor is then notified as well as the student; if necessary, the student is asked to set up an appointment with the academic dean. Finally, as does William Penn University, Wilmington College has an Academic Resource Center to help students individually and in groups. We believe that our programs are reflective of programs at most of our Quaker colleges.

Unprepared Students in "Content Courses"

There are several things you can do in your class to help unprepared students. Unprepared students can greatly benefit from a personal relationship with a mentor. You might initiate a mentoring relationship by requiring students to meet in the office or over coffee. You also can help students get to know each other in your classes. Remember that students often are not culturally ready for college and don't understand how the system works. Therefore, set and communicate clear expectations and require attendance and participation. At Wilmington College the best predictor for who will receive a failing grade in a course is attendance. Contact with students who skip class any time during the first few weeks is important. Give both formative and summative assessment early and often. Think about ways you can use formative assessments not only to identify learning needs, but also to help guide learning. On summative assessments provide feedback and think about having students make an office visit to go over test results. A common comment by an unprepared student after a first test is, "I studied all these hours and thought I was prepared, and I failed this test." Keep in mind that unprepared students have a special need for positive feedback when they do have success.

In our work with first year courses that enroll unprepared students, we have learned that the most important thing is to not lower standards while unprepared students "catch up." It is important to have high expectations. Students have a tendency to respond and to work to set expectations. Unprepared students have the ability to catch up rapidly if they are motivated. Always remember that "unprepared" does not mean incapable. Introduce students to learning styles and have them use this information to discover study strategies that match their learning style. Encourage student ownership and responsibility for learning. One current buzz phrase in higher education is *Learner Centered Instruction*, the core idea of which is that the student takes ownership and responsibility for his or her education, an essential value for the unprepared student who commonly lacks motivation and commitment. Graham Gibbs in an Orientation to College states:

> Encouragement to 'try harder and do better' by developing better study skills may have limited value without directly addressing student motivation and attitudes toward learning (Gibbs, 2004).

Diego James Navarro has developed a program at Cabrillo College to help unprepared students succeed in a community college setting. In the first semester of his program, students take a four-unit, three week foundations course that at its core addresses motivation. This program is designed, according to Navarro, to "rekindle the fire within for learning."[5] We agree that *the most important thing in working with unprepared students is supporting and rewarding ownership and motivation of a student for their learning.*

What Can FAHE Do?

What can FAHE do to support and improve education of unprepared students? We envision the possibility of providing online resources that would be centered on a Friends' pedagogical orientation in working with unprepared students, collecting materials on best practices and reviews of the literature, and developing an online community that can enable people to interact in discussions and to share insights and questions. Another possibility for exploration could be an online mentoring network for students.

Concluding Remarks

As we seek to provide higher education to an increasing number of people, we need to accept the challenge of working with unprepared students who have the ability to succeed, but may not be in the position to do so without appropriate intervention and assistance. In our post-industrial society, higher education is considered the minimal certification for entry into the economic market place. As a consequence we find growing numbers of unprepared students taking their place in our classrooms. Given the economic and social ramifications associated with educational attainment, as Quakers we should recognize that education of these unprepared students involves issues of social justice.

In this article we identify the dimensions of the challenge unprepared students pose to higher education in academic, emotional, and cultural terms. We suggest that the most important dimensions

---

[5]Diego James Navarro. Personal Communication.

are the emotional and cultural–particularly the emotional dimension in that developing commitment and motivation to succeed are critical to a foundation for academic success. We have described what is being done at two of our Quaker institutions of higher learning. Our institutions have made progress in developing and providing resources to meet the academic needs of unprepared students. A need that we have identified is the linkage between the "remedial" curriculum and content curriculum. Finally, we explore future FAHE plans to address this important need and challenge.

Bettinger, E. P. and Long, T. (2005). Remediation at the community college: Student participation and outcomes. *New Directions for Community Colleges*, 129:17–26.

Downing, S. (2007). *On Course: Strategies for Success in College and in Life (5th ed)*. Houghton Mifflin, New York, NY.

Gibbs, G. (2004). Changing concepts of learning. In Steltenpohl, E., Shipton, J., and Villines, S., editors, *Orientation to College: A Reader*. Wadsworth, Belmont, CA.

Greene, J. and Foster, G. (2003). *Public high school graduation and college readiness rates in the United States*. Manhattan Institute, Center for Civic Information, New York, NY. Education Working Paper, No. 3.

University Halls Not Prison Walls

by Diego James Navarro

> The salvation of this human world lies nowhere else than
> in the human heart, in the human power to reflect, in
> human meekness, and in human responsibility.

-Vaclav Havel, addressing the US Congress

Since 1999 I have been under the weight of a concern for young
adult students affected by poverty. Many of these young people
come from marginalized communities and experience poverty in its
many manifestations. Inadequate schools, crime and violence are
three primary examples. My calling is simple: I am a community
college teacher trying to reclaim the lives of young people too often
lost to juvenile hall, prisons, and drug-treatment programs before
entering or after dropping out of a community college.

There is a Friends Committee on Legislation-California bumper
sticker that reads, "University Halls not Prison Walls." That is
what my program, the Academy for College Excellence (ACE), provides students at risk of not completing college.

To understand why I designed ACE the way it is, and the students whom we serve, one must first understand my own experience
growing up in a marginalized community where I was a victim of
inadequate schooling, neighborhood violence, and family trauma. I
was raised in Pomona, California. People unfamiliar with the area
often assume that my hometown houses Pomona College, but they
are mistaken. Pomona College is located in Claremont where the
Claremont Colleges reside; the City of Pomona is on the "other
side of the tracks." In grade school I was placed in the highest English and math classes, but in junior high my last name, Navarro,
preceded me and I was tracked into wood shop, metal shop, and
electric shop. I started getting lost in the education world in junior high school. In Pomona, the community would not pass school
bonds. As a result, by the time I reached high school classes were
down from seven periods to five.

Living in Pomona, I witnessed a lot of violence. Many families
moved to Pomona during the reconstruction period that followed
the Watts riots in 1968. We had the Bloods and the Crips gangs
in our neighborhoods. Some of my friends kept guns in their lock-
ers, retrieving them at the end of the day so they could protect
themselves as they walked home.

I remember Pomona High shutting down for a week every year
due to student riots. My junior high school was just two blocks

down the road, and between classes we would dodge rioting high schoolers running through our hallways. I saw a friend who lived across the street from our home getting jumped by what looked like twenty-five people on the school grounds. As you might imagine, I was hyper-vigilant as a kid, always watching my back. I had to be.

As I was witnessing this physical violence in school, my parents were fighting verbally at home. In ninth grade, my mother was diagnosed with cancer for the second time. This time it turned out to be bone cancer, and she died when I was fifteen and a half. It was 1972, a time before pain control and hospice services were widely available. Towards the end of her life I would wake up at night to her screaming in pain.

School became irrelevant to what I was experiencing in my life, to my experiences at home. I started drinking in ninth grade, and no one at school noticed. It was a way to cope, and it wasn't uncommon for youth my age. In our neighborhood, if you didn't have a strong family, or if you were living in the midst of a traumatic situation, you were left up to the influence of the dominant youth culture, the strip mall culture. This was the early 70s, after all, in the suburbs of Southern California.

Though my parents were members of Claremont Meeting and I attended well into my early teens, I never felt truly connected there. The Meeting members didn't seem to know the struggles facing my family. I didn't receive solace or support during these times. It wasn't until high school when I attended JYM (Junior Yearly Meeting) at Pacific Yearly Meeting (Pacific YM), where I bonded deeply with my peers, that I felt safe and free. I experienced an alternative "universe," one far away from my life in Pomona. Leaving Pacific YM each year, I would feel a deep ache in my chest, already missing my community of Junior Friends.

When I graduated from Pomona High, I could not read or write at the college-level. I went to Pasadena City College for my first years of college. Fortunately, I also experienced numerous Young Adult Friends' gatherings. In December 1975, during my first year of college, I attended the first New Year's Gathering at Ben Lomond Quaker Center. Following this initial gathering, the Western Young Friends met together every New Year, sometimes with over one hundred Young Adult Friends in attendance. In 1978, I attended my first Young Friends of North America gathering. Coming from a liberal Yearly Meeting, YFNA was an eye-opening experience. I was introduced to Meeting for Worship with a concern for business. We were serious about worship, about connecting deeply with each other and letting the Spirit inform our community.

At each gathering of Young Adult Friends, I was able to go

beyond the pain and suffering of my youth and teenage years. I felt I was not alone and, perhaps more importantly, felt like I was a part of a community that was "in this together." I realized that a lot of us from urban environments were deep in the trenches. We were "living in the world" but not always successful at "not being of the world." Our Quakerism, our faith, was informed by some truly horrible situations, and a lot of our families were unable to support us, both economically and emotionally. For many of us, our parents were not aware of how our life circumstances in our neighborhoods and schools were affecting us.

At these Young Adult Quaker gatherings we would bond and connect at a very deep level. The suffering created an authenticity among us and through this community we allowed our wounds to heal. We formed Worship Fellowship groups, men and women support groups, pre-business meetings, and held interest groups where we invited Yearly Meeting elders to seed our discussions. We experienced our deep, wounded places together and, through caring for one another, filled them with hope and love.

Unfortunately my students don't have the loving support of a Quaker Young Adult community. However, they have found the ACE program, whose design was informed by my experiences growing up among Friends. Many of my students come with wounds caused by earlier educational experiences and rough lives, yet they have woken up to the possibility of what higher education can offer.

I have found that there are times when an individual is forced to look at themselves and make new choices because of the convergence of particular circumstances. For some of us, the convergence occurs because of a death, a family break up or an abusive relationship. For others, it is when they are in the midst of an intense social situation, like being expelled from school, getting busted and kicked off a high school sports team, exiting prison, or being forced to enter a drug treatment program.

At these times, we can be reached in a way that is not always possible before that point. These circumstances may cause the beginning of a thirst to understand oneself, to wake up from the trance, to notice routines and habits. Early Friends might call it the "lifting of the veil" or see it as the beginning of the convincement process. One begins to see the power of the Light in one's life. These negative situations are the opportunities to experience the power of "being in the world but not of the world" and begin to examine deeply one's sense of self.

One opportunity where this type of self-inquiry happens is the first time an individual goes to the county jail, where they begin to question their ways and begin to think about changing their lives for the better. We need to find a way to capture these individuals and provide them with alternatives to the prison industrial complex.

I see young people come into my class every year with signs of enduring significant stress, including post-traumatic stress disorder, or something like it. They're hyper-vigilant, unable to focus, and are multitasking a lot. When I first decided to help students with teenage lives similar to mine, I knew that recognizing and witness-ing to our wounds was important, as was working on reflection and building of authentic community, just as I had done with Young Adult Quakers. This is the vessel that would help to build the capacity for healing, growth, and, ultimately, success.

My experience with Young Friends served as my guide for the design of the Academy for College Excellence's Foundation Course, a two-week intensive orientation course. During the development and piloting of the program, I sought ways to provide students with experiences similar to the ones I had helped to create as Clerk of Pacific Yearly Meeting's Young Adult Friends group and the New Year's gathering, but in a secular collegiate environment.

It wasn't easy. One of the first things I realized during the pilot phase of the ACE Foundation Course curriculum–after sev-eral forty-hour curriculum pilots, mind you–was that the behaviors developed for survival in violent and traumatic situations do not apply well to the academic environment of college. (They do help in graduate school, however!)

How do you get students to believe they can succeed in college when they did poorly in high school and still carry the wounds from that and other experiences?

We begin with a Foundation Course, which is a two-week long, three-credit course. Students start the day at 9:00 AM and end at 5:30 PM for eight days. In this high-intensity, high-intimacy setting, they rediscover that they are smart, that they can think, and that they can grow and change. They begin to soften. I call this transformation "lighting the fire within." It only works if students attend full-time, are accountable to each other, and stick together. Additionally, high expectations and group accountability will make or break the group.

These students, though often written off by the educational world, are not dumb; many, in fact, are brilliant. Sometimes high school was too simple. Always the behaviors and habits of the street, and misunderstandings of academic cultural cues–so neces-sary for success in college and professional careers–lead to attrition.

Our student support model, embedded in curriculum, is one that promotes persistence, accelerates remedial learning, and helps students accumulate college transfer credits. Research shows that if you get students to fifteen academic credits they have much higher levels of completion. Get them to thirty credits, and the level of completion is even more dramatic. A nine-semester longitudinal research study of the ACE program, conducted by Columbia University's Community College Research Center, indicated that students enrolled in the ACE program had 140% greater chance of completing associate-level English and over an 80% greater chance of completing transfer-level English as compared to the 11,500 students from the comparison group.

Like the two-week Foundation Course, the entire ACE semester is very intense. Students take 16.5 college credits, a staggering amount for those in remedial education. In this first semester we set up the college experience culturally, giving students a taste of what is to come and providing them with the tools to face it when it does come. Because of the cohort community, which moves together from the Foundation Course and into the ACE semester, students are supported by one another to complete those 16.5 college credits and continue to hold each other accountable throughout their college experience. In some ways, we put them on a spiritual journey–the college journey–and make sure that it is done in a supportive and thoughtful way.

Let's take a step back to look at the larger issue. On a nationwide basis, 60% of enrolling community college students enter college underprepared for college-level math or English. While unfortunate, the real tragedy is that over 60% of them leave before completing remedial English, and over 80% leave before completing remedial math. Unfortunately, given the conditions of our society they may end up in jail or prison. To add insult to injury, 25% of ACE's incoming students received their high school diplomas from continuation schools, meaning they had been dropped from their comprehensive high schools, and 22% do not have a high school diploma.

Community colleges were designed for the students of the 1950s and early 60s: people who were college-ready and had lives that were different than students attending today. With 60% of incoming community college students underprepared for college-level academics, a great deal of stress is placed on remedial programs, many of which are not helping. In fact, most community college remedial programming mimics the remedial programs found in high schools. Einstein's definition of insanity, "If you try to do the same thing over and over again and expect different results," certainly applies here.

So the ACE program does things differently. We build community, we foster new behaviors, and we remind the students that they do have academic expertise, grounded in their life experiences; they just don't know it yet. They have huge strengths in persistence and survival. They have had to overcome significant obstacles in their lives, yet they do not easily translate those strengths to the academic environment.

To help them realize this knowledge, we incorporate a project-based social justice course into the ACE semester curriculum, based on primary research. We have found through extensive piloting that students with low literacy skills are perfectly able to conduct primary research, rather than synthesize multiple sources as traditionally done in lower division courses. We utilize a graduate school pedagogy for low-literacy students entering college. Experientially, my students are PhDs in social injustice, having lived through countless inequalities, whether they are aware of them or not. We build on this expertise. Together we brainstorm about the social justice issues that have affected them, whether in their own lives, in their communities, or in their families. Students fill the white board with issues and prioritize those they feel most passionate about. In the end, four to eight issues are chosen. The class is then formed into teams, and over a thirteen week period they investigate the issue in their community, going through all the steps of research, and then building a community action plan to resolve their issue of choice.

Students in the ACE program also spend time learning about compassion and non-violent communication over the course of the semester. In our first program pilot in 2002, we had students from Youth Build, a program that takes students who did not graduate from high school and puts them into a construction program while they work to get their GED. Usually these students are adjudicated youth, sometimes from a gang background. For our first class of this pilot, the students came into class a half-hour late because of a fight in the parking lot. I did not know it at the time, but our college happens to be in a Norteno neighborhood, and a group of our Youth Build students, from a Sureno neighborhood, were sitting in their car in the school parking lot when the fight broke out. In the fight one of these students got sliced with a knife. From this experience, I realized the ACE curriculum needed to have a more explicit focus on giving them tools to address the violence in their lives. Later that summer I was introduced to the Alternatives to Violence Project at Pacific Yearly Meeting and incorporated it into the Foundation Course curriculum.

There are other Friends-influenced aspects of the program. In order to support student performance, we developed, for the ACE semester, a Team Self-Management class designed to help students reflect on their lives. It gives them a chance to identify the behaviors that keep them from attaining their goals and being successful in school. It makes their implicit choices explicit. In ACE we call this reflection time "focusing," but Friends might see it as going inward. Students sit together in silence and share with each other from a set of queries, providing space in between for reflection. It is a secular form of worship sharing.

University Halls not Prison Walls is a call for social justice. Instead of fostering success in our disaffected youth, our society is building prisons for these young people. As the Religious Society of Friends, we have a long history of testimonies around prisons, and we have an equally passionate commitment to education. By addressing the needs of these young people who live in difficult situations, building a bridge for them to higher education, we can utilize the existing community college system to foster significant social change. There are over 1,200 colleges in communities nationwide. If we can harness those colleges to full advantage, we can make a difference. Prisons will never harvest the potential of these young adults, but meaningful and relevant experiences in higher education can transform communities of poverty.

Chapter 8

Activism and Community Initiatives

A core concern for modern Quakers is demonstrating their faith through their actions within the wider community; thus, Friends are known for their activism. But living the activist's life is always challenging, and Friends continue looking to history for inspiration regarding how to proceed in our present, complex, daunting world. The authors in this chapter, all responding to the question, "Holistic Education: to What End?" They examine the college teaching implications of this quest for living a truthful life, while being especially aware that the substantial majority of their students are not Quakers.

First, Jay Case from Malone University considers students as both thinking and desiring beings, with the thinking part being less prominent than we, as faculty, would hope. As Friends often do, Jay turns to the example of John Woolman for insight regarding how to chart a way forward through conflicting demands; in this case between the expectations of our materialistic, utilitarian society and wisdom of our Quaker spiritual and intellectual traditions. Following Woolman's lead, Jay sees a path to a richer, enduring university community by addressing students' spirituality–encouraging them to be people "...guided by wisdom, justice, and mercy... who learn to love learning... desire to be people of integrity... care about others...(and)...demonstrate wisdom." He challenges them to engage with issues that are bigger than themselves, transcending their own selfish desires.

Next, Tracey Hucks draws on her experiences as a member of a line of African American professors at Haverford College to illustrate how becoming "Quakerly" involves embracing challenges of diversity, moving education beyond our classrooms, and deeply affecting our students', and our own, lives. Tracey reminds us that "...Quakerism is not only a set of values to be espoused and embraced, but it also functions as the source and subject of sound critical intellectual research and reflection." She shares how the teaching and learning environment at Haverford College has freed her "...to teach on the cutting edge of social justice, to bring intellectual value to the silenced, muted, and marginalized of American society, and to cultivate a student atmosphere of expansion, risk, and voice." Her compelling example of a deeply reflective assignment applying James Baldwin's intellectual thought to one's own condition illustrates how faculty can foster students' personal transformation.

Concluding the chapter, Steve Chase draws on the teachings of Martin Luther King, Jr., as well as his own extraordinary field experiences with his students at Antioch University New England, to show how we might educate activists who are, in the best sense, *"creatively maladjusted"* to the injustices of the world. Citing the "Call for Peace and Ecojustice" issued by the Sixth World Conference of Friends held in April 2012 at Kabarak University in Kenya, Steve convincingly argues that, "...we should ultimately be in the business of nurturing the habits of head, heart, and hands that will equip our students to become ever more effective, wise, and loving participants in fostering the 'peaceable Kingdom of God' in their personal, professional, and public lives." While doing so, he reveals the tragic environmental and racial injustice in the stretch of Louisiana along the Mississippi River, between Baton Rouge and New Orleans, known as "Cancer Alley," and he introduces us to the courageous, retired school teacher, Margie Richards, who battled Shell Oil for just settlement for the displaced residents of Diamond, Louisiana. Furthermore, he tackles the issue of how we, as Quaker educators, should respond when confronted with academic resistance to pursuing our calling.

Students are not Simply Thinking Beings

by Jay Case, Malone University

Just about everybody in our society, it seems, believes that the primary purpose of college is to train students for jobs. For those of us who understand the importance of holistic education and for those of us who hope to teach in a way that instills Quaker ideals in our students, this is a serious problem. How are we to encourage our students to seriously consider peace-making, for instance, if they think that the primary reason they are in college is to obtain skills for computer programing, physical therapy, or marketing?

I used to think that the answer was pretty straight-forward. I had to figure out how to get students to think about significant issues in life and embed those issues in my history curriculum. By getting them to read, write, and discuss these issues in my history classes, they could also see that there is more to higher education than job training. If I could get them to think critically about racism, and economic inequality, and the role of mass media, they would start to see why these things matter.

At this point in my career, however, I am not convinced that this approach really gets at the heart of the matter. Maybe this way of looking at human beings doesn't quite get it right.

Maybe, at the core of who we are, we aren't really thinking beings. Yes, we think (some of us less clearly than others), but perhaps there is something that goes deeper than thinking, something that directs how we think and why we think about those things we think about. Maybe it is more accurate to consider humans as fundamentally desiring creatures.[1] I use this word "desire"–though other terms can be used, such as "affections" or "love"–terms that I use interchangeably in this article, though some philosophers would make distinctions between these words.

I need to be clear that when I use the term "desire," I am *not* simply speaking of an emotion. This is important, because I am working with a definition that differs from much of the Western intellectual tradition from the last three centuries. Enlightenment thinkers had a tendency to describe human nature in terms of two competing characteristics: rationality and emotion. The result of this intellectual arrangement was that there has been a strong tendency in modernity to divide human qualities into one of these two

---

[1]Most recently, Smith (2009) has made this point. However, this idea about human nature goes back at least as far as Augustine and has influenced Christian thought at different times through history. As I show in this article, it deeply influenced Quakers like John Woolman.

categories. Desire and love were often considered to be emotions, which were seen to be a detriment to the dispassionate, calculating, and critically thinking methodologies of higher education.

There is good reason, though, to consider desires to be something that are neither quite the same thing as emotion or rationality, but something deeper that influences and drives both. For instance, the most dispassionate, objective, rationalistic scientist is still driven by desires: she has a desire to discover what is true, a desire to analyze the data accurately, and a desire to prevent biases from influencing her analysis.

Undoubtedly, we desire certain outcomes from our teaching. We want our students to love learning. We want them to love all humans equally. We want them to love God. We want them to desire social justice.

But I'm not sure we recognize how deeply the modern practices, habits and structures of higher education still affect us. The reality is that we are deeply ensconced in an academic culture that assumes that humans are fundamentally thinking beings. Without realizing it, perhaps, we often act as if critical thinking, problem solving and a certain kind of rationality will lead students to act and live in the way we would like them to.

For example, I am an instructor in our required first-year orientation course here at Malone, which we call "The College Experience." It is a great and important class, with its own particular set of challenges. One of the things we try to do in this course is to help first-year students consider more carefully what college ought to be about. We raise questions about whether college should just be about job training. We talk about how at Malone we believe that college is more about what students will become, rather than what they will do. We discuss how general education classes fit into this philosophy and why we think these classes are just as important as the classes in their major. We hit them with this right from the beginning of the semester. Students engage these themes through readings, discussion, and papers.

Last fall, I led a class through these ideas in the first weeks of the semester. Sometime after midterm we had moved to the topic of academic performance and discussed how the students were doing at that point. To facilitate discussion, I asked the students to identify what sort of things helped their academic performance and what sort hindered them. The students, unsurprisingly, eventually came to the problem of what they called "boring" classes. As we discussed what sort of factors made a class boring and how to handle this, somebody mentioned that it was difficult to get interested in classes that weren't in their major–general education classes. Another student then asked why we had to take general education classes in the first place. Shouldn't we just be taking classes related to our major, he asked, since those were the classes that were preparing us for jobs?

To review: this student had already read several articles about this topic. He had been in class when, on more than one occasion, we had discussed this idea. He had even written a paper that dealt with this issue. Now, three weeks later, this student showed that these ideas still did not sink in.

Why not? Well, the *idea*, in and of itself, was not enough. If students don't have a desire to consider, weigh and analyze ideas, simply presenting them with a new idea will not compel them to take that idea seriously, even if we require them to discuss and write about it. Surely you have had the disquieting experience of reading a paper or an exam in which a student is repeating or mimicking an idea that you have talked about in class, but you realize that there is no conviction behind the writing. Students have learned how to pick up and wear an idea for a short period of time, like a costume in a play, and then cast it away after the final curtain comes down.

But if you are rather dense, like me, you keep trotting out newly designed costumes every semester, thinking that this particular wardrobe will have staying power. If you are like me, you think that by the virtue of wearing these ideas long enough, our students will become the characters that they have been acting out during the semester.

A qualification: we know that some students are not acting. Some of my students in that college experience class really did get it. We know that some students show up in our classes primed to get engaged with the Quaker principles. With those students, we can really go places.

But most of these students already arrive at college with many of these desires in place. My focus here, then, is not about students who already love learning or already have a deep desire to serve the world. My concern is with that conglomeration of students whose desires run in different directions. For some, the desire for education is driven by a desire of an imagined "good life" of consumerism and entertainment. Some love one subject, like biology or sociology, but do not desire a holistic education. Some are conflicted by competing desires: a desire to live a life pursuing consumerism and entertainment (which is driven by a basic selfishness) and the desire to be a good person in life (which requires the opposite of selfishness–service and selflessness).

To more effectively engage these students, let us briefly think about ourselves. There is a reason why we think that our ideas, or critical thinking tasks, our problem-solving exercises–as well as our desires for social justice, Quaker testimonies and holistic education– will hold our students' interest: these are the things that we love, that we desire. That's what makes us academics and intellectuals. We care about ideas, higher education, about our students, about our society and about the Quaker heritage. We are pretty sure they are all related to one another somehow and we want to figure out how. But we should recognize that this also means we live our working lives amongst practices, habits and dispositions that subtly but powerfully lead us to believe that humans are first and foremost thinking beings, rather than desiring beings.

This is a legacy of higher education from the past three centuries.[2] For instance, consider how we do assessment–both our grading system and the accreditation system that encourages us to establish assessment procedures. In the 17th century the Scientific Revolution made huge strides in our understanding of the natural world through empirical observation and measurement. By the late nineteenth century, higher education, especially in the newly created disciplines of the social sciences, had institutionalized the sense that human societies could be best understood through measurable processes. The result is that today we assume that the most important things we do in higher education are those things that can be measured, and that these measurements tell us what we need to know about how education works.

There is a strong pull here to see assessment and measurement as the same thing (though good assessment does not have to be measurable). The problem with this idea of measuring everything is that it is actually difficult, and sometimes impossible, to measure the desires that we want to cultivate in our students. I can measure how effectively my students can say what I want them to– like whether my first year students write that college is not just about getting a job–but that does not mean they really believe them or will implement them in their lives. Could you create a tool that accurately measured increases in students' love for the Quaker testimonies? Will you ever find yourself in a committee meeting saying the following, "Ah, I see from this spreadsheet that the desire for peacemaking among our sophomores has risen 13.4% this semester?"

Secondly, the compartmentalization we have created in higher education has fragmented and undermined any consensus about

---

[2]Intellectual history is actually a long and complicated story, which I cannot fully capture here, so these points are necessarily simplified. For a fine overview of these themes in higher education, see Marsden (1994).

the purposes of college or even how to engage the most significant questions of life. Since the late 19th century, academics have created disciplines and majors and courses that are very good at isolating tasks and methodologies, a system that works well if, say, you want to teach students how to build a bridge. In the late 19th and early 20th century, it was assumed that this sort of scientific education would naturally produce graduates whose work would be good for society. In the terminology of the day, the "progress of civilization" could be seen in tasks of building electric dynamos and analyzing statistics on poverty and researching diseases.

But here is the rub: while many of these tasks truly have produced good for society, the technical processes underlying them could also be used for more pernicious ends. And so during the twentieth century, higher education also produced college graduates who have built nuclear weapons, who have analyzed financial statistics to cheat others out of their money, and have used African Americans as unknowing experiments for testing diseases. It is difficult to develop a sense of justice in all areas of learning when higher education has compartmentalized and isolated tasks without an accompanying overarching and robust discussion about significant human questions related to those tasks.

We attempt to address this problem by requiring students to take general education or core courses that engage important issues. But this system doesn't address these matters as well as we hope. If, for instance, questions of social justice only appear in separate courses and are not integrated across the curriculum, they end up getting framed as consumer goods–optional sort of items that I can add to my life if I want to, like a particular major or a job. In effect, our students are led to adopt the attitude, "Oh, so you like social justice? That's great. Good for you. I'm really excited about information technology myself."

Finally, it became increasingly clear in the late twentieth century that the entire project of grounding education in empirically-based investigation, scientific objectivity, and the assumptions of Enlightenment rationality did not produce widespread agreement on issues of what is good or true or important (Marsden, 1994, p. 430). Without consensus, we have fallen back, almost by default, onto ideals of individual autonomy and freedom of choice as the way to function in a society when we can't agree upon larger human questions.

As a result of this ethic of individual autonomy, we not only give students more and more options for shaping their own education, we tell them in countless ways, that they should study and do whatever they like. Having been shaped as consumers from that pre-school

267

day when that they first got excited about commercials for Trix cereal and Disney movies, this system of thinking that they should just choose what they want in education comes naturally to them. To our students, it seems like common sense that they should study whatever they want. And here is our problem: If this is so, why, then, should they be compelled to study topics that they don't like? What if they don't like political science, literature, economics or chemistry? What if they don't really care about integrity, or social justice?

This is a serious set of challenges that we face. But I believe there is hope for those of us who wish to cultivate desires toward the good. I am encouraged when I consider the efforts of John Woolman, a Quaker who lived in colonial New Jersey in the mid-eighteenth century. He was an active campaigner for many causes, though he is most famous for campaigning against slavery. Given what he was up against, I am amazed at what John Woolman and his fellow Quakers were able to accomplish in their lifetimes. Woolman began campaigning against slavery in 1746. By 1784 (ten years after his death) every single one of the Quaker yearly meetings in America had eliminated slaveholding among their members. Furthermore, this campaign formed the impetus for the small but growing antislavery movement in America and Great Britain. That is no small accomplishment.

This may be an odd historical event to compare to higher education, but I think it can provide some interesting insights for us. Just as John Woolman hoped to encourage his fellow Quakers to act and live in a just and compassionate way for the good of society, so we hope to encourage our students to live and act in a just and compassionate way for the good of society.

I daresay that Woolman had the harder task. He was deeply engaged in cultivating desires–desires to do what was just and good and right. In the first sentence of his opening paragraph of his influential antislavery pamphlet, "Some Considerations on the Keeping of Negroes," Woolman spoke to his readers about the "treasures of the soul" (Woolman, 1818, p. 176).[3] He then immediately launched into a discussion of human affections–or what I have been calling desires. An interesting way to begin a persuasive tract.

These themes permeated his work. At the London Grove Quarterly Meeting in Pennsylvania in 1758 he told listeners that they were to be "careful to have our minds redeemed from the love of

---

[3]This is an allusion to the New Testament passage from the Sermon on the Mount where Jesus says, "Where your treasure is, there your heart will be also."

wealth." He later observed that for slave-holding Quakers, "the desire of gain to support" the practices of slavery "has greatly opposed the work of truth" (Woolman, 2010, pp. 56, 58, 73). These were not simply emotional appeals. Woolman was very much committed to the business of getting his audience to think clearly. But he believed that in order to think clearly, to grasp what he called the "infallible standard (of) Truth"–to be truly rational, as it were– human desire needed to be directed toward loving the right things (Woolman, 1818, p. 176).

Let me use John Woolman as a touchstone to suggest a few principles for how we might help cultivate proper desires in our students. First of all, John Woolman understood that we are spiritual beings, and that spirituality is deeply related to our desires. He prayed often. He believed that God changed hearts. He wrote about promoting a spirit of meekness, heavenly-mindedness, sympathy and tenderness. He believed that God was actively at work in the process of understanding. "In infinite love and goodness he hath opened our understanding from time to another concerning our duty towards this people," he wrote (Woolman, 2010, p. 57).

I realize universities are not meeting houses or churches. What we can do in the realm of spirituality in our classes varies widely. And I realize that those who are associated with different branches of the Friends tradition have different ways of thinking and speaking about spirituality. But at a fundamental level, we share a belief that all persons have a deep spirituality to them. We can all gain confidence and encouragement from the conviction that this spiritual quality of humanity means that what we do in education can truly encourage and cultivate desires for what is good.

Secondly, when reading Woolman's journal, I was struck by how he did not just encourage people to do certain kinds of things, but encouraged listeners to become certain kinds of people. In other words, Woolman did not simply focus on the task of giving up slave-holding. He encouraged listeners to be people who demonstrated a life guided by wisdom, justice, and mercy. This is important. He believed that if Friends truly and fully desired these things, then they would give up slave-holding. Despite the compartmentalization and task-oriented structures of our institutions, I believe we can tap into deep seated spiritual desires to encourage students to *be certain kinds of people*: people who learn to love learning, who desire to be people of integrity, who care about others, who demonstrate wisdom.

Thirdly, John Woolman kept pointing his listeners to something bigger than themselves. "When self-love presides in our minds, our opinions are biased in our favor," he wrote in his antislavery pamphlet. We should "apply to God for wisdom, that we may thereby be enabled to see things as they are." Suffused in a culture of consumerism, entertainment and entitlement, many of our students are trapped by a certain kind of self-absorption and they are rather adrift. But if they find a purpose higher than their own selfishness, then their desires for what is good in education will be deepened.

Let me suggest, then, that we keep in mind what role the cultivation of desires has to do with our teaching. And let us enter into our teaching with the hope and encouragement that, despite everything else our culture throws at us, what we do is important, it is good, and it will endure.

Marsden, G. M. (1994). *The Soul of the American University: From Protestant Establishment to Established Nonbelief.* Oxford University Press, Oxford.

Smith, J. K. A. (2009). *Desiring the Kingdom: Worship, Worldview and Cultural Formation.* Baker Academic, Grand Rapids, MI.

Woolman, J. (1818). *The Works of John Woolman, in Two Parts.* Benjamin and Thomas Kite, Philadelphia, PA.

Woolman, J. (2010). *The Journal of John Woolman.* General Books, Memphis, TN.

Becoming 'Quakerly': The Legacy of Social Justice and its Challenges

by Tracey Elaine Hucks, Haverford College

Social justice at Quaker educational institutions has always been in a dialogical relationship with the wider society. Throughout major historical moments in North American history, Quaker institutions of higher learning have struggled to maintain their commitment to tolerance and community while seeking to deepen their ties to social justice. Today, in contemporary contexts, we grapple with what it means for academic institutions with Quaker roots to live and to learn in multicultural educational environments, while negotiating the challenges of a sustained enduring commitment to co-existence across difference. Haverford College has been no exception.

Lucius Outlaw, the esteemed African-American philosopher and scholar, taught at Haverford College for over two decades, into the 21st century. At a major Haverford forum in honor of Martin Luther King Jr. Day, he once remarked that if you teach long enough at a place like Haverford, even if you do not become Quaker, you will "become *Quakerly*."[1] Becoming *"Quakerly"* is an important metaphorical and transformative trope in the lives of non-Quaker academicians who live out their professional lives at intellectual institutions with Quaker heritages. I found these words quite probing and insightful as I reflected on how the institutional values of Quakerism influenced my and other colleagues' expressions of our professional/ethical identities and the impact of these values upon the students we teach at Haverford College.

My own initiation into the unique ways of Haverford College and its Quaker academic culture began with my unequivocal embracing of its expressed core values of "testimonies of peace, simplicity, equality, integrity, and justice."[2] Initially, its student Honor Code challenged my Harvard-trained sensibilities, where proctors were in high demand and handsomely compensated each semester to monitor and supervise young undergraduates engaged in the taking of exams. Over time, I came to appreciate and to acclimate to an educational practice that assumed student honesty and academic integrity as institutional norms.

---

[1] Lucius Outlaw, "MLK in the Age of Obama," Speech given at Haverford College, February 16, 2011.

[2] As articulated on the college web site: `http://www.haverford.edu/abouthaverford/quaker/religion.php`

Most helpful in facilitating this transition was learning more of Haverford's historical consistency in seeking to live out, even when imperfectly, its highest ideals. For most scholars of American religious history, knowledge of historical Quakerism has been closely associated with contested, yet consistent, campaigns against slavery and with frequently quoted citations from the 1688 Petition Against Slavery. This petition (drafted by Francis Daniel Pastorius) is often heralded as the earliest denominational anti-slavery literature from a religious body, clearly articulating, "Now tho they are black we cannot conceive there is more liberty to have them slaves, as it is to have other white ones. There is a saying that we shall doe to all men like as we will be done ourselves; making no difference of what generation, descent or colour they are."[3]

This historical Quaker campaign against slavery was not just localized in North America but extended throughout the larger Atlantic world. For example, I recall two summers ago conducting research at the British Museum Library in London on slavery in the Anglophone Caribbean colonies. I discovered numerous pages of microfilmed Quaker documents regarding their abolitionist efforts in the British West Indies. At one point, the museum librarian was unable to locate one of the requested microfilms on Quaker abolitionism in the Caribbean and apologized that there was only a single original copy of the document that existed in the world. Much to my surprise and delight, it was located in Haverford College's Quaker Special Collections and rare book archives, which boasts a holding of approximately 40,000 books and materials on or about Quakers.

It is the distinguishing social behavior of Quakers that weaved itself throughout Atlantic world history and sought educational distillation in the formation of Haverford College in 1833. Today, the faculty, staff, and student body of Haverford can perhaps be divided into two groups: the 'formally Quaker' and the 'practicing Quakerly.' Collectively, this body has both spearheaded radical innovation and weathered internal challenges. For example, one important and momentous occasion in the history of the institution's hiring practices was the employment and retention of University of Chicago-trained Dr. Ira De Reid, a Quaker, and the first tenured African-American faculty member at Haverford from 1946-1966. Reid was hired under Gilbert White, the sixth president of Haverford College and a Convinced Friend who worked for

---

[3] Garret Hendricks, Derick Op den Graeff, Francis Daniel Pastorius, and Abraham Op den Graeff, "The Germantown Protest," February 2, 1688. Available online at http://www.yale.edu/glc/aces/germantown.htm

the AFSC in France during WWII. White pledged as his vision for Haverford a "balanced concern for the intellectual, emotional, and spiritual" (Oliver et al., 2007, p. 13).

Ira Reid became the first African-American chair of sociology and anthropology in 1947. This was a monumental moment for racial diversity at the institution. I locate myself within a narrow lineage of African-American tenured presence on Haverford's campus that began with Ira Reid's early Quaker presence and continued in more recent years with Quaker colleague, Emma Lapsansky-Werner, Professor Emeritus, former Curator of the Quaker Collection and the first African-American woman awarded the rank of Full Professor at Haverford.

In the 21st century, Haverford has had to navigate the challenges of racial diversity and the creation of a tolerant atmosphere that accepts it. In 2004, the institution (under the Quaker leadership of President Thomas Tritton) was severely confronted on these issues when two white male Haverford seniors adorned in minstrel blackface and Afro wigs, confessedly dressed like Black women, attended the Bryn Mawr College annual Halloween Party. Eventually tried under Haverford's Social Honor Code, this event shattered two campuses for well over a year. Haverford wrestled internally with how students were being trained; students openly challenged the curriculum and the failure of the social justice requirement to comprehensively address matters of American racial difference; the Honor Code and system of student self-governance were structurally strained and challenged as a result.

Spearheaded by the then Dean of Multicultural Affairs, Sunni Green Tolbert, Quaker faculty member Doug Davis, and Lucius Outlaw, the first Unity Fest was collectively launched in 2005 in an effort to bring restorative and healing measures to two communities fractured by an egregious act of racial and gendered consequence. During Unity Fest, Davis offered his reflections on the occasion of this event, "I've been at Haverford for 33 years. I came the year after Haverford experienced a major crisis of confidence in its ability to commit itself to diversity."[4] In his observations of over a half dozen crises the institution had weathered over the years, Davis surmised, "They all have certain features in common. They all involve the Honor Code. They all involve issues about social responsibility. They all challenge our notions of who we really are, whether we are what we claim to be [as a Quaker-founded institution], whether we can pay off on the noble claims that we make."

---

[4] "Haverford College Unity Fest," Haverford College Field House, October 20, 2005.

In concert with Davis' efforts, Lucius Outlaw offered sharply critical reflections and located Haverford as part of a larger national body of elite educational institutions that perpetuate what he called "the systematic production, validation, justification and mediation of ignorance." He offered a hypothetical example to elucidate his point more emphatically,

> No candidate for an open position in philosophy... is going to be hired if all they know are literatures regarding people of African descent because you will not be regarded as sufficiently competent to be hired in such a position... No white person applying for a position in... philosophy will be *denied* a position because they know *nothing* about people of African descent. You can be thoroughly systematically ignorant and your competence will never be questioned if you know *nothing* about people who are fundamental to this nation-state.

Furthering his point, Outlaw discussed his current institutional affiliation and stated "You can... get a PhD in Philosophy with a specialty in American Philosophy [and] you never have to read a history book; you never have to look at any literature not produced by three or four white males and be certified with a PhD and go off and teach at colleges and universities..." He concluded, "this is both intellectually bankrupt and morally grotesque" and "inexcusable." It complements the "structures of emotions, of passions, and attitudes and of sentiments that ill prepares us for living in a social order increasingly made up of people of a variety of racial and ethnic cultural backgrounds, economic class, religious convictions, sexual orientations."

At the close of his address, he posed a critical question to the larger Haverford audience, "How are we going to deal with this?" This question is a fundamental challenge for many institutions of higher learning, inclusive of the many institutions associated with FAHE, as we reflect on how Quaker resources will be a part of these greater efforts of inclusion. What will be our institutional representation to the world as we do so?

In recent years at Haverford we have struggled, particularly as a faculty, with how we should represent ourselves to a wider public in relationship to Quakerism. Today, you will find on our website, "Haverford was founded in 1833 as Haverford School by a group of New York and Philadelphia Quakers who sought to create an institution of learning grounded in Quaker values. Though we are nonsectarian today, our Quaker roots influence many of our values and processes."[5] These representational challenges are closely linked to broader issues of institutional identity–are we a Quaker college? Are we a *historically* Quaker college? Are we a college with Quaker roots and Quaker elements? These questions become increasingly critical and relevant as liberal arts colleges navigate the demands and pressures of a growing culture of pre-professionalism among undergraduate students across the nation. Perhaps the time is ripe for faculties of Quaker-inspired institutions to revisit the lengthy challenges Lucius Outlaw posed in 2005 when he queried:

> Is this education really and truly deeply devoted to pro-
> ducing young people who will go forth as leading citizens
> in a nation-state increasingly made complex by racial
> and ethnic and other kinds of diversities? Or is the cur-
> riculum really a collage of deep commitments within the
> near silos of disciplines that is designed more and more
> to make of our young people apprentices in the spe-
> cialization of our disciplines? Do we have the courage
> to look deeply at what we are doing educationally for
> young people and really take up the issue of no longer
> being involved in any way possible in the systematic
> production of ignorance? ...Do we have the courage to
> fashion an education of young people at Haverford that
> is as courageous as were those crazy Quakers who broke
> the deal in the 1790s and simply went in [to Congress]
> and said on behalf of this nation we must stop this slav-
> ery business, if we are really about these values... But
> they were not crazy, they [were visionaries]. Is that a
> legacy that we could tap [in] to take a look at educa-
> tion of young people at Haverford? ...Do we have the
> courage to do it?[6]

Resolved in his ultimate belief in the virtues of Haverford College, Outlaw concluded, "I happen to think that this is one of the few places of higher education in this country where in fact, it could be done."

In 1997, I accepted a tenure-track position in the Religion Department at Haverford (turning down a position from my undergraduate alma mater) because I, too, believed it could be done at Haverford College. My experience in teaching at an institution that

---

[5] As articulated on the college web site at
http://www.haverford.edu/abouthaverford/history.php
[6] "Haverford College Unity Fest," Haverford College Field House, October 20, 2005.

privileges its Quaker heritage has enabled me to be bold in pushing the boundaries of my intellectual goals and pedagogical approach to student learning. In my own discipline of religious studies, Quakerism itself has been a symbolic boundary-pushing entity within a normative Protestant historiography. Teaching at an institution that embraces and privileges this spirit of boundary pushing has cultivated an even greater boundary-pushing commitment in me with regard to curriculum.

Although many religious studies curriculums have tended to focus on tradition-based approaches to understanding the discipline, I have found a freedom at Haverford to shape the contours of my curricular offerings. This sense of freedom is undergirded by an institutional educational mission to cultivate the "process of discovery," ask "difficult questions," and challenge injustice. More specifically, the mission states:

> ...Quakerism and liberal arts education both see the pursuit of new insights as being relentless. Truth is contestable–it can be expected to continually evolve. And the process of discovery is not constrained by any established authority... Haverford is one of America's leading liberal arts colleges, a close-knit intellectual community that combines the Quaker values of dignity, tolerance and respect with a rigorous academic program... Today, Haverford's Quaker elements are dynamic and evolving, and they correlate with an attitude of openness–asking difficult questions, resisting dogma, and challenging injustice.[7]

This is a tall order to fill as it encourages me to be bold and innovative in my teaching.

Teaching aspects of Quakerism within the Haverford curriculum–as in my semester-long course on Harriet Beecher Stowe's *Uncle Tom's Cabin*, or entire courses such as the *History and Principles of Quakerism* taught by Emma Lapsansky-Werner–has had tremendous impact upon Haverford students. Quakerism is not only a set of values to be espoused and embraced, but it also functions as the source and subject of sound critical intellectual research and reflection.

To illustrate this impact, I mention that Haverford students are required to produce a senior thesis or senior project equivalent. In the past year alone, the Religion Department has seen a tremendous

---

[7] As articulated in a Haverford College pamphlet, http://www.haverford.edu/abouthaverford/quaker/elements.pdf

increase in the number of student majors who have chosen some aspect of Quakerism as the subject of their senior thesis. Recent titles of 2013 senior theses in the Religion Department included: "State and Religion: Austrian Quaker Nazi Identity in World War II;" "Levi Coffin's Abolition Crusade: A Narrative of Moral Disagreement and Ethical Practice;" and "Inwardly Outward: Quaker Representation in Uncle Tom's Cabin."

Thus, given this historical legacy of human service, collective risk taking, and the espousal of these Quaker values at an institutional level, I have felt unfettered as a faculty member at Haverford College to teach on the cutting edge of social justice, to bring intellectual value to the silenced, muted, and marginalized of American society, and to cultivate a student atmosphere of expansion, risk, and voice. Perhaps only in the context of Haverford College could I have experienced teaching the single longest class in my career from 1:30-8:00 p.m. Over the duration of seven and a half hours, we debated a series of sensitive and contested issues, compelling us all as culturally Quakerly to remain open and engaged, stand firm through the discomfort, and work through our collective deliberations. It is in this academic space that I have had the confidence to add to the Haverford curriculum a semester-long course on intellectual history featuring one of America's brilliant thinkers, James Baldwin, who never received an advanced degree beyond Dewitt Clinton High School in NYC.

Finally, I convey to my students that in addition to shaping course content, the radical pedagogical challenge for me is not whether or not I can get students to discuss the great social issues of race and gender and sexuality within the boundaries of the classroom, but whether or not I can instill in them and model for them as an educator the necessary courage and risk-taking to discuss these issues beyond the safety of the classroom and in their own homes, in their own families, and to those who look like them in their own communities.

It is at this powerful juncture where academic knowledge must leave its ivory towers and be exported into the personal world of family and identity that I become most aware of the dichotomous lives our students often lead. At Haverford, students fearlessly travel the world in service to unknown others supported by the Center for Peace and Global Citizenship, yet they find one of the hardest things to do is to travel home and be in service to their own families and communities regarding issues of justice and equity. I express to the students enrolled in my courses that my ideal course environment would not be in the Margaret Gest Center in room Gest 101 but traveling each week as a class to their hometowns, to their living rooms, to their kitchen tables teaching amidst their extended intergenerational families members.

Until such time, I rely on unconventional pedagogy and creative assignments to simulate a boundary crossing and innovative knowledge transmission. One of the most frightening final assignments in my course on the intellectual thought of James Baldwin requires them to write a letter addressed to one of their family members, conveying an analysis of the thought of James Baldwin. Furthermore, an ungraded version of their submission will be mailed to the addressee. From this exercise has emerged some of the most insightful and generative student work where students directly engage the world of ideas within a wider social milieu. I leave you with an excerpt from one student letter written as an example of pushing the learning boundaries through Quaker-inspired intellectual endeavors:

May 16, 2013

Dear Dad,

In 1962 when you were seven years old, and I was not even a possibility, James Baldwin was writing a letter to his nephew called "My Dungeon Shook." He was writing on the one hundredth anniversary of Emancipation and spoke to his nephew about how to continue living in a world where he was still not free. He wrote, "I have begun this letter five times and torn it up five times" (Baldwin, The Fire Next Time,1963,3). I too have written and rewritten this letter to you. Writing to someone you know well is at once easy and comfortable while at the same time incredibly challenging.

I chose to write to you because you know Baldwin; I remember how excited you were when I told you I was taking this course. I also chose to write to you rather than someone else because there were days in class when it felt like Baldwin was speaking to you. I thought of you, of your childhood, and your parents, and I heard your stories in Baldwin's words... Even though Baldwin died in 1987, the thoughts and ideas that emanate from his words resonate in what I see in the world around me. This world that you and I live in Dad, might claim to be more modern and more developed than the world of previous generations, but there is a lingering attribute that has persisted throughout American history. It is something that stares us directly in the face every time we drive down Whalley Avenue in New Haven and pass the invisible line that separates the ghetto from Yale...

But like a stubborn child with an unsatisfactory answer, I am driven to understand why White America needs to pretend this dichotomy exists and the purpose it serves in society I have found in my two years at Haverford that it is surprisingly easy to let classroom discussions remain perfectly separate from myself. In the Passover story that we read every year at Seder, there is mention of the Wicked Son. He is the one who asks his parents what the story of Passover has to do with them, excluding himself from the history and the narrative of the Jewish people. It is too easy to be the Wicked Son, something Baldwin acknowledges. ["It is the innocence which constitutes the crime."] To acknowledge that you and I are also afraid is challenging. However, that is what I am asking of both of us. I want us to better understand where our crime has been committed and in what ways we can strive towards a true self-consciousness within America.

Throughout this course, we worked to fight the mentality of the Wicked Son and to involve ourselves in what we read and discussed. We shared personal anecdotes of family members and our experiences at home and at school. In one class, about half way through the semester, we read Baldwin's essay *Negroes are Anti-Semitic Because They're Anti-White*. This essay reached at a small part of me that had remained distant from all of our class discussions–my Jewish identity... As I hope you can tell from this letter, I am leaving this course with more knowledge and more questions than I would have imagined at the beginning of the semester.

Baldwin was like taking off a blindfold you always knew was there, but you were not sure how to deal with. I was looking at what I knew to be unjust and waited for someone else to come along because I felt defeated by apathy. I often still feel that way; just opening up a newspaper is enough to make me doubt that any change can ever happen. However being able to take my thoughts and my ideas from this class and transport them outside the round table of our classroom makes me feel less doubtful. These conversations cannot stay in our insular group but need to be brought out and discussed among all types of circles of people. I look

279

forward to making your kitchen table one of those circles.

Love always, H

Students like this remind faculty of the impactful potential of teaching in classrooms with permeable borders, of the need to cultivate innovative transmissions of knowledge production, and of the responsibility to inspire students to collectively imagine a world of true *Quakerly* social justice for all.

Oliver, Jr., J. W., Cherry, C. L., and Cherry, C. L., editors (2007). *Founded By Friends: The Quaker Heritage of Fifteen Colleges and Universities.* Scarecrow Press, Lanham.

Educating For Beloved Community:
Cultivating Creative Maladjustment
Within Ourselves and Our Students

by Steve Chase, Antioch University New England

The end is the creation of the Beloved Community.
–Martin Luther King, Jr., August 11, 1956

At the 2013 national conference of the Friends Association for Higher Education, I had the honor of being one of three plenary speakers to address the conference theme "Holistic Education: To What End?" Having a deep dialogue about our purposes as educators is always worthwhile, but it is particularly important in light of our current global predicament, which is urgent and dire.

If you do not perceive this urgency, I encourage you to read the prophetic *Call for Peace and Ecojustice* put forth by the attenders of the Sixth World Conference of Friends held in April 2012 at Kabarak University in Kenya. Sounding like the prophet Hosea, and blasting right through their own lingering denial and complacency, this remarkably diverse group of Quakers shared several hard truths with us:

> We have heard of the disappearing snows of Kilimanjaro and glaciers of Bolivia, from which come life-giving waters. We have heard appeals from peoples of the Arctic, Asia and Pacific. We have heard of forests cut down, seasons disrupted, wildlife dying, of land hunger in Africa, of new diseases, droughts, floods, fires, famine and desperate migrations–this climatic chaos is now worsening. There are wars and rumors of war, job loss, inequality and violence. We fear our neighbors. We waste our children's heritage. All of these are driven by our dominant economic systems–by greed not need, by worship of the market, by Mammon and Caesar. Is this how Jesus showed us to live? [1]

In response, these Friends at Kabarak University echoed Martin Luther King and urged all of us to become ever more faithful, counter-cultural, nonviolent revolutionaries. They declare, "We are

---

[1] "The Kabarak Call for Peace and Ecojustice." World Conference of Friends 2012, April 24, 2012.
http://saltandlight2012.org/kabarak-call-peace-and-ecojustice/

called to work for the peaceable Kingdom of God on the whole earth, in right sharing with all peoples." This is the Quaker way at its best (Guiton, 2012).

It is also my answer to the question, "Holistic Education: To What End?" The *Kabarak Call for Peace and Ecojustice* suggests to me that we should ultimately be in the business of nurturing the habits of head, heart, and hands that will equip our students to become ever more effective, wise, and loving participants in fostering "the peaceable Kingdom of God" within their personal, professional, and public lives. This holistic vision, which is focused on helping our students foster "peace, equality, simplicity, love, integrity, and justice," resonates deep in my heart and soul.

Yet, religious language about the Kingdom of God as the central purpose of our work as educators is only powerful in some academic settings, not all. As a faculty member at a secular school such as Antioch University New England, for example, it does not make much sense for me to talk about the "Kingdom of God" as Antioch's answer to the question "To What End?" In my educational setting, I have had to find other ways to articulate and share this message with people of other faith traditions and with secular–and sometimes even militantly anti-religious–faculty, staff, and students. This effort to find more inclusive language is important, for as the *Kabarak Call* points out, "We are called to cooperate lovingly with all who share our hopes for the future of the earth."

I have found the prophetic words and deeds of Martin Luther King of particular value in this effort, especially his concept of "the beloved community," which was King's favorite way of naming the Kingdom of God when he was speaking to a diverse audience that included secular people and people of different faith traditions. I have also found great value in King's lesser-known concept of "creative maladjustment." Both of these themes have been useful in my educational setting, and maybe they will be in yours.

Cultivating Creative Maladjustment

Do we, as Quaker educators, also believe that fostering "the beloved community" is our central calling–regardless of our different theologies, schools, disciplines, departments, or programs? If so, I think it is very valuable to pay attention to King's ideas on cultivating "creative maladjustment." As King wrote in 1963:

> This hour in history needs a dedicated circle of transformed nonconformists. Our planet teeters on the brink of atomic annihilation; dangerous passions of pride, ha-

tred, and selfishness are enthroned in our lives; and men do reverence before false gods of nationalism and materialism. The saving of our world from pending doom will come, not through the complacent adjustment of the conforming majority, but through the creative maladjustment of a nonconforming minority (King, 2010).

This passage suggests that our institutions of higher education should help as many of our students as possible make the transition from "the complacent adjustment of the conforming majority," what the Jewish prophets would call missing the mark, to the "creative maladjustment of a nonconforming minority," a form of ever-growing faithfulness and adventurous living.

Martin Luther King discussed the issue of creative maladjustment in more detail during a keynote address he gave at the 1967 national convention of the American Psychological Association. In that little-known talk, King directly challenged the notion that the ultimate goal of psychology is to help individuals become "well-adjusted," or conformed, to the social world around them. As King declared in this address:

> You who are in the field of psychology have given us a great word. It is the word "maladjusted." It is good certainly declaring that destructive maladjusment should be eradicated. But on the other hand, I am sure that we all recognize that there are some things in our society, some things in our world to which we should never be adjusted. There are some things that we must always be maladjusted to if we are to be people of good will. We must never adjust ourselves to racial discrimination and racial segregation. We must never adjust ourselves to religious bigotry. We must never adjust ourselves to economic conditions that take necessities from the many to give luxuries to the few. We must never adjust ourselves to the madness of militarism and the self-defeating effects of physical violence (King, 1999).

In his talk to the APA, King also argued that it is actually pathological for any person to become well-adjusted to a world of injustice, violence, and exploitation, even if this reality is often hidden and obscured from our view. He went on to say that if psychologists want to make a meaningful contribution to mental health they should find ways to help ordinary citizens deepen their capacity for "creative maladjustment." As he put it, "It may well be that our world is in dire need of a new organization: The International Association for the Advancement of Creative Maladjustment."

I think many of us would like our campuses or departments to serve as local chapters in this envisioned international association. Does not the cultivation of "creative maladjustment" concern us as educators, as well as practicing psychologists? Parker Palmer and Arthur Zajonc argue in their book *The Heart of Higher Education*, "If higher education is to keep evolving towards its full potential, it needs people who are so devoted to the educational enterprise that they have a lover's quarrel with the institution whenever they see it fall short of that potential–and are willing to translate that quarrel into positive action" (Palmer and Zajonc, 2010, p. 21).

Creative Maladjustment At Antioch

As someone long inspired by King, I have aspired to cultivate a growing level of "creative maladjustment" in my work as an environmental studies professor at Antioch University New England in Keene, New Hampshire. I think these efforts have made a positive difference in my department and in my students' lives–despite the continued existence of both internal and external countervailing forces that seek to keep us all lulled into the "complacent adjustment of the conforming majority."

One good example of this change is that my department has consciously agreed that our purpose is to "train effective local, national, and international environmental leaders working to create a sustainable society that embodies respect and care for the community of life, ecological integrity, social and economic justice, democracy, nonviolence, and peace." Given this vision of social change, we now require courses in "Political Economy and Sustainability" as well as "Leadership For Change." These courses are required for all master's students–whether they are studying to be high school science teachers, field biologists, resource managers, environmental educators, or social movement activists.

For the last twelve years, we have also been the only environmental studies program in the country to offer a master's program concentration in Advocacy for Social Justice and Sustainability. In this concentration, we cultivate creative maladjustment by educating public interest advocates and grassroots organizers working for ecological sustainability, social justice, the democratic control of corporations, and alternative forms of economic development rooted in fair trade, economic relocalization, community ownership, and permaculture principles. As part of my work as director of this program, I get to teach courses in "Organizing for Social Change" and "Diversity, Justice, and Inclusion."

I have also worked with my colleagues to make our extensive field studies program more "creatively maladjusted." For years, our field studies program included wilderness-based, ecological science trips to Costa Rica, Mexico, Alaska, the Pacific Northwest, and the Adirondacks. These were all amazing field courses. They were not the problem. The problem was that there was not a single field studies course in our curriculum that focused on the grassroots environmental justice movement in the United States. This movement emerged in the late 20th century as a popular response to the corporate and government malfeasance underlying the disproportionate pollution impacts that regularly hit poor communities and communities of color.

I worked with a colleague to ensure our students were exposed to–and challenged to understand–corporate power, the capture of government regulatory agencies, urban environmental issues, and, very importantly, racism and white privilege–the latter a topic poorly addressed in most of our nation's environmental studies programs. We also wanted our students to get to know tough and creative people who have resisted these powerful forces and won real victories for their communities. We saw our proposed field studies course on environmental justice issues in Louisiana as a good way to address these creatively maladjusted educational goals within our department's curriculum.

Maladjustment in Action

Most of our fieldwork took place along the 87-mile stretch of the Mississippi River between Baton Rouge and New Orleans, which is now home to 156 petro-chemical plants and oil refineries on both sides of the river. The Louisiana Chamber of Commerce calls this stretch of the Mississippi the "Chemical Corridor," but most of the local people call it "Cancer Alley." This is clearly contested territory.

Before going to Louisiana, our students researched the characteristics of the state they were about to visit. They found out that Louisiana produces about 25 percent of the United States' petrochemicals–a huge source of financial wealth–but that Louisiana is also the second poorest state in the country. This made them think about economic justice. Louisiana also has the worst public health record of any of the 50 states, which is not a surprise given the plague of high levels of industrial pollution, particularly in the part of the state they would be visiting. Furthermore, although African Americans make up around 35 percent of the state population overall, African Americans usually make up 90 to 95 percent of the population in the communities surrounding the many plants along Cancer Alley. As my students concluded, it is very hard to believe that "environmental racism" is a not a variable in this situation.

This became even clearer to us when we arrived in Louisiana and met Margie Richard. Margie is a retired elementary school teacher who used to live in Diamond, Louisiana. She has deep family roots there. Her great, great grandfather, for example, had lived in what is now called Diamond as a slave on the old plantation where a Shell Oil refinery and chemical plant now sits. Margie told us with pride that he was a leader of the largest slave rebellion in Louisiana's history. Margie also explained to us how she led her own community rebellion in Diamond to ensure that the Shell Oil Company paid every homeowner in Diamond enough money to move out of harm's way after just a few decades of its toxic operations had made life there unsafe.

We picked Margie up at her new house, an hour or so from her old community, and drove with her in our rented van to the now abandoned town of Diamond, Louisiana. According to Margie, her organizing efforts did not keep her community in place, healthy, and together, but they still sparked a needed change in Shell corporate policy. As background, she told us about how she and her neighbors used to sleep in their clothes so they could make a quick escape from the town if the plant sirens went off in the middle of the night. She also told us about the increasing number of miscarriages, respiratory diseases, leukemia, and breast cancer cases that she and her neighbors noticed over the years after the plant had moved into town. She even told us how many vegetables stopped growing in their gardens and how people stopped fishing in the river because of how deformed the fish had become.

Now standing with us on the spot where her front porch had once been, Margie pointed across the street to a lot bordering the fence line of the still active Shell plant. She told us about the hot summer day when she was sipping tea and watching a 17-year-old neighbor boy mowing the lawn for her elderly friend. A giant explosion suddenly erupted from the plant. Margie saw the fireball spread across the fence line and engulf the teenager, a young man whom she had taught in elementary school and known for years. She described the terror that swept over her as she watched this young man, still on fire, run away, and she traced his path for us with her finger. Pointing to a tree on her side of the abandoned street, she said that was where he finally fell and died, before the ambulance could arrive.

She told us, too, of her anger and heartbreak when the Shell Oil

Company offered the boy's mother $500 for her son's death–but only if the mother would sign away her right to sue the company for negligence. The mother was poor enough, Margie said, that she felt she had no choice but to take the corporation's offer, just to have enough money to bury her son. The community felt so disempowered back then that they did not feel like there was anything they could do about the situation.

Margie showed us a still-intact playground whose back fence is the fence line of the Shell plant. She pointed to a sign put up by Shell saying, "Parents, Keep Your Children Safe!" and asked, "Is there any way to keep our children safe on this playground?" Several of my students answered that they did not see how. We had only been in Diamond for about a half hour, and all our eyes were watering. Half of us had severe headaches. Several were starting to cough. One student had to go lie down in the van, because she was overcome with nausea.

A student then asked Margie what finally prompted her to start organizing a campaign to pressure Shell to buy out her and her neighbors' homes. Margie explained that as their living conditions continued to worsen over the years, the Shell Company finally offered a buyout deal to the white residents who lived in her town. The corporation refused, however, to offer the same deal to the African Americans living in Diamond. This was too much for Margie. She decided then and there that she had to become a community organizer, had to try to negotiate a fair deal with Shell about buying out *all* the neighbors in Diamond, and had to begin building a national coalition with environmental groups like Greenpeace and the Sierra Club to pressure Shell to do the right thing: to offer the same deal to the African Americans in Diamond that they had offered her white neighbors.

My students sat on the playground's bleachers and listened intently as Margie told them the details of how she organized her community over a period of years–including the heartbreaks along the way, the temptations to give up, and the creeping hopelessness about their chances of changing Shell's racist policies. Margie also told us about her group's very creative strategies and tactics, like raising enough money to buy Margie a few shares of Shell stock and sending her to Europe to attend a corporate shareholder's meeting. There, Margie went up to the table where the corporation's directors were sitting and poured each one of them a glass of water. Margie explained to them that this was water from a well in Diamond, Louisiana, and she encouraged them all to drink up and quench their thirst, if they thought living in Diamond was safe. None of the directors drank from their glasses. It was not long after this that the Shell Oil Company accepted the campaign's demands and offered everyone in Diamond enough money for their homes so that all the residents could move to relative safety.

One of my students then asked Margie how she found the courage to go up against one of the most powerful corporations in the world. Margie looked directly at my student, and said, "Aw honey, if Jesus can die on the cross for me, I can damn well take care of the babies in my community!"

What About Academic Resistance?

Margie's answer to my student brings us all the way back to our spiritual calling as Quakers–to follow the pattern and example of Jesus, to listen to our Inward Teacher, and to strengthen the Kingdom of God within all the spheres of our lives. For Quakers and other people of goodwill working within higher education this means staying professionally focused on the core goal of "education for beloved community," no matter what our theology, department, or discipline. This is our sacred calling.

It is not an easy calling. Palmer and Zajonc document the frequent hostility this educational vision engenders among many conventional and well-adjusted academics who believe that this vision is too messy, value-laden, emotional, controversial, community-based, and spiritual. Happily, Palmer and Zajonc offer several good ideas about engaging these academic critics in meaningful and transformative dialogue, but they also note that there are no easy answers for educators "seeking the insight and skillful means necessary to encourage forms of teaching and learning that honor the complexities of reality and our multiple ways of knowing, weaving it all together in ways that contribute to personal well-being and to the common good" (Palmer and Zajonc, 2010, p. 5). We still have a lot to figure out in practice.

Still, we, and our students, are worth the effort. Miracles do happen. Transformative learning does takes place. Time and time again, education shakes up empires, challenges patterns of injustice, strengthens the beloved community, and nurtures right relationships in our midst. This spiritual enlightenment encourages both faithfulness and skillfulness among those whom God reaches and teaches. In King's words, this helps people "make a way out of no way" (King, 1991, p. 252). I personally cannot imagine a better vocation than educating for beloved community, even when it is so challenging.

Conclusion

I also cannot think of a better way to finish this essay than going back to the *Kabarak Call for Peace and Ecojustice*, which reminds us:

- We are called to see what love can do: to love our neighbor as ourselves, to aid the widow and orphan, to comfort the afflicted and afflict the comfortable, to appeal to consciences and bind the wounds.

- We are called to teach our children right relationship, to live in harmony with each other and all living beings in the earth, waters and sky of our Creator, who asks, "Where were you when I laid the foundations of the world?" (Job 38:4)

- We are called to do justice to all and walk humbly with our God, to cooperate lovingly with all who share our hopes for the future of the earth.

- We are called to be patterns and examples in a 21st century campaign for peace and ecojustice, as difficult and decisive as the 18th and 19th century drive to abolish slavery.

All I can add to this is to shout, "Amen," and note that this is the spirit that should shape what, how, and why we teach.

Guiton, G. (2012). *The Early Quakers and the "Kingdom of God": Peace, Testimony and Revolution.* Inner Light Books, San Francisco, CA.

King, Jr., M. L. (1991). *A Testament Of Hope: The Essential Writings And Speeches Of Martin Luther King, Jr.* Harper Collins, New York, NY. Edited by James M. Washington.

King, Jr., M. L. (1999). Kings challenge to the nations social scientists. *APA Monitor*, 30(1).

King, Jr., M. L. (2010). *Strength To Love.* Fortress Press, Minneapolis, MN.

Palmer, P. and Zajonc, A. (2010). *The Heart Of Higher Education: A Call To Renewal.* Jossey-Bass, San Francisco, CA.

Index

Pacific Yearly Meeting, 255
Palmer, P., 10, 31
Pasadena City College, 255
Penington, I., 109
Penn, W., 44
Piaget, J., 235
Plato, 135, 208
Pogo, 20
Pollock, J., 130
Pope John XXIII, 216
Potthoff, S., 36
Presbyterian College, 189
Punshon, J., 116

QHE, 2
Quaker Earthcare Witness, 5, 26

Redding, E., 148
Rediehs, L., 102, 134
Reynolds, D., 67
Richard, M., 286
Roberts, J., 8
Rockefeller, J. D., 202
Roose, K., 49
Rowe, D., 29

Sawruk, T., 207
Shaw, D., 62
Shell Oil, 286
Shiva, V., 10, 13
Simmons, M., 211
Smith, D., 231
Smith, S., 111
Socrates, 135, 208
Spencer, C., 32
St. Augustine, 72, 263
Sterling, S., 27
Stowe, H. B., 276
Supreme Court, 219

Teresa of Avilla, 81
The College of New Jersey, 7, 31

Thomas à Kempis, 103
Tolbert, S. G., 273
Tritton, T., 273
Twombly, C., 130

University of Chicago, 202
University of Central America, 225
University of Chicago, 26
University of Connecticut, 6
University of Hartford, 190
University of Michigan, 219
University of Phoenix, 179
University of San Salvador, 225
Upholt, W., 25

Valentine, L., 213
Viola, W., 132
Vygotsky, L., 235

Walsh University, 189
Weinholtz, D., 27, 178
Western Yearly Meeting, 172
White, G., 272
William Penn University, 250
Wilmington College, 6, 250
Wilmington Meeting, 172
Woodbrooke, 73
Woolf, V., 76
Woolman, J., 45, 62, 107, 108, 268
Wright State University, 6

Young Adult Friends, 257

11984544R00188

Made in the USA
San Bernardino, CA
04 June 2014